AIDING
PEACE?

 *A project of the International Peace Academy*

AIDING PEACE?

The Role of NGOs in Armed Conflict

Jonathan Goodhand

ITDG
PUBLISHING

Intermediate Technology Publications Ltd.
Schumacher Centre for Technology and Development
Bourton on Dunsmore, Rugby,
Warwickshire CV23 9QZ, UK
www.itdgpublishing.org.uk

© Jonathan Goodhand 2006

First published 2006

ISBN 1 85339 632 X
ISBN 978 1 85339 632 8

Intermediate Technology Publications Ltd is the wholly owned publishing company of
Intermediate Technology Development Group Ltd (working name Practical Action).
Our mission is to build the skills and capacity of people in developing countries
through the dissemination of information in all forms, enabling them to improve
the quality of their lives and that of future generations.

Index preparation: Indexing Specialists (UK) Ltd.

Contents

Tables and Figures

Tables

Figures

Foreword

Terje Rød-Larsen
President, International Peace Academy

The International Peace Academy is pleased to be associated with this volume by Jonathan Goodhand, which brings an invaluable perspective to current international discussions about peacebuilding. Since its entry into international policy and practice in the early 1990s, peacebuilding has come a long way. While there are continuing debates about its exact definition, scope and boundaries, peacebuilding has come of age with the establishment of dedicated units, departments and programs in various organizations, culminating in the decision to create a Peacebuilding Commission at the 2005 World Summit at the United Nations (UN).

There are many reasons that peacebuilding captured the international imagination in the decade following the end of the Cold War. The 1990s started with the hope that the end of East-West antagonism would bring a peace dividend throughout the world. After years of relative paralysis, the UN Security Council began to play an active role in addressing a range of conflicts throughout the world, and international efforts were instrumental in ending several of the protracted proxy wars of the Cold War era. Meanwhile, development agencies, which had traditionally shied from working on conflict issues, saw an important role for themselves in supporting the transition of war-torn societies from conflict to sustainable peace and development. Importantly, the 1990s also saw the growing role of non-governmental actors in conflict contexts as humanitarian, development, environmental and human rights organizations grew in number, scale and scope of involvement. Within a short decade, the conceptual, institutional and operational parameters of international efforts to promote peace and development changed in ways that were unthinkable during the Cold War. Many of these innovations were, naturally, experimental and required a steep learning curve on the part of governments, non-governmental organizations and international institutions. By the turn of the new century, there was growing interest in taking stock of the cumulative effects of this proliferating activity in the name of peacebuilding.

The International Peace Academy (IPA) has been in the forefront of efforts to analyse the nature of the peacebuilding challenge and to assess international peacebuilding efforts since the early 1990s. This has taken a variety of forms, including early work on post-conflict operations in Cambodia and El Salvador, comparative assessments of international strategies to implement peace and 'end civil wars', pioneering work on war economies (which also involved Jonathan Goodhand) and statebuilding, and, most recently, a major research program on the 'security-development nexus'.

Jonathan Goodhand has written an exceptionally timely and relevant book. The volume sheds light on a much-debated but little researched topic: the role of non-governmental organizations (NGOs) in peacebuilding. From the International Convention to Ban Landmines to the establishment of the International Criminal Court, NGOs have come to play an increasingly prominent role in international affairs. While NGOs' role in advocacy and agenda-setting is fairly widely accepted, their peacebuilding activities are more controversial and have come under increasing scrutiny—not least from the NGOs themselves. As the number of NGOs, and their role in conflict situations, has grown exponentially, they have found themselves increasingly strained to find an appropriate balance between competing demands for relief, development, human rights and peace work, and between their own roles and that of other international and national actors.

In this important study, which is firmly grounded in seven case studies, Goodhand ably situates the role of NGOs in peacebuilding within the dynamics of contemporary conflicts and the evolving complexities of international peacebuilding. His study promises to become a valuable resource for the Peacebuilding Commission and other practitioners in their interaction with civil society. It also stands to make a significant contribution to current debates about the appropriate role of external actors in peacebuilding and our collective understanding of what it genuinely takes to build peace.

IPA is pleased to bring this work to the attention of policymakers, practitioners and scholars as a result of a creative partnership between Jonathan Goodhand, our Security-Development Nexus Program under the direction of Neclâ Tschirgi, INTRAC and ITDG Publishing. We are grateful to the governments of Australia, Belgium, Canada, Denmark, Germany, Luxembourg, Norway, Sweden and the United Kingdom as well as the Rockefeller Foundation for their support of our Security-Development Nexus Program and its publication series.

Acknowledgments

I started this research eight years ago, and numerous people have provided support and encouragement along the way. It has taken many forms and come from different sources. In the first instance I would like to thank the Economic and Social Research Programme (ESCOR) of the Department for International Development (DFID), which funded part of the field research, and the Conflict and Humanitarian Affairs Department (CHAD) of DFID, which provided support for the preparation of the manuscript.

I would also like to thank the International NGO Training and Research Centre (INTRAC), which has provided institutional, intellectual and management support for the duration of the study and publication process, and particularly Brian Pratt and Jackie Smith for their patience in the face of several delays in the production of the book.

I owe a particular debt to the following: David Hulme of University of Manchester and Henry Bernstein of SOAS for their academic guidance over the years and comments on parts of the manuscript; Tania Kaiser of SOAS for her valuable feedback on earlier drafts and ongoing support; Neclâ Tschirgi, formerly of the International Peace Academy, for her intellectual engagement and encouragement of the project; and Toby Milner of ITDG Publishing for his perseverance in seeing this project through, in spite of its various twists and turns en route.

I have been fortunate to work with many people who study, write about, or work on conflict and peacebuilding. They are too numerous to all be mentioned here, but I am particularly thankful to Philippa Atkinson, Haneef Atmar, Anthony Bebbington, Jo Boyden, Neil Cooper, Chris Cramer, Debi Duncan, Mark Duffield, Mark Hoffman, Tim Jacoby, Nick Lewer, Peter Oakley, Michael Pugh and Rob Walker. All in different ways have challenged my thinking and provided encouragement.

I would also like to thank Tom Feeney and Alan Martin, who conducted background research at different stages of the book's preparation.

This research would not have been possible without the engagement and support of many people living and working in extremely difficult circumstances in seven conflict-affected contexts. I am deeply indebted to them for the numerous ways in which they have contributed to this study.

Finally, I would like to thank my friends and family for their support, particularly Tania and my parents, Bill and Marion.

—Jonathan Goodhand

AIDING
PEACE?

1

Introduction

NGOs in a Conflictual World

The 20th century was one of the bloodiest and most destructive on record. More than 140 civil wars around the world since 1945 have killed approximately 20 million people and displaced 67 million (Sambanis, 2003). However, in recent years there has been a decline in global armed conflict. Since the early 1990s there has been a 40 per cent drop in the number of armed conflicts around the world (Human Security Report, HSC, 2005). With the end of the Cold War there has been an explosion of international concern to respond to and resolve violent conflicts. The decisive shift towards interventionist policies was accelerated further by the events of 11 September 2001.

As international inhibitions to intervene in other people's wars have declined, so the role of non-governmental organizations (NGOs) has grown. Historically, their primary function has been confined to mitigating the effects of war by providing humanitarian aid and protection on the peripheries of violent conflict. In theory, humanitarian action is guided by the principles of neutrality towards political and military objectives, proportionality in distribution of help and independence from the political agendas of states and international organizations (MacFarlane, 2001: ix).[1] The classical humanitarianism that was born in the 19th century was perhaps never as pure or as neutral as some writers and many humanitarians would have us believe.[2] Moreover, the conventional wisdom that the fall of the Berlin wall marked a radical departure from the years that preceded it can be questioned, and there are continuities between the contemporary humanitarian landscape and earlier periods (Minear, 2002: 2–3). But two trends are clearly associated with the Cold War era. First, there has been a growth in the size and reach of the humanitarian system due to increased funding for relief activities.[3] NGOs have been one of the chief beneficiaries of increased official aid for emergencies. Second, NGOs have been encouraged to extend their activities into developmental relief and peacebuilding. In many of today's conflicts NGOs find themselves integrated into multidimensional peace operations, a hybrid response involving diplomatic, military, developmental and humanitarian actors. This has occurred through a

1

combination of the mandate expansion of relief and development NGOs and the proliferation of specialized conflict resolution or peacebuilding organizations. As a consequence, NGOs have become central to the international response to war, in part because of the limitations of traditional diplomacy in contemporary conflicts and in part due to a belief in their comparative advantages. NGOs have come to symbolize everything that governments are not: they are unburdened with large bureaucracies and they are seen to be flexible and able to respond to grassroots needs (Richmond, 2003).

Whether NGOs live up to these supposed comparative advantages and whether they can and should play a significant role in peacebuilding have been the subject of debate in practitioner and academic circles. Broadly two schools of thought have emerged; one arguing that NGOs should stick to their classical role as providers of relief and protection, a minimalist position, and the other arguing for an expanded role, which incorporates developmental relief and peacebuilding to meet the complex challenges of contemporary conflict, a maximalist position (Goodhand with Atkinson, 2001). The debate has tended to be normatively driven and based more on ideological orientation than empirical evidence. Until recently limited attention was paid to the impact of NGOs' activities on the origins and dynamics of conflict and peace (MacFarlane, 2001: ix).[4] This is surprising given the resources increasingly funnelled through NGOs and the roles and responsibilities that they have taken on.[5] The question of what impact they have individually or cumulatively cannot be answered with any degree of confidence. The levels of accountability demanded of NGOs in developmental contexts are in general far higher than for emergencies.[6]

This is changing, however. In recent years there has been a growing focus on the impact of humanitarian aid in general and to a lesser extent on the impact of aid on conflict and peace dynamics (Le Billon, 2000; White and Cliffe, 2000; Collinson, 2003). This coincides with and is partly the result of reforms in the West's public sectors, which have seen the introduction of new management systems focusing on results (Duffield, 2001; Macrae et al., 2002; Cooley and Ron, 2002). This concern about impact is illustrated in a speech given by Andrew Natsios, Administrator of USAID, in 2003 in which he stated: 'Doing good is not enough. We have to show what kind of good we're doing, in which sectors, in which communities and whether good has bad consequences, or bad side effects that no one anticipated' (cited in Hoffman et al., 2004: 5). In other words, good intentions are no longer sufficient. NGOs must be able to demonstrate that they are achieving positive outcomes and also that they are consciously adjusting their activities to minimize potential harm. If one reads Natsios's statement as a plea for improved technical performance on the part of NGOs, few would disagree. But what constitutes a harmful or 'good' consequence depends also on one's moral and political framework. And in the post-9/11 environment, many fear that such statements are a coded language, disguising strong covert (and sometimes overt) pressures on NGOs to act as force multipliers in the Global War on Terror (GWOT).

Rationale for This Book

Donors provide funds and NGOs engage in peacebuilding activities largely as a leap of faith. There is very limited systematic empirical evidence to either support or refute the claims of minimalists or maximalists. This book aims to provide an empirical grounding to these debates, by exploring two primary questions. First, what impacts do NGOs have on the dynamics of conflict and peacebuilding in areas affected by armed conflict? Second, what are the main factors (contextual and organizational) which determine NGOs' ability to work effectively in or on conflict? These questions are addressed by combining a selective analysis of the literature on this topic with a distillation of key findings from two research projects conducted by INTRAC and the Institute for Development Policy and Management (IDPM), University of Manchester. These studies involved comparative analysis of seven contexts that have been affected by armed conflicts—Afghanistan, Armenia-Azerbaijan, Kyrgyzstan, Liberia, Moldova, Nepal and Sri Lanka—with a particular focus on the interactions between aid, NGO interventions and the dynamics of peace and conflict.

Drawing upon the research as well as contemporary writing on armed conflict, NGOs and peacebuilding, this book provides an overview of key theoretical and policy debates on the changing role of NGOs and donors in conflict, and outlines their implications for improving policy and practice. One of the main conclusions of this book is that universal solutions or frameworks for best practice have a limited value given the astonishing complexity and specificity of conflicts currently taking place around the world. This variety is reflected in the seven case studies, and although there are no universal recipes for success, one requirement across the board is improving understanding. What kind of understanding has proven useful for policy-makers and practitioners and how it can be applied in practice is an important theme of this book. Although it is not possible to engage with the details of operational matters across the seven cases, this book does examine the ways in which theory and policy interact with everyday NGO practice. Given the growing external pressures on NGOs mentioned above, it is argued that an awareness of and an ability to engage with these wider theoretical and policy debates may be critical in terms of both their survival and effectiveness.

Engaging with Practice

My interest in these issues goes back a long way and this book has had an extended germination period. It dates back to the period 1987–90 when I was an NGO worker based in Peshawar on the Afghan–Pakistan frontier. This was my first and formative experience as an aid worker. I turned up with a rucksack and some rather naïve views about helping the Afghan cause. I soon found a voluntary position with an international aid agency teaching English to Afghan refugees. Within a year I was working on crossborder relief and rehabilitation programmes, monitoring projects implemented by NGO partners. It involved being smuggled across the frontier (this still being Soviet-occupied Afghanistan), then couriered from one commander to another until we reached our destinations, usually rural areas in eastern and southern Afghanistan, to monitor the projects. This was at a time when crossborder and refugee assistance programmes were part of the West's 'non-lethal aid' to the Afghan resistance. Aid was highly politicized. Some solidarity NGOs were explicit about this: they were part of the jihad to get the Soviets out of Afghanistan. Others were less comfortable with this position and stressed their humanitarian rather than political role. But in practice we were all compromised, at least in the eyes of most Afghans who saw how we accepted the controlling influence of the mujahideen political parties in the camps, how we built alliances with commanders inside Afghanistan to gain access, and how we naïvely allowed ourselves to be colonized by hiring Afghan staff from one political party or another. I left Afghanistan with extremely ambivalent feelings towards the 'humanitarian international' (de Waal, 1997). It was hard to tally the intelligence, commitment and talent of the people who worked for aid agencies with the apparent dysfunctionality of the enterprise as a whole. The question for me was a familiar one to aid workers who came back from stints in Afghanistan, Rwanda or Kosovo in the 1980s and 1990s: are we doing more harm than good?

After this, a two-year NGO position in northern Sri Lanka followed. I was again living and working in the middle of violent conflict, managing an NGO relief and rehabilitation programme in the Jaffna peninsula. Though the context was very different, the dilemmas on the ground were familiar. This time, instead of having to do deals with warlords, it was necessary to negotiate with the Liberation Tigers of Tamil Eelam (LTTE) or the Sri Lankan armed forces. Again there were concerns that aid was doing harm, or at best not doing as much good as it should do. Although some of these dilemmas may equally apply to developmental contexts, violent conflict brings them out much more starkly. The costs of a bad decision may be literally one of life or death.

Having this comparative experience—and observing at first hand the continuities in terms of aid-conflict interactions and agency behaviour—persuaded me of the need for more systematic reflection. The two research programmes mentioned above were a product of this realization. My motivations were twofold: first, to better understand what was going on, having been a (hopefully) reflective but confused practitioner for several years; and second, to generate research findings that could be shared with fellow practitioners and contribute to efforts to improve practice. There is inevitably a tension between the objectives of academic rigour and policy relevance. But research on humanitarian and peacebuilding practice which does not actually engage with practice is unlikely in my view to be either very rigorous or very relevant to the needs of practitioners and policy-makers. This kind of research cannot be done from a distance: 'at some level to be able to discuss violence, one must go to where violence occurs [and] research it as it takes place' (Robben and Nordstrom, 1995: 4).

Making Difficult Choices: Working in Areas of Armed Conflict

This book is concerned with the world of practice and NGO practitioners.[7] For the purpose of this book, the term 'practitioners' is understood to mean a broad range of NGO actors from a country desk officer in head office to the fieldworker operating 'at the coalface'. Though their type of engagement is quite different, it is argued that violent conflict poses common challenges to practitioners wherever they are located in the aid system. Practice is also taken to mean more than simply the implementation and management of projects. Development and peacebuilding outcomes can be achieved in many ways and projects are only one of them. This book also explores other ways of working beyond direct implementation, including building the capacities or seeking to influence other agents of development and peacebuilding.

Humanitarian and peacebuilding practice is necessarily about making tough decisions. It is about engaging in a messy world. Often it involves choosing between least-worst options in highly politicized (and compromising) environments. Although the same applies to more stable development settings, conflict tends to bring into sharp relief the dilemmas associated with making difficult choices. There is no such thing as best practice when every context is different and circumstances change over time. It will be argued that skilful practitioners learn to match responses to contexts (White and Cliffe, 2000) rather than try to apply a best-practice template from one place to another. This takes us towards a pluralist orientation, in which good practice is about increasing probabilities rather than creating certainties. However, merely to say that everything depends on context and timing is not very helpful. There is sufficient accumulated experience to suggest that applying certain principles of good practice may support the conditions that make success more likely. This book aims to explore some of the success stories (as well as the failures) in order to understand what has worked in certain circumstances, why it has worked and what we can learn that can be applied or adapted elsewhere.

If NGO practice is about making decisions, these decisions are never made in a vacuum. They are shaped by a range of interconnected factors. Broadly there are three types of filters that shape decision-making processes, which span the macro, meso and micro levels: these are the political context, the organizational environment, and individual values and preferences.

The Political Context

Violent conflict is a game of high stakes. Intervention by aid actors inevitably affects the calculus of those involved in conflict; there is always an impact. War may be the product of previous interventions, or intervention may have contributed to new forms of contention. The idea of neutral, third-party interveners who stand above the fray should be discarded. Practitioners intervene in highly political contexts and will be seen as political actors themselves. Even the International Committee of the Red Cross (ICRC), perceived by many as the archetypal neutral humanitarian organization, is acutely aware of this. As one ICRC fieldworker commented to me once, 'To be neutral you have to be extremely political.' Decision-making is shaped by both the politics of the emergency and the politics of the response. The intrinsic links between Northern politics and economic interests, on the one hand, and Official Development Assistance (ODA) and humanitarian action, on the other, are not new. But Kosovo, Afghanistan and Iraq signify a growing politicization of international assistance, leading some to argue that the 'quality of mercy is now strained to breaking point' (Donini, 2003b: 12). In increasingly polarized contexts where one is forced to choose sides—'you are either for us or against us'—practitioners must consider where they position themselves and the extent to which they can create political space or room for manoeuvre.

The Organizational Environment

Although a great deal has been written about political constraints, organizational questions have been a blind spot in the literature on armed conflict and intervention. As the Brahimi report (UN, 2001) highlights, political will is crucial, but so too is institutional performance. Practitioners work within organizations, from small niche NGOs to large multi-mandate NGOs. These organizations and the wider institutional environment in which they are situated influence (and constrain) practitioners' choices. Good practice involves a constant tension between what is desirable and what is possible. Frequently, organizational and operational matters such as funding, capacity or management, force practitioners to make pragmatic choices based upon what is possible rather than what is necessarily the most desirable course of action.

Organizational capacities may be one bottleneck, organizational interests are another. Practitioners work in messy organizational environments in which they have to balance competing interests and forms of accountability. On the one hand, there are the soft interests in terms of declared mission and primary constituency; on the other, there are the hard interests related to funding, profile and market share. Within organizations there may be competing constituencies, for example, between the relief and development sections or the Africa and Asia desks. Competitive relationships between organizations are also likely, particularly in high-profile, multi-mandate peace operations.

Therefore, how problems are framed and responded to is influenced by a range of organizational factors that are independent of the problem itself. For instance, two NGOs, one with a human rights mandate and another with a relief focus, working in the same context may define the problem and respond to it in very different ways: one focusing on the denial of rights and the other on the lack of basic needs.

Practitioners almost never have a free hand in deciding what is to be done—organizational mandates and biases limit the range of options and approaches. But although organizations may be limiting, and using Chambers' (1997) phrase, 'self-deceiving', they can also be empowering. This book, as well as highlighting cases of the former, looks at positive examples of organizational learning and adaptation by agencies that have worked effectively in and on conflict.

Individual Choices

Finally, the personal dimension tends to be another blind spot in debates on intervention in armed conflicts. Practitioners are often viewed as the unwilling agents of wider political and institutional interests. Structures are seen to operate in a deterministic way so that there is no space for individual agency. Yet my personal experience suggests otherwise. Individuals do have agency and for better or for worse, they can make a difference. Although we operate within the limitations of structural constraints, such constraints are mediated through people. To take an actor-oriented approach, as this book does, is not to deny the importance of structures. Practitioners' room for manoeuvre is clearly limited by the wider political environment and this must be part of their frame of reference. But the biases, values and capacities of practitioners also have an impact on how problems are framed and responded to. Organizations vary from country to country and policies are implemented differently in different contexts. Often this is because of the individuals involved on the ground. An over-structuralist analysis misses the diversity of development and peacebuilding practices. Research highlights the importance of human agency and particular policies, which is good news for those seeking to influence violent conflict in a positive direction. Although this does not mean that situations and events can be socially engineered by outsiders, it does indicate that the probabilities of peace or violent conflict can be influenced through particular policies and interventions.

At the heart of this book is an exploration of the question of agency, and more specifically the agency of NGOs and NGO workers in contexts of armed conflict. Practitioners can and do create room for manoeuvre, leading to alternative discourses, practices and development outcomes. This study explores actually existing practice and the processes through which practitioners make choices in a messy, conflict-ridden and constantly changing world. As outlined above, choices are shaped by the wider sociopolitical environment, the organizational context, and individual biases (conscious and unconscious) and values. This is not to adopt a voluntaristic view of decision-making, which gives insufficient attention to examining how individual choices are shaped by larger frames of meaning and action. Agency is composed of social relations and can only become effective through them (Long, 1992: 23).

Paradoxically, one of the key arguments of this book is that the agency of NGOs and NGO workers has been overestimated by both their supporters and critics. In order to arrive at a more realistic assessment of their impacts it is necessary to examine in some detail the conflict and peacebuilding contexts in which NGOs operate and the role of other agents or drivers of change within these contexts. Therefore, much of this book is about trying to understand war, by looking at the empirical evidence from the case studies and drawing upon a related body of theory.

Research Approach

This book draws upon fieldwork conducted between 1997 and 2001 which focused on NGOs, conflict and peacebuilding.[8] This involved a combination of fieldwork in the case study countries and background research drawing on the relevant literature and secondary material. In each country a team of international and national researchers conducted a combination of studies that focused on different levels of analysis and intervention. These consisted of: macro studies, which provided both an overview of the history, sources and dynamics of violent conflict and a typology of the various responses to conflict; organizational studies, which focused on individual NGOs with a view to identifying and learning from examples of good practice, which covered different types of interventions, from conflict-sensitive relief to explicit attempts to build peace, including community-based reconciliation or conflict resolution; and community studies, which aimed to capture 'the view from the village', to complement and ground in truth 'the view from the agency'. Clearly in each case there were multiple views, but the idea of the community studies was to develop further our understanding of how aid agency interventions impacted upon the lives of individuals, households and communities living in war-affected areas. Taken together, the aim of these studies was to build up a multilevel picture of conflict and intervention. Particular attention was paid to teasing out the linkages (and disconnects) between these different levels, as this is key to understanding how conflict escalates and spreads and how it may be managed and resolved. The approach meant that the research produced thick qualitative case studies. This made it possible to generate fine-grained analyses of particular cases which captured many of the complexities and the dilemmas involved in working in or on conflict. Of course, one should be cautious about generalizing from a relatively small number of cases. Furthermore, these case studies represent snapshots of particular conflicts at particular moments in time.

Evidently conflicts move on and analysis quickly becomes dated. But even if the specific configuration of conflict structures, actors and dynamics changes, this does not negate the value of the analysis. A clear finding of the research is the need to think much more historically about conflict and intervention; the time frames of analysts and policy-makers are often far too short.

Although this book draws heavily on the above research, its analysis and findings are not limited to these two projects. The book incorporates and discusses a wider body of thinking and writing about NGOs, conflict and peacebuilding. It is hoped that this will provide practitioners with an understanding of the broad contours of current theoretical and policy debates, and their relevance and applicability to humanitarian and peacebuilding practice. Since events have moved on quite dramatically in a number of the case study countries since the time of the research, I have attempted where possible to update the analysis.

Finally, as a book written by a former aid practitioner, there is a danger of bias and consequently an 'aid-centric' view of the world. Much of the data for this book is derived from interviews with women and men involved at different levels and in different capacities in the aid system. However, I am conscious of the danger of bias and have attempted to counter this by capturing the perspectives of a range of non-aid actors, including government officials, journalists, conflict entrepreneurs, community members and businesspeople. My own personal bias and experience also need to be mentioned. Having greater field experience in Afghanistan and Sri Lanka, I have drawn more extensively on case study material from these two countries.

Being Careful with Words

Unsurprisingly, debates on NGOs, conflict and peacebuilding are characterized by the contested use of language and terminology. The same words may be used in different and often contradictory ways, reflecting distinct moral discourses and political positions. These complex definitional debates will not be rehearsed here, as they have been well covered elsewhere (Fetherstone, 2000; Wallensteen, 2002), but how the most important terms are understood and used in this study is briefly elucidated below.

Conflict and War

War is killing for some collective purpose. (Keegan, 1998: 72)

War is the organized pursuit of interest by means of force. (Hirst, 2005: 51)

The focus of this study is on violent militarized conflict rather than conflict per se. The terms 'armed conflict' and 'war' appear to be relatively unproblematic and are often taken for granted. But several points of ambiguity can be highlighted. First, although there has classically been a firm distinction between international and internal conflicts, this is becoming increasingly blurred.[9] Many of today's wars are hybrid affairs which dissolve clear distinctions between the domestic, regional and international spheres: they are neither introverted civil conflicts, nor classical inter-state wars. Whereas in the past such wars were viewed as domestic affairs, state and inter-state actors increasingly assert the right to intervene or the right to protect, based on hard-security or human rights criteria.

Second, there is ambiguity about the distinction between war and other forms of collective violence. Wallensteen and Sollenberg (1998) define wars as conflicts with more than 1,000 battle-related deaths in a year.[10] But the idea that war can somehow be neatly separated out, and viewed as distinct, from other forms of collective violence may be challenged. Wars rarely have clearcut beginnings and endings and they are often preceded or followed by other forms of collective violence, including riots, scattered attacks or chronic political instability. These interconnected 'ecologies of violence' (Sambanis, 2003) are characterized by different combinations of settings and causal processes but are not distinct species of social interaction (Tilly, 2003: 23). The boundaries between them are porous, and one form of collective violence can mutate into another, depending on the activation or cessation of causal processes (ibid.). War is conventionally understood to be conducted for political purposes and crime for economic purposes. As Clausewitz famously wrote, 'war is the continuation of politics by other means' (Clausewitz, 1982). However, in contemporary (and earlier) wars the distinction is rarely so clearcut, since war may frequently provide the cover for the institutionalization of crime (de Waal, 1997; Keen, 1998; Reno, 2000).

Third, there is ambiguity about the relationship between war and peace. As Stepputat (1997: 21) notes, 'The habitual association of violence with disorder and peace with the return of order is an oversimplification.' This stereotype is often based upon both a demonization of war and romanticized notions of peace. The apparent lawlessness of civil war is often supported by the state (Keen, 2000). As Richards (2005: 5) argues, war is a social project among other social projects and therefore 'to understand war we must first deny it special status' (ibid.: 3). This means recognizing the links between war and peace. As Keen (2000: 8) notes, 'it may be difficult to account for mass violence or civil war without examining the violence embodied in peace'. Rather than seeing peace and conflict as mirror images of one another, they might better be conceptualized as relative conditions, in which we see variations in degrees rather than absolute differences. Conflict may involve the amplification or acceleration of pre-existing social and political processes. In Sierra Leone, for example, Keen (1998) highlights the similarities between the 'sell game' arrangements of warring factions and the peacetime patterns of corruption.

How wars are defined and how they are represented are important, as the dominant discourses can shape responses. Some conflicts remain hidden as the countries concerned resist the label 'civil war'. The Sri Lankan government, for instance, often referred to the conflict as a 'terrorist problem' rather than a civil war. Countries at war are subject to a form of international triage where the most strategically important, resolvable or visible conflicts are selected for international attention at the expense of others that are less deserving or amenable to peacebuilding efforts (Gurr, Marshall and Khosla, 2001). The process of triage has clearly been shaped since 9/11 by the GWOT, with attention increasingly focused on the regions and countries where the 'terrorist' threat is perceived to be greatest.

Various terms have gained currency in recent years, in order to distinguish between new wars and old wars.[11] This study will stick to the classical terms 'armed conflict', 'war' and 'intra-state war', as in my view the analytical centre of gravity has shifted too far towards stressing the newness of modern conflicts while failing to recognize the historical continuities with earlier wars. Whichever term is used, ultimately every conflict is unique, with its own configuration of power, structures, actors and beliefs or grievances, and this highlights the need for detailed analysis and exploration of context.

Peace and Peacebuilding

Peace is commonly conceptualized as the antithesis of war, the 'beating of swords into ploughshares', a situation in which physical violence does not occur. The formal ending of a war, however, does not necessarily mean the end of violence. In Latin America and South Africa, for instance, there has been a shift from militarized conflict to widespread social conflict. The signing of peace agreements between elites may leave wider societal tensions unaddressed. The transition from war to peace may involve re-establishing hierarchies that had been transformed by conflict. For instance, in some post-conflict contexts there have been strong social pressures for women who played an active role in the military and political struggle to revert to their pre-conflict roles (Pankhurst, 2003).

Development and peace are both value-relative and are likely to be defined by the most powerful in society. Particularist interests and agendas may be masked under the guise of pursuing peace (as may also be the case under the cover of war).[12] Conflict resolution tends to normalize particular ways of thinking about violent conflict and excludes others (Fetherstone, 2000: 198). At a global level, Duffield (2001) argues that Western powers pursue stability in the global South in order to protect their own core interests and to promote the expansion of liberal capitalist institutions. In this sense peacebuilding is about manufacturing and policing consent.

There are, however, alternative readings of peacebuilding. Arguably, Galtung's (1969) notion of 'positive peace' (the absence of structural violence) and the concept of 'human security' open up the promise of more emancipatory approaches to peacebuilding. Both ideas recognize that human insecurity is not only related to the existence of physical violence, but to a range of other interlocking factors which increase or decrease the risks and vulnerability of individuals, households and communities. These risks and vulnerabilities may be political (e.g. the denial of rights, incomplete citizenship, lack of participation), economic (e.g. livelihoods opportunities) and social (e.g. social prejudice, discrimination). Positive peace therefore involves the lowering of risks and vulnerability in these interlocking areas, in other words building higher levels of human security for the society as a whole, including minority groups. Although recognizing this is broad-term and open to many different forms of interpretation, I intend to examine debates on peacebuilding through the lens of human security. The concept usefully shifts the analytical focus from realist, state-centric notions of security to a multidimensional analysis of communities and households living in areas affected by insecurity.

While peacebuilding is sometimes conceived of as a post-conflict activity, here the term is used more broadly to include any activity undertaken with the purpose of preventing, alleviating or resolving violent conflict:

> Peacebuilding is the effort to strengthen the prospects for internal peace and decrease the likelihood of violent conflict. The overarching goal of peacebuilding is to enhance the indigenous capacity of a society to manage conflict without violence. Ultimately peacebuilding aims at building human security a concept that includes democratic governance, human rights, rule of law, sustainable development, equitable access to resources and environmental security. (Government of Canada, 2000, cited in Ball, 2002)[13]

The following points are intended to further refine and clarify the approach taken in this study to peacebuilding, and to make explicit underlying assumptions.

First, peacebuilding is fundamentally a political task. It involves explicit recognition of the political causes and dynamics of armed conflict at the heart of which are questions of state contestation and/or breakdown. It also involves making visible the political framework of the peacebuilders. The political baggage associated with peacebuilding is made invisible because of its seeming 'rightness' (Fetherstone, 2000: 197). But blindness to its normative underpinnings increases the risks that peacebuilding will become an instrument of hegemony rather than of transformation. This applies particularly in the post-9/11 environment, in which peacebuilding is increasingly associated with a discourse of counter-terrorism, homeland security and nation-building.

Second, just as conflict is multi-layered, so must be efforts to build peace. Commonly, conflict resolution and peacebuilding are divided into different mediation 'tracks' involving different actors and different processes.[14] For

the purpose of this study Track One diplomacy is defined as official negotiations between political and military elites, in other words top-down efforts at
peacemaking. Track Two is defined as non-official mediation, which may be
between civil society actors as well as communication behind the scenes between political elites. Track Three is defined as humanitarian and development
assistance which may or may not have explicit peacebuilding objectives but
will have an effect on the context in which peace negotiations are occurring.
Aid is delivered into a political environment and inevitably affects incentive
systems one way or another: 'Aid affects not only the size of the economic pie
and how it is sliced but also the balance of power among the competing actors
and the rules of the game by which they compete… the political impacts of aid
can help to decide whether the peace endures or war resumes' (Boyce, 2000:
367). The focus of this study is on Tracks Two and Three, which are primarily
bottom-up approaches to peacebuilding based on civil society. To an extent they
are less concerned with the high politics of the state than with the low politics
of society, an approach sometimes referred to as 'peacebuilding from below'
(Woodhouse, 1999). I do not assume, however, a neat distinction between high
politics and low politics, state and civil society.[15]

Third, one should differentiate between peace as the ultimate objective and
the intermediary stages for getting there. My aim is not to assess the efforts of
NGOs to end war—in other words to build peace 'writ large' (Anderson and
Olson, 2003). It would be unrealistic and unfair to judge NGOs by such standards. Instead, questions are asked about the different kinds of impacts they have
had—positive and negative, direct and indirect, intended and unintended—in
different contexts and time periods and at different levels on different kinds
of processes, structures, institutions and individuals. Peacebuilding (like war)
is a process which does not have a precise beginning and end and it is likely
to be the result of multiple and cumulative efforts. In the same way that there
are separate but overlapping ecologies of violence, there may be distinct but
interconnected ecologies of peace, which NGOs can influence for better or
for worse. Their efforts may often be invisible, involving everyday forms of
resistance—something that James Scott (1997) refers to as 'infra politics'—to
the rationality and culture of war.

Fourth, peacebuilding can be seen not only as a discrete project but as the
impact of any activity on a particular set of relations—in this case peace and
conflict dynamics. It is viewed as a lens through which aid agencies can assess
the outcomes and impacts of policies and programmes. Although my focus is
on NGOs, it is possible to apply this lens to a range of other policy instruments,
such as wider aid policy, trading relations and diplomatic measures. Whether
NGOs' activities taken together have a cumulative effect on peace processes
depends to a great extent on both the nature of the conflict and whether the
wider policy environment is conducive to such efforts. It is, therefore, as already
mentioned, important to avoid an analytical framework that is too aid-centric.

NGO activities should be located in relation to the wider policy environment and other external actors.

NGOs, Intervention and Peacebuilding

Two approaches to the analysis of NGOs are adopted in this study: from the outside in and from the inside out. The first focuses on the contextual factors that shape and influence NGOs, ranging from global trends in conflict or aid provision, for example, to variations in operating environments at the micro level. The second focuses on the internal dynamics of NGOs. Although they are shaped by wider, often more powerful forces, NGOs also have agency. To understand them, one also needs to appreciate NGOs' diversity and how their individual identities, organizational structures and cultures can contribute to different types of activities and outcomes. NGOs are instrumental organizations in that they seek to get things done (or they may be used by other actors to achieve certain goals), but they are also expressive organizations in that they seek to embody a particular set of values or way of thinking about the world (Lewis, 2002: 378). These two complementary approaches are applied in this study to the analysis of NGOs, the first drawing heavily on a political economy approach, and the second adopting an organizational perspective.

In this study NGOs are situated first as actors within multi-mandate, multi-actor peace operations, and second as part of an aid system that has increasingly reorientated its goals and approaches towards conflict prevention and peace-building. Both the wider international response and the aid system which NGOs are part of are analysed through a political economy framework. An assessment of peacebuilding efforts must be built upon a solid understanding of both the political economy of conflict and the political economy of the response. Aid is not delivered into a political vacuum and nor does it come out of a political vacuum. Responses to contemporary conflicts have been shaped by perceived national interests, while aid is similarly politicized, with allocations being determined by political interests, public opinion and media images. The idea that third-party intervention in conflicts is essentially a neutral and altruistic exercise must therefore be problematized, if not altogether abandoned.

Three more terms require further clarification as they are used frequently in this study: 'intervention', the 'international community' and the 'aid regime'. First, there is some controversy over 'intervention' because of the potential width of activities the term covers, from coercive military interventions to sanctions to development assistance and humanitarian aid (ICISS, 2001: 8). This study is primarily concerned with the interventions of aid actors that have the stated purpose of protecting or assisting people at risk. Second, strictly speaking there is no 'international community', there are only international institutions (Rieff, 2002: 326), since the word 'community' implies shared values and common convictions (Weiss, 2001: 423).[16] In this study the term is used to include the broad range of intergovernmental, governmental and non-governmental organizations that have an influence on peace and security. These institutions are arenas in which member states make decisions and pursue national interests. But they are also, as Weiss (2001) argues, operational actors with a semi-independent identity capable of making choices and of doing the right or the wrong thing. Third, my focus is on the 'aid regime', a subset of actors within the international community. This term encompasses development and humanitarian actors, including the UN, multilateral and bilateral donors, the International Red Cross and Red Crescent, and international and local NGOs. A further subcategory is the 'international humanitarian regime', sometimes referred to as a 'system' or perhaps more appropriately, as Hilhorst (2003: 205) argues, a complex: 'There is no humanitarian system in the sense of an assembly of parts that fit together and feed each other with complementary roles and responsibilities. Rather one faces a humanitarian complex consisting of shifting actors, diffuse boundaries, partly conflicting interests and values, and a high level of diversity of relations, organizational forms and work styles.

NGOs are therefore just one group in a much wider family of organizations.[17] NGOs are clearly not a homogenous group. One way of subdividing them is according to their historical roots. Stoddard (2003) identifies three historical strands: the religious, the 'Dunantist' and the 'Wilsonian'. The first has its antecedents in missionary work, the second emerged from the Red Cross movement and the third comes from a largely US tradition of close identification with government policy. Another way of categorizing NGOs is according to what they do. Broadly NGOs working in the international sphere operate in four different areas of work (Anderson, 1996):

- the provision of humanitarian relief in emergencies;
- the promotion of long-term social and economic development;
- the promulgation, protection and monitoring of human rights;
- the pursuit of peace through support for conflict resolution.

Some NGOs may specialize in only one of these areas, for instance Amnesty International with its focus on human rights, while multi-mandate organizations such as Oxfam simultaneously work in several areas. Broadly, three different working modalities may be employed:

- direct intervention, that is, delivery of assistance, implementation of projects without working through intermediary organizations;
- capacity building, that is, working with and developing the capacity of individuals or intermediary organizations to sustain the effects of projects/programmes;
- advocacy, that is, influencing policy-makers and decision-makers to engender changes at the macro level.

While some NGOs may favour one particular way of working, most pursue different combinations of all three, depending on activity and context. Table 1.1 provides a typology for mapping NGOs in terms of their areas of work and ways of working. The study aims to capture a range of different types of international and local NGOs working in different areas.

Table 1.1   NGO Areas of Intervention and Modalities

	1 Relief	2 Development	3 Human rights protection/advocacy	4 Conflict resolution
Direct intervention				
Capacity-building				
Advocacy				

In practice the dividing lines between the different columns are likely to be blurred and categories merge into one another. For instance 'relief' and 'development' are not clearly bounded categories. Development agencies are frequently involved in a range of activities which span columns 2 and 3, from support for good governance to poverty alleviation.

Although the table is not meant to denote a hierarchy, as one moves from the left to right the focus on peace and conflict dynamics becomes more direct and explicit; similarly, the greater the involvement in sensitive areas such as the judiciary and the security sector, which directly impinge upon questions of sovereignty. Conversely, as one goes in the other direction the peacebuilding impacts are likely to be more indirect and to be perceived as less politically sensitive. Activities in columns 3 and 4 are likely to be high-risk, but high-opportunity. They include Track One and Track Two peace mediation, peacekeeping and security sector reform, all of which have a direct focus on peace and conflict dynamics.

Some organizations like the Quakers and Mennonites have a long history of involvement in conflict resolution and peacebuilding. However, there has been a proliferation of new actors in this field, including humanitarian organizations which have expanded their mandates and newly created niche organizations with a specific peacebuilding focus. This study includes both multi-mandate and niche NGOs.

Broadly three different approaches to conflict and peacebuilding can be identified among NGOs and donor agencies (Goodhand with Atkinson, 2001), as follows.

1. *Working around conflict.* This treats conflict as an impediment or negative externality that is to be avoided. Conflict is viewed as a constraint on development, and if any form of linkage is recognized it is the lack of development

which contributes to conflict. It is a common reflex action of many policy-makers and practitioners to argue that development by definition promotes peace (Uvin, 2002: 6).

2. *Working in conflict.* NGOs working in areas of active conflict have at-tempted to mitigate conflict-related risks and also minimize the potential for programmes to fuel or prolong conflict. Attempts have been made to conflict-proof programmes by avoiding large-scale insfrastructural projects and focusing on low-profile, quick-impact initiatives.

3. *Working on conflict.* Policies and programmes have an explicit and pri-mary focus on conflict prevention, management or resolution. This may involve a broad range of activities, though in practice much of the work focuses on rec-onciliation and human rights issues, primarily through civil society groups.

Case Studies

This research is based on fieldwork in seven conflict-affected areas. All have been affected to varying degrees by violent conflict and all have involved NGO responses to the effects and sources of conflict. But these cases were not selected as a result of a deductive approach in which ideal types of conflict were identified and then cases chosen to fit the model. Real-world research in conflict zones, which involves extended periods on the ground, rarely works like this. Case study selection was largely an inductive, iterative and to an extent opportunistic process. Although it was important to examine a range of different types of violent conflict involving contrasting peacebuilding ecolo-gies, ultimately the choice of individual cases came down to factors such as the availability of researchers with relevant skills and experience, security and access, demands from collaborating agencies, political constraints, etc. Table 1.2 provides a comparative overview of the different case study coun-tries in terms of the broad dimensions of violent conflict and intervention.

It is a truism to state that no two conflicts are alike, though this is often not sufficiently appreciated by those who intervene. Although the case study countries shared a common experience of violent conflict, this manifested itself in very different ways in each country. Each conflict had its own unique configuration of structural tensions, dynamics and actors. Each, at the time of the research, was at a different stage in the trajectory of its conflict. Broadly they could be arranged according to a bell-curve representing the continuum of peace–war–peace (Richards, 2005: 13), from structural tensions (Kyrgyzstan), to emerging organized violence (Nepal), to open warfare (Afghanistan, Sri Lanka), to frozen but unresolved conflicts (Moldova and Armenia-Azerbaijan), to post-conflict recovery (Liberia). Evidently the status of three of the cases has changed significantly since the research period. Nepal has shifted from emerging conflict to open warfare, although Sri Lanka and Afghanistan have at

Table 1.2 Summary of the Case Study Countries

Afghanistan

Dimensions of Conflict	International Peacebuilding	Aid and Conflict	NGOs and Peacebuilding
1979–2001 evolved from a Cold War proxy conflict into a regionalized civil war. 1.5 million died and 5 million became refugees. Emergence of warlordism and a war economy based on drugs, smuggling and regional power support. Virtual collapse of the Afghan state after Soviet withdrawal leads to fighting between mujahideen factions. The Taliban emerge in the ensuing vacuum, while the country becomes a sanctuary for radical Islamic groups including Al Qaeda. Following 9/11, US-led support for opposition forces leads to the fall of the Taliban. The Bonn Agreement of Dec. 2001 provides for the creation of an Afghan Interim Administration (AIA), the development of a new constitution and the holding of elections. In the context of a fragile transition from war to peace, threatened by various spoilers including neo-Taliban, Al Qaeda and regional warlords, presidential and parliamentary elections are held in 2004 and 2005.	Soviet and US support for proxies in 1980s. Geneva Accords in 1989 and Soviet withdrawal lead to the decline of Western interests and faltering UN efforts to negotiate a peace settlement. Regional states also act at various times as both spoilers and mediators. The Taliban regime is not recognized by Western states and UNSC sanctions are imposed in 1999 and 2000. After the fall of the Taliban and the signing of the Bonn Agreement, an International Security Assistance Force (ISAF) is established. But their area of operation is limited to Kabul. In parallel, a US-led coalition (Operation Enduring Freedom) continues its military operations with the objective of countering 'terrorism'. In order to address the problem of insecurity in the countryside and facilitate DDR, Provincial Reconstruction Teams (PRTs) are formed. By the end of 2004 there are 19 such teams around the country.	Pre-war aid from the Soviet Union and the US contributes to the creation of a rentier state. There are three generations of aid during the conflict: first generation—relief assistance to refugee camps and crossborder aid that is part of western 'non-lethal' assistance to the mujahideen; second generation—rehabilitation and development-oriented assistance in rural Afghanistan following Soviet withdrawal; third generation—peacebuilding and human rights, operationalized through the UN-led Strategic Framework process. After Bonn, US$4.5 billion is pledged in Tokyo in 2002 for reconstruction assistance. This is followed by a donors' conference in Berlin in 2004 at which $8.2 billion is committed. But these figures are dwarfed by the $12 billion that is spent annually by the US on ongoing military operations.	Though objectives change with each generation of aid, donor funding is primarily short-term and relief-oriented. Third-generation strategy, principally through the Strategic Framework, involves developing stronger links between the political and assistance strategies to support peacemaking and peacebuilding. UN agencies and NGOs experiment with community-based peacebuilding but impacts are limited and transitory due to lack of progress on the central political track. After the fall of the Taliban, NGOs find it increasingly difficult to operate in the south and east of the country due to insecurity. Concerns grow about the securitization of aid and the blurring of the line between humanitarianism and the military, particularly in relation to PRTs. MSF withdraws from the country in 2004. NGOs are learning to adapt to a new institutional environment in which there is a recognized government and a growing private-sector role in reconstruction activities.

Table 1.2 continued

Dimensions of Conflict	International Peacebuilding	Aid and Conflict	NGOs and Peacebuilding
		Azerbaijan-Armenia	
Southern Caucasus is linked to a wider regional conflict system. Situated on a geopolitical faultline with international and regional powers competing over strategic and economic interests, primarily oil. The Nagorno-Karabakh (NK) conflict has existed since the end of the First World War, but it only becomes a fully fledged war following the collapse of the Soviet Union and the emergence of nationalist groups in Armenia and Azerbaijan. In 1992 Armenia annexes NK which is in Azeri territory. A war ensues 1992–4, in which 20,000 are killed and close to 1 million displaced. The Bishkek protocol of 1994 establishes a ceasefire and means the creation of a de facto second Armenian state. A no-war, no-peace, 'frozen conflict' has ensued. Both are militarized but weak states, which are dominated by old elites.	Competing Russian and Western interests in the Southern Caucasus undermine efforts to negotiate peace. Partiality of external powers to negotiate peace. Partiality of external powers, e.g. US adopt sanctions against Azerbaijan so long as it maintains a blockade against Armenia. 1994, Russian-brokered ceasefire. Track One negotiations through the OSCE Minsk Group (co-chaired by Russia, the US and France). Despite a 'peace offensive' in 2000–1, followed by several rounds of peace talks in 2004–5 (the Prague Process) an agreement remains elusive. Azerbaijan argues for territorial integrity and Armenia for self-determination.	Aid provision has reflected geopolitical interests. Armenia has received roughly 50% more aid than Azerbaijan. Aid primarily focused on the goal of economic liberalization with secondary priorities of government reform, social protection and humanitarian aid. Structural reforms consolidate economic power in the hands of the elite. Arguably they indirectly impede the peace process as weak, incoherent states are less willing and less able to negotiate for peace.	NGOs are actively supported by donors such as USAID and the Soros Foundation in order to support democratization and/or work in the area of welfare provision. There is some support for Track Two processes, e.g. regional initiatives related to the media, youth, business development. But they tend to be ad hoc, involving brief encounters rather than sustained, strategic linkages. Very limited NGO activity in NK itself. Some NGOs work on longer-term questions of governance and providing citizen voice, in the belief that while the conflict is frozen this constitutes their main contribution to peacebuilding. Since 2003 a multi-NGO peacebuilding initiative has been supported by the UK government.

continues

Table 1.2 Continued

Dimensions of Conflict	International Peacebuilding	Aid and Conflict	NGOs and Peacebuilding
		Kyrgyzstan	
Conflict has been largely latent but with sporadic outbursts of armed violence, for instance, violent inter-ethnic conflict in the southern city of Osh in 1990 (500 killed) and militarized incursions from the Islamic Movement of Uzbekistan (IMU) in 1999 and 2000. Ferghana Valley in southern Kyrgyzstan an incubator of various sources of tension, including: inter-state tensions over water resources, land and borders, inter-ethnic tensions between Uzbek and Kyrgyz, north–south political conflicts, Islamic radicals, conflict over control of criminal activities including drugs and human trafficking. Political and social tensions continue to build up after flawed parliamentary elections in 2005 and mass protests lead to the ousting of President Akaev in the so-called Tulip revolution. The violent suppression of an uprising in Andijan in neighbouring Uzbekistan leads to displacement across the border and increases tensions in the south.	No widespread militarized conflict, therefore no perceived need for mediation. Number of international organizations, notably the OSCE, involved in conflict monitoring. Talks between regional governments on strengthening borders, counter-terrorism and narcotics measures. Regional security arrangements through the Shanghai Cooperation Organization. After 9/11 the geostrategic importance of the region to Russia and Western powers is heightened. The US establishes a military base in the north of the country, and the Kyrgyz government opens a new military base in the south in 2005.	Cutting-off of Soviet subsidies after 1991. Transition model of aid donors which involves a push towards rapid economic liberalization and democratization. Privatization policies create opportunities for political and economic elites. Land privatization especially destabilizing in the south. Growing focus on conflict prevention, for instance the UN Ferghana Valley programme.	Primarily civil society support, particularly from the US, for democratization, human rights, the environment. There is a growing NGO presence in the south, whose development activities are viewed by donors as a form of conflict prevention. Some niche peacebuilding NGOs with a focus on early warning and conflict resolution around resources issues such as irrigation systems and land use. In spite of accusations that NGOs were behind the Tulip revolution, to a great extent Western-funded civil society is sidelined by the events (ICG, 2005a: 19).

Table 1.2 Continued

Dimensions of Conflict	International Peacebuilding	Aid and Conflict	NGOs and Peacebuilding
		Liberia	
Pre-war roots in the patrimonial state dominated by Americo-Liberians. 1980 military coup followed by deepening economic mismanagement, corruption and political repression. This leads to the outbreak of civil war at the end of 1989, which lasts until 1996 and in which 25,000 people are killed. Charles Taylor emerges as leader of the most powerful faction, presiding over a collapsed state and a regionalized war economy. Over 200,000 conflict-related deaths and 1 million refugees, with the same figure internally displaced. Taylor is elected president in 1997 and many of the dimensions of the war economy persist into peacetime. After renewed fighting and a series of battles for Monrovia, Taylor is forced to step down in 2003. Presidential elections are held in 2005 and are won by Ellen Johnson-Sirleaf.	ECOWAS acts as mediator in a long succession of peace negotiations, including the Cotonou Agreement of July 1993 and the Abuja Accords of 1995 and 1996. Various other non-official mediation initiatives including the Inter Faith Mediation Council and The Carter Center. ECOWAS also sets up ECOMOG in 1990, which finally withdraws in 1998. Initial anti-Taylor sympathies damage its reputation as a neutral peacekeeper. UN works with ECOMOG through UNOMIL till 1997 after elections. UNSC arms embargo is imposed on Taylor because of his support for the RUF in Sierra Leone. The lack of a robust international response to the crisis in 2002–3 compels ECOWAS to intervene. A Comprehensive Peace Agreement is signed in 2003 and UNMIL (with 15,000 peacekeepers) is charged with restoring security and assisting the transitional government to prepare for elections.	Until the late 1980s the state was dependent on US development (and financial/military) assistance. Declining aid contributes to elite infighting and the outbreak of war. Specialist UN agencies and INGOs' emergency assistance programmes from 1990. Insecurity hinders aid programmes and during the peak of the conflict feeds into the war economy, leading to innovative responses by humanitarian actors, including PPHO and JPO. During the post-election phase the main dilemma is one of balancing humanitarian with rehabilitation goals. A number of donors apply aid conditionality to limit funding to Taylor's government. In 2004 at an international reconstruction conference in New York aid donors pledge $522 million.	A major humanitarian programme is mounted by NGOs during the war years. After 1997 there is an increased focus on reconciliation and peacebuilding. But the effects of such micro-level projects are limited by wider aid conditionalities. After Taylor's departure civil society organizations become increasingly vocal and active on issues related to human rights, corruption and the environment.

continues

Table 1.2 Continued

Dimensions of Conflict	International Peacebuilding	Aid and Conflict	NGOs and Peacebuilding
		Moldova	
The emergence of Moldovan-Romanian nationalism following the collapse of the Soviet Union leads to escalating tensions with the Slav population of Russian-speaking Transdniestria, the country's richest region. In 1990, backed by the Soviet 14th Army, Transdniestria secedes from Moldova. Armed clashes intensify, leading to a large-scale military battle in 1992 in which several hundred are killed and 100,000 displaced. Transdniestria remains unrecognized internationally. But like NK it is a frozen conflict, involving regional interests, notably Russia and the Ukraine, and a political elite which has a limited interest in negotiating for peace. A criminalized shadow economy develops across the Transdniestria border, which means there are strong vested interests in the status quo.	Ceasefire, brokered in 1992 with Russia and Ukraine as guarantors along with the OSCE and the US, since February 1993. International peacekeepers monitor the border. OSCE Contact Group facilitates mediation efforts (Tracks One and Two). In the Moscow Memorandum of May 1997, Moldova agrees to the eventual formation of a common state, but there is subsequently limited progress towards this proposal. In November 1999 the Istanbul Declaration commits Russia to removing or destroying Russian military equipment and ammunition from Transdniestria. In 2003 a Russian attempt to break the deadlock, the Kozak Memorandum, founders due to disagreements over the proposed constitutional set-up and Russia's continued military presence in Transdniestria.	The economy has fallen to one-third of the pre-independence level. International policy has arguably played a role in this impoverishment. IFI structural adjustment policies have contributed to high indebtedness, state capture and the erosion of safety nets. Aid has been unevenly distributed, heightening tensions with regions like Gaguauzia. World Bank has no specific strategy towards Transdniestria. Slow realization that there are strong links between conflict, corruption, bad governance and poverty, leading donors to place a greater emphasis on social protection, poverty and governance.	There is a growing, though relatively embryonic, LNGO sector, with INGOs primarily involved in service delivery and welfare provision. There are some Track Two activities through civil society, notably MICOM and JCDC, an INGO and LNGO respectively, which have supported work with parliamentarians, including study visits to Northern Ireland. But generally, links to the Track One process have been limited. A few isolated Track Three initiatives, for instance EU/TACIS bridge-building programme between Moldova and Transdniestria. Like NK, there has been limited international support for civil society in Transdniestria.

Table 1.2 Continued

Dimensions of Conflict	International Peacebuilding	Aid and Conflict	NGOs and Peacebuilding
		Nepal	
The Maoist insurgency is rooted in long-standing grievances, the result of political and socio-economic exclusion and heightened by the inability of democratically elected governments to deliver on their promises. The 'People's War' is declared in 1996 by the Maoists. The insurgency escalates, with its epicentre in the mid-west, which in turn generates growing state violence. A state of emergency is declared in 2000 and the Royal Nepalese Army takes over the counter-insurgency functions of the police. In 2001 Crown Prince Dependra murders his father, King Birendra, and most of the members of his immediate family. The King's brother, Gyanendra, accedes to the throne. In 2001 an interim ceasefire is declared but lasts only four months. By 2004 up to 9,000 have been killed (more than 5,000 in 2003–4). Large swathes of the country are controlled by Maoists and widespread human rights abuses are committed by both sides. A complex three-sided struggle emerges which involves the Maoists, the palace and parliament. A royal coup in February 2005 marks the latest stage since the outbreak of the conflict of the systematic dismantling of democracy (ICG, 2005b: 3).	The Nepalese government resists offers of external mediation, but lacks the internal political stability to negotiate a settlement. Initially, international donors continue providing development aid and military assistance to the government, in spite of the resurgence of an authoritarian monarchy and the growing militarization of the state. Though there has been no direct international mediation, increased pressure from Indian, US and European officials is thought to have been a significant factor in bringing both parties to the negotiating table. A ceasefire holds for seven months in 2003, but it subsequently breaks down as the Maoists' demands for a Constituent Assembly are turned down. This is followed by another three-month ceasefire declared by the Maoists in September 2005 that again breaks down. In April 2006 mass demonstrations against palace rule lead to the King retreating from direct rule and to the restoration of parliament. The Maoists subsequently call a ceasefire, and talks between them and the political parties begin over plans for elections to a constituent assembly.	Historically, a highly aid-dependent economy. Development assistance has contributed to corruption and uneven development patterns, concentrated in the Kathmandu valley, feeding growing grievances. Rural development projects outside the capital, such as the USAID Rapti programme, raise expectations but create a thin layer of wealthy beneficiaries (Lieten, 2002: 435). As the conflict escalates, the large multilateral and bilateral aid programmes implemented through governmental partners are forced to withdraw from conflict-affected areas. In many areas the state no longer has a presence and the role of NGOs as service providers becomes increasingly important. Some of the European donors are vocal in their displeasure at the suspension of democracy, and a number of them cut or reduce aid programmes to the government. There is also a freeze of military aid to the government.	Growth of civil society activism and the NGO sector following the restoration of the multiparty system in 1990. But the lion's share of funding is funnelled through development NGOs, which up until 2000 tend to be conflict-blind. After the conflict escalates, increased efforts are made to adapt programmes so that they are more conflict-sensitive. Human rights NGOs and activists become an important conduit to the Maoists and in 2001 a nongovernmental peace team facilitates talks. There is also a growing peace movement in society, but its impact is limited by its fragmented and Kathmandu-centric nature. However, in 2005 following the royal coup, demonstrations in Kathmandu are led by the Citizen's Movement for Democracy and Peace (CMDP), making a powerful statement against autocracy, royal or Maoist (ICG, 2005b: 6).

continues

Table 1.2 Continued

Dimensions of Conflict	International Peacebuilding	Aid and Conflict	NGOs and Peacebuilding
		Sri Lanka	
Structural roots of conflict in the colonial and post-colonial state. Following independence the state becomes progressively 'Sinhalized', reflecting the interests of the majority group. Uneven development patterns lead to growing grievances and challenges to the state in the form of two Marxist/Sinhala nationalist (JVP) uprisings in 1971 and again in 1987–90. 1983 marks the outbreak of the secessionist conflict with the LTTE fighting for a separate Tamil homeland in the northeast. 120,000 are killed as a result of the JVP uprisings and secessionist conflicts. There are three phases of conflict, interspersed with fragile ceasefires and peace talks. The fourth and latest round of peace talks begins in 2002, but breaks down the following year. However, a fragile ceasefire continues to hold in spite of changes of government and the emergence of an LTTE splinter group in the east. Trust between the two sides is further undermined by their failure to reach an agreement on a post-tsunami reconstruction mechanism.	Notwithstanding the failed IPKF of 1987–9, the Sri Lankan government manages to resist international intervention, preferring to treat the conflict as an internal terrorist problem. But direct mediation and peace talks fail on four occasions (Bhutan, 1984; Indian Peace-Keeping Accord, 1987; Colombo, 1989; Jaffna, 1994). By 2002 the conflict has reached a hurting stalemate and both sides agree to an internationally monitored ceasefire and Norwegian-facilitated peace talks. Six rounds of talks are held, but after breaking down in 2003, there are no more direct negotiations. Track Two activities continue and help to keep channels between the two sides open. But a change of government and the absence of cross-party unity in the south mean that the requisite settlement stability is lacking.	International donors have historically supported large-scale, state-led projects such as the Mahawelli dam. Such projects tended to sharpen inter-group and core–periphery tensions. The liberalization of the economy after 1977 exacerbated uneven development processes, with the northeast and south falling further behind the southwest region. Conflict and donors' responses to it further widen these disparities. Although the south continues to receive development aid, assistance to the northeast is limited to humanitarian projects. This begins to change before the ceasefire, with the World Bank supporting reconstruction activities in the conflict-affected areas, and accelerates in the aftermath of the ceasefire. But major projects are held back, because of the lack of agreement between the LTTE and the government on the institutional modalities for reconstruction. In June 2005 aid donors pledge nearly \$3 billion for post-tsunami reconstruction.	A strong and vibrant NGO sector in the south focusing on a range of issues including development, human rights, political reform and advocacy. Because of the conflict and limited political space in the northeast, there is less scope for independent LNGOs. During the conflict NGO programmes are broadly divided between those delivering humanitarian and rehabilitation projects to the northeast and those working on development or human rights and policy issues in the south. During the 1990s there is a growing peace lobby in civil society, including the National Peace Council and a number of faith-based organizations, attempting to build links between the north and south. After the 2002 ceasefire, peace groups, with external assistance, further expand their activities.

least notionally become post-conflict. It is also possible to identify a spectrum of conflict in terms of the intensity and destructiveness of the violence, from inter-household and inter-communal violence, to widespread criminality and looting, to low-level skirmishes, to setpiece battles involving regular armies.[18] It is not possible to draw precise boundaries between different forms of violence, both within and between countries. For example, the Afghan conflict is part of a wider regional conflict formation whose faultlines stretch westwards into the Caucasus and connect with the conflict in Azerbaijan.

All the conflicts have been subject to international interventions of varying kinds, though for much of their life cycles they have been forgotten conflicts. Apart from Afghanistan in the 1980s and after 9/11, they have received limited international attention. The nature of the conflict and the framework of international intervention provide the backdrop and set the parameters for NGO interventions. The history and responses of NGOs have differed as a result of the varying challenges set by individual contexts. It is hoped that through studying and comparing NGOs' responses in conflictual environments, one can move towards identifying how best to match responses to contexts.

Structure of the Book

The book is structured around an analytical framework that was developed as part of a DFID Conflict Assessment project. This conflict assessment framework contains three key elements: an analysis of conflict; a mapping of policy responses with a particular focus on aid; and an analysis of strategies and options for working in and on conflict (Goodhand, Hulme and Lewer, 2000a). This is illustrated in Figure 1.1.

This provides a framework for systematically examining conflict responses and strategies for working more effectively in or on conflict. This framework deliberately places NGOs within a wider context in order to understand where NGOs fit in relation to conflict writ large and the international response. This should lead to a more realistic assessment of both their potential and limitations in relation to peacebuilding. The book is divided into three sections and eight chapters. The first section focuses on conflict analysis (stage A), the second on

Figure 1.1 The Stages of Conducting a Conflict Assessment

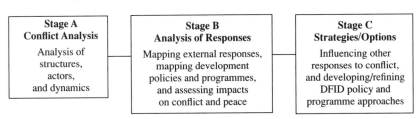

Stage A Conflict Analysis	Stage B Analysis of Responses	Stage C Strategies/Options
Analysis of structures, actors, and dynamics	Mapping external responses, mapping development policies and programmes, and assessing impacts on conflict and peace	Influencing other responses to conflict, and developing/refining DFID policy and programme approaches

responses (stage B) and the third on possible strategies and options (stage C). The first section selectively examines different theories of conflict (Chapter 2) and is followed by a comparative analysis of armed conflicts, drawing from the seven cases (Chapter 3). The second section begins with an overview of international engagement with war over the last 15 years, and positions NGOs within this emerging model of intervention (Chapter 4). This is followed by an examination of NGOs' impacts on conflict and peacebuilding processes (Chapter 5). In the light of these findings, the exogenous factors which limit or enhance the scope for peacebuilding are examined (Chapter 6), focusing on the nature of peace processes and international aid regimes. The final chapter in this section moves inside NGOs to explore the internal factors that determine organizational effectiveness and the potential for NGOs to build peace (Chapter 7). The third section examines the implications of the foregoing analysis in terms of improving policy and practice. Three key challenges are highlighted: those of understanding, funding and action (Chapter 8).

2

Armed Conflict in Theory

This chapter first examines the costs and characteristics of violent conflict. This is followed by a selective overview of some of the most important theories on the origins and dynamics of war. Finally, some of the implications for policy-makers and practitioners are highlighted.

Contemporary Conflicts: Characteristics and Costs

> In absolute terms—and probably per capita as well—the twentieth century visited more collective violence on the world than any century of the previous ten thousand years. (Tilly, 2003: 55)

Armed conflict patterns are being mapped continuously by several research projects.[1] Although there is no universal agreement, since different projects have adopted different classification systems and forms of data analysis, there is a level of consensus. First, as Tilly (2003) notes, the last century was an extremely violent one. Between 1900 and 1999 there were about 250 new wars, international or civil, in which battle deaths averaged 1,000 per year. These wars caused about 1 million deaths per year (Tilly, 2003: 55). Between 1946 and 1991 the number of state-based armed conflicts trebled (HSC, 2005: 3). Second, contrary to the popular view, the numbers of armed conflicts globally declined during the 1990s. As already mentioned, the occurrence of war declined by more than 40 per cent after the early 1990s. Between 1991 and 2004, 28 armed struggles for self-determination started or restarted, while 43 were contained or ended. There were just 25 armed secessionist conflicts under way in 2004, the lowest number since 1976 (HSC, 2005: 1), whereas in 1950 nearly 700,000 were killed in armed conflicts around the world, compared with 20,000 in 2002 (ibid.: 4). Third, the overwhelming majority of conflicts since the Second World War have been in the third world. Eight out of 10 of the world's poorest countries are suffering from or have recently suffered from large-scale violent conflict (Stewart, 2002: 342). Armed conflict has declined to historically low levels in Europe, the Middle East and the Americas. In Asia it has fallen but remains at a high level, while in sub-Saharan Africa there has been a sustained increase.

At the turn of the 21st century more people were being killed in wars in sub-Saharan Africa than in the rest of the world (HSC, 2005: 4). Fourth, most armed conflicts have been primarily intra-state or have possessed an important intra-state dimension. Of the 96 armed conflicts which took place between 1989 and 1996 only five were between states (Wallensteen and Sollenberg, 1998). Fifth, although the number of armed conflicts have decreased, in the main it has been the minor conflicts that have ended. Of the 24 armed conflicts active in 2000 at least 17 date their origins to the period before 1989. The trend, according to Wallensteen and Sollenberg (1998), is one of fewer conflicts but more complexity. The degree of complexity is a function of the conflict duration, negative experiences of peacemaking and the regionalized dimensions of many conflicts. Sixth, such long-term conflicts are likely to also have long-term costs for the affected countries. 'Poor societies are at risk of falling into no-exit cycles of conflict in which ineffective governance, societal warfare, humanitarian crises, and the lack of development perpetually chase one another.' (Gurr, Marshall and Khosla, 2001: 13). Moreover, in the case of regional conflict complexes the costs are often widely spread, with neighbouring countries suffering from the spillover effects.

The costs of conflict are both direct and indirect. The direct impacts, including battlefield deaths, disablement and displacement, have long-lasting costs for societies. However, many more people die from wars as a result of lack of basic medical services, the destruction of rural life and transport, and the collapse of the state, than from direct battlefield deaths. Indirect deaths receive little media attention as it is impossible to distinguish them from deaths caused by malnutrition and disease (HSC, 2005: 7).The costs of conflict are not accidental: wars involve the systematic and deliberate violation of individual and group rights to produce and secure an adequate livelihood (Macrae and Zwi, 1994: 21).

According to Stewart (1993: 357) between 1950 and 1990 around 15 million deaths were caused (directly or indirectly) by war in developing countries. The mean GDP per head in countries affected by civil war at any point in time from 1960 to 1999 is less than half that of countries with no civil war experience, and countries with no war experience grow much faster than war-affected countries (Sambanis, 2003: 1). The effects of violent conflict are likely to be experienced long after the fighting has stopped. Societies which have experienced violent conflict are in a sense geared up for war, and are more vulnerable to future violence than pre-conflict societies with similar risk factors (Collier, 2000: 18).

A Framework for Analysing War

In order to build peace one must go some way towards being able to answer the question of why people go to war. To what extent does academic theory help us answer this question? Broadly, contemporary research on conflict tends to be divided between studies which have adopted a quantitative econometric approach—involving multiple countries and the identification of risk factors which leads to general prescriptive advice—or a qualitative approach involving individual country studies, leading to detailed diagnosis of individual cases (Mack, 2002). Both approaches face methodological problems: the lack of reliable data; the problem of establishing appropriate counterfactuals and the difficulty of disentangling the effects of conflict from other forces active at the same time (Luckham et al., 2001). It has been argued that conflict itself has fundamentally changed and therefore research approaches and their associated theories of conflict may no longer be relevant. Although the simplistic distinction between old wars and new wars can be questioned, there may be some truth in the idea that contemporary conflicts provide new challenges for those seeking to understand and respond to them. In a sense this has led to a crisis of theory as well as a crisis of practice. Findings on the underlying causes of conflict often contradict one another. Even when similar methodologies or data sets are used, researchers may come to different conclusions. Some, for example, have found a high correlation between inequality and conflict, while others have found it to be insignificant. The same can be said about a number of different factors such as democracy, ethnic fragmentation or levels of poverty. Therefore contemporary research often generates contradictory findings. This makes theory confusing for policy-makers and practitioners. Many questions remain unanswered even at a theoretical level. As a consequence policy-makers and practitioners often continue to rely on rules of thumb.

In the rest of this chapter some of the principal theories of war are examined. The DFID conflict assessment methodology provides the analytical framework. This involves examining three elements in detail:

- the structures or the underlying sources or root causes of violent conflict;
- the actors or conflict stakeholders and their motivations, incentive systems and capacities;
- the dynamics of violent conflict, including the key trends, triggers and potential scenarios.

Each of these three areas has its own set of internal divisions, as shown in Table 2.1. This framework is used to structure the analysis below.

Conflict can rarely be understood in terms of one simple cause, which makes it critical to recognize connections and overlaps between sources of tension in different areas and at different levels. Although recent writing on conflict questions the relevance of 'root cause analysis' (Duffield, 2001), it is still important to start from an adequate understanding of the historical and structural antecedents of violent conflicts (Cliffe and Luckham, 1999). The following section provides a selective overview of theories and debates that have particular relevance to this study.

Table 2.1 A Framework for Conflict Assessment

Structures	Actors	Dynamics
Analysis of long-term factors underlying conflict: • security • political • economic • social	Analysis of conflict actors: • interests • motivations • relations • capacities • peace agendas	Analysis of: • long-term trends of conflict • triggers for increased violence • capacities for managing conflict • likely future conflict scenarios

Structural Dimensions of Conflict

Security Dimensions

Analysis and writing on hard security issues have traditionally been the preserve of international relations specialists, security analysts or military advisers. This has changed as notions of security have broadened, thus opening up the field to a range of new actors, including specialists in peace research and development studies as well as development donors and NGOs that draw explicit links between security, development and peacebuilding.

Broadly, three different but interconnected notions of security can be identified (Freedman, 2004). First, there is the traditional idea of national security, in other words, what dangers threaten the survival of the state? Second, there is security as international order, based on the conviction that decisions taken collectively are likely to be better judged and carry greater legitimacy. Third, there is security conceptualized more broadly as justice or human security, as defined in Chapter 1. These different notions of security can be seen also as values or objectives, the relative weightings of which have changed according to structural changes in the international system as well as particular events (ibid.: 249).

There is usually a hierarchy of values when it comes to security, with national security trumping order and justice. As Bobbitt (2002: 7) notes, it is the 'axiomatic requirement of the State to survive by putting its security objectives first'. Whether we are talking about dynastic rulers or modern states, the struggle for survival and protection against external threats (perceived or real) take precedence. Insecurity and the changing demands of war were the motive forces for the creation of states (Tilly, 1985; Bobbitt, 2002). States emerged and sustained themselves through success in war, which depended on mastering the appropriate techniques, including the weapons systems and financial underpinning (Howard, 2002: xvi). Security was achieved through military innovation, but as states proliferated the question of international order became increasingly important. The Peace of Westphalia in 1648 addressed the need for a common structure for reciprocal acceptance and mutual recognition, by constituting a 'society of states' (ibid.: xvii). The two golden rules of the sovereignty game are non-intervention and reciprocity, the former meaning the right to conduct the affairs of the state without external interference and the latter involving the symmetry of giving and taking for mutual benefit (Sorensen, 2000: 10).

Those studying questions of national security and international order tend to come from a Western ethical tradition of political realism and utilitarianism. Realists, applying the analytical tools of power politics, focus on the international or systemic level. Their core assumption is that relations within this system are characterized by anarchy, meaning the absence of an overarching global government; essentially the social contract that at least nominally ensures accountability in the domestic sphere does not exist at the international level. The core problem of the Westphalian state system is seen to be the so-called security dilemma. This is the tendency for states in a context of uncertainty to defect from cooperative arrangements if they perceive other states' security preparations as threatening (Cerny, 2000). As Mack (2002: 516) notes, the 'tragedy of anarchy is that states acting both rationally and defensively in pursuit of security often achieve its opposite.' Whether international order is more precarious in the post–Cold War context has been much debated. Cerny (2000: 645), for example, argues that new sources of uncertainty have affected the underlying logic of the security dilemma, with defection becoming a more viable option, which may involve defection from above, for example, US unilateralism or the actions of rogue states, or defection from below, from substate, transnational actors, including international terrorists.

Policy prescriptions which derive from this type of analysis have traditionally tended to be top-down and assume that there is a well-defined leadership which acts in predictable ways. Game theory logic may be applied to model the conflict and possible solutions to it. This may be a point of convergence between realists and writers from a peace studies background such as Zartmann (1996), since both focus on the rational calculations of the conflicting parties and how these might be influenced using sanctions and rewards. Finding a formula for peace or a way out is more likely when there is a hurting stalemate and the costs of continuing war outweigh the benefits of peace.

Realism continues to focus most of its attention on the interstate system, even though interstate wars constitute less than 10 per cent of the total number of armed conflicts (Mack, 2002: 516). Therefore as a discipline it may have limited utility when it comes to explaining the causes of intra-state conflicts. So in recent years the analytical focus has shifted towards questions of security and insecurity at the domestic level. Against wider concerns about weak and failing states, there has been a growing interest in first, the security sector and its relationship to questions of governance and development, and second, a broadening of the notion of security beyond a narrow focus on physical violence. Development policy has traditionally steered clear of questions about the military because they touch upon the sensitive questions of sovereignty. The need for states to be able to concentrate the means of coercion and have strong policing capabilities has been under-recognized by development actors. Earlier research in this area tended to focus on questions around military expenditure (MILEX) and its relationship to development and underdevelopment and the likelihood of violent conflict. There is now a growing body of research which analyses processes of state failure (as discussed in the next section) and the nature of non-state military formations. This work is beginning to generate insights about warlordism, fighter mobilization and non-state transnational networks (Reno, 2000; Kalyvas, 2000; Keen, 1998; Duffield, 2001). In spite of this increased interest, more is known about how the state deals with the non-state than vice versa. The growing focus on the internal affairs of weak and failing states reflects what Sorensen (2000) describes as a shift in the regulative rules of sovereignty. Arguably in an international system in which there is a diminished degree of substantial statehood (see next section), the golden rules of non-interference and reciprocity are seen to be more conditional.

The most recent growth area is research on terrorism and the globalization of insecurity. The attacks of 9/11 brought out in sharp relief the interconnectedness of security and insecurity. No country or region can be dismissed as irrelevant to security, particularly since the threats emerged not from strong states, but from weak states (Freedman, 2004). But it is as well to remember that although international terrorism is the focus of enormous attention, it has killed fewer than 1,000 people per year on average over the past 30 years (HSC, 2005: 6). The GWOT has meant that small wars are viewed less in terms of their local causes, than their relations to global conflict formations, in much the same way as local disputes were infused with superpower rivalries during the Cold War period. As Freedman (2004: 258) notes, victim status is becoming a prized commodity for insecure regimes looking for external support: 'will a cry of terrorism be used as a cry of communism was in the past, by inadequate and repressive governments to suppress any inconvenient dissent?'.

In the face of the real and imagined threat of terrorism, there has been a reassertion of state power. The war on terror has recast the relationship between security and justice, as the US administration chose to focus on security to the exclusion of order and social justice (Freedman, 2004). Some argue that there was a brief interlude in the 1990s when human security and social justice provided the normative underpinning for peacebuilding and the international order (Tschirgi, 2004). The GWOT appears to have changed the normative climate; with the shift in emphasis from human security to homeland security, peacebuilding increasingly looks like an imperial rather than a cosmopolitan endeavour. As Howard (2002: xviii) argues, we are living in a unipolar world not seen since the Roman empire. Hirst, among others, questions whether empire can be the solution to the disorder caused by anti-systemic terrorism and he draws a striking parallel between earlier colonial struggles and the contemporary situation in Iraq:

... colonial regimes were difficult to legitimate at either end of the chain of imperial power: democratic publics in the metropoles were unwilling to bear the costs of colonial policing and war against insurgents, and colonized peoples sought self determination rather than a foreign rule, that was at best patronizing, and at worst brutal. Little has changed, except that the rhetoric 'legitimating empire' has now shifted to 'nation building'. (Hirst, 2005: 47)

Political Dimensions

State formation and the social contract. Social stability is seen to be based on a hypothetical social contract between the people and the state (Stewart, 2002: 343). Tilly (1985) examined the link between the processes of warmaking and statebuilding and the forging of this social contract, based upon a historical analysis of European states. Developing military capability and waging war were central to the task of establishing a monopoly of force over a territory, protecting borders and generating revenue.[2] Gradually, due to the fiscal demands of war, institutions developed in order to mediate between the rulers and the ruled. These enabled the ruler to raise taxes but at the expense of his autonomy. Therefore checks and balances, which characterize the social contract, emerged as a result of the ruler's need to wage war. People accept state authority so long as the state delivers services and provides reasonable economic conditions. Without political legitimacy there can be no social contract: 'Legitimacy must cloak the violence of the State, or the State ceases to be' (Bobbitt, 2002: 17).

It took four or five centuries for European states to establish themselves by concentrating the means of coercion. Unfortunately for third-world statebuilders, they cannot afford the luxury of prolonging the traumatic and costly experience of statemaking (Ayoob, 1995: 41).[3] What are considered to be the norms of civilized state behaviour including the human rights of individuals and groups, in many contexts may contradict the imperatives of statemaking. States produce rights and rightlessness, deciding who is included and who is excluded (Duffield, 2004). As Clapham (2002: 791) notes: 'It is salutary to remember that core states of the modern global system that rejoice in peace, democracy and high levels of human welfare were themselves for the most part created and for a long period maintained in ways that fell far short of the standards now expected by that system.'[4] The institutions of modern states were founded on, and continue to depend upon, violence; as Foucault (2003) argues, politics may be understood as the continuation of war by other means.

State-building led to the 'bifurcation of violence', with the monopolization of coercion by the state and the consequent decline of societal violence (Tilly, 1985, 2003). The wars of the 19th and early 20th centuries were about state-based violence. Arguably, however, in the late 20th century, the state's monopoly of force was weakened by globalization and non-state violence has again become more prevalent (see below). This is particularly the case in what Tilly (2003) calls 'low-capacity undemocratic regimes'. High-capacity regimes, whether democratic or authoritarian, generally leave little space for disloyal oppositions to accumulate military power. They monitor, contain, co-opt or destroy nongovernmental specialists in violence (Tilly, 2003: 67).

International policies may have a significant influence on state–society relations and the development of a social contract. External aid flows represent a form of unearned income which may decrease the incentives for governments to tax their populations. As Moore (2000: 3) notes, 'bad governance (political underdevelopment) is made not born and "we" (in the North) play a part in creating and maintaining it.'

State failure and crises in governance. A defining feature of contemporary wars is state contestation or failure. This is part cause and part consequence of the armed conflict. The causes of wars 'are not only to be found in the issues around which conflicts are politicized, such as ethnicity or regional identity, but also in the prior trend towards a failure of governance' (Cliffe and Luckham, 1999: 32). State failure and state collapse are not necessarily the same things. For example, the Rwandan genocide may have been a manifestation of state failure but not state collapse, since the regime was able to mobilize groups and organize the killing with terrifying efficiency.[5] Milliken and Krause (2002) argue that failing states are those which are unable to perform their three core functions of providing security and protection, representation and legitimacy, and wealth and welfare. The lack of effective statehood has led to what Jackson (1990) has termed quasi-states in the third world, which are the precursors of failed or collapsed states, potent examples being Somalia, Afghanistan and the Democratic Republic of Congo (DRC). An emphasis on state failure, however, fails to grasp that certain groups may have helped the state to fail and may have derived benefits from its weakness or elimination. As Reno (2000: 4) argues, shadow states use conflict as a tool of governance: 'a shadow state ruler will minimize his provision of public goods to a population. Removing public goods, like security or economic stability, that are otherwise enjoyed by all, irrespective of their economic or political station, is done to encourage individuals to seek the ruler's personal favour to seek exception from these conditions.'

Defects in or the absence of democratic processes are highlighted by a number of writers as an underlying cause of conflict. Democracy is seen by many as a conflict prophylactic.[6] Rummel (1995) argues that democracies are unlikely to go to war with one another and they have the lowest levels of internal violence.[7] However, research findings on the links between democracy and conflict are contradictory and contested. Hegre (2003), for example, found that democracy is correlated to peace only in highly developed countries and goes on to argue that poor democracies tend to be unstable and cannot provide effective conflict resolution mechanisms. Snyder (2000), like Mann (1999), points to the dark side of democracy, arguing that democratizing countries may be prone to war; it is the transitional or middling states which are neither autocracies nor inclusive democracies which have the highest levels of violence.[8] What this debate on democracy and conflict does tell us is that it is best approached by examining specific contexts at particular times. Snyder's analysis of democratization and violence in the former Yugoslavia, for instance, highlights the nature of the regime and the political system. These in turn shaped the opportunity structures that guided the choices of different ethno-political leaders. Therefore, one has to look below the level of the state at the underlying norms, material interests and the real politics of elites and their followers.

Globalization and conflict. Globalization can be defined in many ways, but it is taken here to mean the ascendancy of transnational activity at both supranational and substate level and the increasing political and economic interdependence between states. The idea that today's wars are new in the sense that they are fundamentally different from the old wars of the Cold War period has gained currency in recent years (Kaldor, 1999; Duffield, 2001).[9] It is argued that contemporary wars are linked to the processes of declining nation-state power and the intensification of transnational commerce. First, the end of the Cold War period and the effects of globalization have led, particularly in the South, to a decline in the competence and capacity of the nation-state. Second, today's conflicts are characterized by expanding networks of parallel (illegal) and grey (semi-legal) economic activities. Such networks are significant in their size and reach: 'It is not a study of individual people operating in the shadows, but a study of vast networks of people who move goods and services worldwide—networks that broker power comparable to and in many cases greater than a number of the world's states' (Nordstrom, 2000: 36). While liberalization may not have caused these new forms of instability, market deregulation has made it easier for warring parties to develop the grey or parallel international linkages necessary for survival. In today's wars domestic and international relations become analytically integral to one another (Duffield, 2001).

The literature on new wars tends to exaggerate the hollowing out of contemporary states, and perhaps underestimates the continuities between the Cold War and the post–Cold War world period. As Kiely (2005: 161) notes, there has been an 'exaggeration of state power in the past, accompanied by an underestimation of state power in the present'. Furthermore, just because liberal states now use their power to promote the market, this does not mean that the market must hollow out their power (Hirst, 2005: 42). Non-state actors such as corporations or NGOs, which are supposedly supplanting the state, actually need state power, whether it is to bail them out of a financial crisis or to enforce human rights legislation. Territorial states are still the key locus that ties together the various levels of governance and, according to Hirst, remain our main source of accountability and democracy in a complex system of governance.

Although the new wars literature perhaps exaggerates their newness, it does yield some important insights. It shows that conflict is not the irrational breakdown of societies and economies: rather 'it is the re-ordering of society in particular ways. In wars we see the creation of a new type of political economy, not simply a destruction of the old one' (Keen, 1998: 7). The value of such political economy perspectives is that they highlight that violence may serve important functions and confer benefits on certain groups and individuals. A political economy approach is essentially about analysing the production and distribution of power, wealth and destitution during violent conflict, in order to explore the motives and responsibility of those involved (Le Billon, 2000: 1). This encompasses the domestic and international dimensions of conflict. Arguably a political economy approach has not gone far enough in examining the regional dimensions of armed conflicts. Civil wars have important contagion and diffusion effects (Pugh and Cooper, 2004). Regional-conflict complexes are characterized by crossborder spillover of violence, together with the empowerment of borderlands as sanctuaries for combatants and nurseries for recruits, and also as centres of shadow economic activity (ibid.: 2).[10]

Economic Dimensions

Marxism and war; the disruptive transition to capitalism. Writers with a Marxist perspective such as Scott (1976), Moore (1966) and Wolf (1971) have yielded valuable insights about the causes of war. Their approach is based upon an analysis of material interests, processes of capital accumulation, class formation and, importantly, class disintegration. Historically, processes of development involving a hesitant transition to capitalism have rarely been smooth and conflict-free. They have involved bitter struggles between competing groups over material interests. The language of development is often used to legitimize dominance over marginal groups. Such processes have been accompanied by violent conflict with war-making often being the midwife for wider economic and societal changes. Such a tragic view of history, that violent conflict may be an inevitable and necessary phase in the transition to capitalist society, challenges the liberal assumption that all good things come together, or in other words, that the diffusion of capitalism and liberal democracy will lead to the Kantian ideal of perpetual peace. Such views are ahistorical, although they are deeply ingrained in the thinking and policy prescriptions of the international financial institutions (IFIs). Finally, a Marxist approach also helps us understand capital and capitalism as an international phenomenon, something that is often missing from some contemporary analytical approaches which tend to focus almost exclusively on the internal causes of civil wars. None of the so-called civil wars can be explained without reference to international capital linkages (Cramer, 2003).

Orthodox economics and war. Orthodox economics has arrived rather late on the field of conflict (Cramer, 2002: 1845). Economists saw conflict as irrational and temporary: 'Economists… often associated sectarian conflicts with pre-capitalism and expect these to fade away with the development of markets, modern technology and capitalist institutions' (Bardhan, 1997). Conflict in a sense was treated as a 'black box', an irrational but temporary distortion that was likely to be alleviated through trade and industry. There is a level of con-currence among researchers that economic growth is an important predictor of violent conflict. All other things being equal, as GDP rises, the incidence of war falls (World Bank, 2003). However, there is a paradox in the fact that although income per head has risen in most of the developing world over the last 50 years, the number of armed conflicts—at least until the early 1990s—has increased steadily (Mack, 2002: 521). Economic growth therefore cannot be relied on to remedy the problem of civil war.

Broadly, economic analyses of war can be divided into models which focus on structural conditions and inequality and models which draw upon rational choice theory. As a shorthand, the former are referred to as grievance-based models and the latter as greed-based models.

Structural conditions: grievance models. It is argued that uneven develop-ment processes lead to inequality, entitlement[11] failures and poverty. Recent research has extended Sen's (1981) work on entitlements, which tended to marginalize the role of war and violence in its analysis of famine, by not rec-ognizing the relationship between famine and violations of legality. Stewart and Fitzgerald (2001) added the concept of 'extra-legal' entitlements (commodities acquired outside existing legal frameworks), including for instance resources gained through raiding, protection rackets, trade in illicit commodities and the diversion of relief supplies.[12]

The erosion of people's entitlements contributes to growing grievances, particularly when they coincide with ethnic, religious, language or regional boundaries—'horizontal inequalities' or 'relative deprivation' as Stewart (1993) and Gurr (1970) respectively call them. These underlying grievances may ex-plode into open conflict when triggered by external shocks (such as a sudden change in terms of trade) and mobilized by political entrepreneurs. Writers on the economic antecedents of conflict tend to highlight the role of historical develop-ment patterns, for instance colonial and post-colonial development strategies which led to the marginalization of certain groups.[13] These structural factors are exacerbated by particular domestic and international policies: for example, state bias towards certain groups—such as land colonization and education policies in Sri Lanka which ethnicized entitlements and heightened interethnic tensions—or state repression, as for instance in Latin America (Booth, 1991).[14] Furthermore, international policies, such as privatization and trade liberalization, may lead to the exclusion of certain groups and generate grievance.

Poverty is seen to be a significant factor in this model. As Geremek (1973, cited in Hobsbawm, 2001: 10) notes, the rhythm of hunger determines the rhythm of brigandage. Similarly, in Sierra Leone a chronic shortage of employment opportunities was matched by a contraction in educational opportunities, leading many youths to turn to rebellion as a shortcut to wealth and status (Keen, 1998). The ideology of development and modernity sit dangerously alongside a failure to deliver it (Keen, 2002: 7). Few argue for a direct causal relationship between poverty and conflict, but many see it as a powerful predisposing factor, and the combination of horizontal inequalities, a failing state, disaffected elites and external shocks is likely to be a combustible cocktail.

Rational choice: greed models. Rational choice models of conflict build upon the idea of players making choices: basically actors will choose conflict when it is more profitable. War happens when the expected utility of war is greater than the expected utility of peace.[15] As Hirshleifer (1994) argues, 'appropriation' may be favoured over 'production' by rent-seeking rebels. In this model disputes are generated by opportunities rather than objective grievances. According to Collier (2000), although conflicts may generate loud discourses of grievance, they are actually motivated by greed—in other words it is the feasibility of predation which determines the risk of conflict. For rebel leaders, war offers opportunities to profit on the margins. For the poor war involves low opportunity costs: they have a comparative advantage in violence as they have nothing to lose (Hirshleifer, 1994).

Grievance-based models tend to be state-centric, whereas greed-based models are rebel-centric. Rebel groups face three hurdles: finance, group mobilization and group cohesion. First, access to primary commodities, such as diamonds or timber, provides military groups with finance. Collier and Hoeffler (1998) found that a typical developing country whose exports are heavily dependent on primary commodities is 20 times more likely to experience violent conflict than one that has no primary commodity exports. Second, to mobilize, rebels need a cause. Rebels therefore generate a loud discourse of grievance around poverty and injustice in order to rally the masses. Third, rebels use social capital, based for instance on ethnicity or clan, to build group identity and cohesion. As Collier (2000) argues, rebels generate group grievance by manufacturing both the grievance and the group.

According to this model, today's wars have been freed from ideology. Keen (1998), adapting Clausewitz's famous dictum, argues that today's internal wars may now be better understood as the continuation of economics by other means. If economic agendas and criminality are the framework for understanding today's wars, this leads to a very different set of policy choices from grievance-based models. 'The finance of war is often a decisive factor in who wins, and therefore international action to reduce war finance and increase its cost may be one way to encourage peace' (Addison, Le Billon and Murshed, 2001: 962). A critical question, however, is whether people go to war to loot or loot in order to keep fighting.

The debate on whether conflicts are caused by greed or grievance has become rather sterile. Greed and grievance are conceptualized as binary opposites, with different camps arguing for competing frameworks and contrasting policy prescriptions. However, greed and grievance may be more usefully viewed as being internally related to one another. As Sambanis (2003: 2) convincingly argues, 'greed and grievance are hues of the same variables and it is often impossible to distinguish between these overlapping and mutually reinforcing motives for political violence'. If one understands them as being essentially relational this leads to an analysis of the interactions and synergies between them.[16] Greedy behaviour, for instance, may either give rise to, or arise from, grievance. Indeed we often see more political greed and economic grievance than the other way round (Sambanis, 2003: 57). If state failure or government illegitimacy turns domestic politics into a near anarchic world, then what Collier and Hoeffler (1998) call greed is really synonymous with the pursuit of survival (Sambanis, 2003: 57). Grievances are themselves transformed by conflict and popular support is shaped, won and lost during the war, rather than being immutable and fixed once and for all (Kalyvas, 2000: 18). Therefore it is important not to lose sight of the social contexts in which greed and grievance dynamics play themselves out.

Social Dimensions

Although in a market-driven world economic rationales are important, one also needs to see how conflict makes sociological sense.[17] Hunger for identity and social order in a disintegrating world have provided the humus in which effective political forces can grow (Hobsbawm, 1994). One cannot understand the rise of the Taliban in Afghanistan without analysing the social context of the *madrasas* or religious seminaries from which they emerged. The meanings that people attribute to events, institutions, policies, motives and appeals for support are as important as the phenomena themselves (Uphoff, 1992). Wars may be caused or sustained by a particular type of political economy, but they are also driven by an emotional economy that cannot just be explained away in material or political terms. Greed as conceptualized by Collier (2000) is related purely to commodities rather than to other people. This fails to recognize that the economic should be embedded in the social, relational and historical (Cramer, 2002). If violence is socially and culturally defined, this implies that the search for peace will need to build upon local cultural resources (Richards, 1996).

Social relations: resistance, trust and energy. A 'functions of conflict' approach tends to focus on the winners and marginalizes the losers. It also views power relations and modes of domination as stable and fixed. The work of Foucault (2003) and Scott (1976) provides an alternative perspective about the agency and capacity for resistance of those facing disadvantage. Rather than taking an exclusive and amassed view of power, they view it as something which is decentred and circulating. Power itself is ambivalent; it can be either good or bad.[18] Foucault shows that acts of domination produce the impetus for resistance. Similarly, for Scott politics is encapsulated in everyday practices, the unseen forms of resistance of subordinate groups, something he calls the 'weapons of the weak'. In the context of violent conflict this may mean resistance to the dominant discourse of ethnic nationalism and religious hatred. And it may mean the emergence of moral economies as well as predatory ones. Relatively little research has focused on why people choose not to fight and ways in which they seek to live in defiance of the domination that surrounds them (Gilgan, 2001). Mary Anderson's (1999) work on local capacities for peace encourages aid agencies to understand and support the pro-peace constituencies in society, that is, groups that have chosen to disengage from war. But Gilgan (2001) argues that it is less about supporting disengagement than supporting forms of resistance. This places social relations within an ineluctably political framework.

Anderson's work and that of others illustrate that social assets, the mutual trust and cooperation within and between families, kin and neighbours, are a crucial response for survival and offer opportunities for building peace in the future. In the fields of economics and development studies there is a burgeoning literature on social capital and networks of civil engagement, which are perceived to be the principal determinants of development. Social capital is defined by Putnam, Leonard and Nanett (1993: 167) as 'features of social organization such as trust, norms [of reciprocity], and networks [of civic engagement] that can improve the efficiency of society by facilitating coordinated actions'. The term has been picked up by social scientists and policy-makers for many reasons, but many were attracted to social capital as it provided 'a language to help bring together discussion of the social, political and economic without ultimately elevating just one of these spheres as the most causally implicated in the production of the other two' (Bebbington, 2004: 348).

Social capital theory has had little to say about violent conflict, first because of its positivist thrust and emphasis on cooperation and second, because of its conceptualization of conflict as a non-violent activity, that is, a lack of trust. However, recent work has attempted to make conceptual links between violent conflict and social capital.[19] In a study of Hindu–Muslim conflict in India, Varshney (2002: 3) found that 'Associational and everyday forms of civic engagement, if robust promote peace; contrariwise, their absence or weakness opens up space for communal violence'. A number of writers distinguish between bonding (social capital that builds intra-group solidarity) and bridging (social capital that builds inter-group solidarity) and build upon this distinction to hypothesize that violent conflict is less likely where there are high levels of generalized trust between groups (bridging social capital). Conflict entrepreneurs may utilize the idea of bonding social capital to mobilize support and consciously undermine that of bridging social capital. However, there has been limited empirical research on violent conflict and social capital and what has been done tends to ask questions rather than provide definitive answers.

Social capital is not a concept that should be used uncritically. First, it sidesteps considerations of power.[20] Second, it ignores the fact that the consequences of organization or social capital can be negative for many members of society, especially those who are relatively powerless. Perhaps the term 'anti-social' capital (Goodhand and Hulme, 1997) should be applied to forms of engagement and networks which do not accrue endowments of capital for the benefit of society as a whole, but foster factionalism. One could hypothesize that anti-social capital can be whipped up by conflict entrepreneurs fairly quickly in comparison with the long-term and incremental process of building up 'pro-social' capital.

Even if one tries to refine Putman, Leonard and Nanett's (1993) concept of social capital, it still carries considerable linear development baggage along with it (Christoplos, 1998). According to Uphoff (1992), the traditional focus of the social sciences has been on power and equilibrium, with much less attention paid to energy and 'adhocracy'. Hirschman's (1984) idea of social energy, though rarely applied to violent conflict, may provide a useful additional analytical lens for understanding the often ephemeral and mutating nature of collective action in war zones.

Identity conflicts. Collective violence involves the activation and reinforcement of boundaries (Tilly, 2003). Any individual or population has multiple identities and thus multiple boundaries, but boundary activation singles out one of these shared identities and its opposition to other identities. Ethnicity is one source of identity that often appears to be singled out. Views on the relationship between conflict and identity are diverse and contested. Broadly three positions can be identified. First, there is a narrative popularized by the likes of Kaplan (1994), in which the fall of the Berlin wall and collapse of authoritarian rule are seen to have removed the lid on ancient rivalries, allowing people to settle long suppressed grievances. This back to barbarism narrative assumes that identity is primordial and fixed and has a central role in contemporary conflicts. Second, a number of political scientists and economists argue that identity is constructed and instrumentalized by political elites. In this sense it is a dependent variable: it is seen as a symptom rather than an underlying cause of conflict. Collier (2000), for example, argues that ethnic diversity lowers the risk of violent conflict as elites find it more difficult to mobilize significant numbers to rebel. Certainly a historical analysis supports the view that identity is constructed. Ethnic identities in Sudan, for example, were largely invented by the colonial powers for administrative purposes.[21] Conflict may become ethnically patterned, as has been the case in Afghanistan, but this is different from saying it is ethnically caused. Third, writers such as Gurr (1970) agree that ethnic boundaries are generally fluid, but argue that identity can become a salient factor, in other words an independent variable that cannot just be argued away in political or material terms. Central to Gurr's analysis is the idea of a 'frustration-aggression nexus': if people feel a discrepancy between what they have and what they expect to have, this may trigger violent conflict. Group identity varies in salience but if a group is disadvantaged and subject to active discrimination its sense of collective identity and common interest tends to be high. Groups feeling relative deprivation[22] are more likely to be mobilized by ethno-political leaders.[23] Whether conflict becomes violent depends on a range of other factors, including the nature of the political system and the international context. Gurr's treatment of identity is more sophisticated than the other two positions in the sense that it recognizes the complexity of contemporary conflicts and the interactions between the political and emotional economies.

Psychosocial models. War serves important psychological as well as economic functions (Keen, 1998). Factors such as group pressures, regard for comrades, respect for leaders, concern for reputation and the urge to contribute to the success of the group (Kalyvas, 2000: 10) may be at least as important as economic or political calculations. There is a growing literature which focuses on the psychological roots of violent conflict (Grossman, 1996; Das et al., 2000; Keen, 2002). A number of models have been developed in relation to interpersonal conflict rather than war, but they may still provide important insights into why people choose violence. Of more interest than the biological models, which argue that people are inherently disposed to violence, are those which examine psychological factors in relation to social processes. Violence may be a response to a sense of shame (Gilligan, 2000) or powerlessness (Arendt, 1969). Violence may arise from an impulse to restore self-respect, for example the Taliban can be seen as an attempt to reverse the historic domination of the countryside by the city in Afghanistan. Girard's (1996) theory of envy, scapegoating and mimetic rivalry roots conflict within specific relational structures and histories.

As already mentioned, conflict generates and is sustained by a certain type of emotional economy. Violent struggles may provide a language that is meaningful and empowering for those involved. Central to Al Qaeda's ideology is the idea of cosmic struggle, the history of mankind being seen as a 'perpetual war between belief and unbelief' (cited in Burke, 2004: 25). Violence, language and symbols are skilfully deployed to build emotional bonds between 'brothers in arms'.

> Seeing the world as a battlefield enables an individual to deploy a whole series of mythical, cultural and religious references. This is hugely empowering. Those who take part in the cosmic struggle are holy warriors, strong, deserving of respect and prestige. (Burke, 2004: 26)

Conflict resolution approaches often draw upon psycho-social models. However, a common criticism is that they tend to focus on the individual and interpersonal levels, aiming at behavioural change rather than wider structural transformation (Duffield, 1997; Voutira and Brown, 1995).

Gender Analysis

Gender has been placed outside the above schema since it is an overarching and crosscutting issue. It is an analytical lens that must be employed, whatever one's theoretical approach. Gender analysis has recently been introduced to the study of wars (Nordstrom, 1999; Jacobs, Jacobson and Marchbank, 2000; Moser and Clark, 2001; Pankhurst, 2003), although there is a longer history of the study of domestic violence and gender relations (Macmillan and Gartner, 1999; Schuler et al., 1996). It is beyond the scope of this chapter to examine this literature in detail. The gender analysis of wars has illustrated the different ways in which women and men are caught up in struggles over power and resources and the ways in which gender relations may be profoundly altered by conflict. While gender analysis has an economic dimension, for example the economic roles of women and men are often changed during armed conflict, it also has social and cultural dimensions, for example in the construction and reproduction of the identity of 'warriors'.[24] The latter varies enormously from place to place. In Afghanistan the warrior is invariably male and women's roles are largely confined to the private sphere.[25] By contrast, in Sri Lanka the LTTE developed a feared cadre of female fighters and suicide bombers, and the government also deploys female soldiers. Women are not simply victims, as has commonly been assumed, but are also active agents: their roles range from being effective perpetrators of violence and fearless combatants to being the main force behind initiatives to promote peace.[26] In the post-conflict moment there may be strong pressures for a return to normalcy in terms of gender relations: 'the challenge posed to traditional gender relations during times of war becomes too great for patriarchal societies to accept in times of peace' (Pankhurst, 2003: 161).

Conflict Dynamics and Actors

In his novel *Anil's Ghost,* Michael Ondaatje nicely captures the complexity and dynamism of civil conflict in Sri Lanka. The war manifests itself in many different ways, involves multiple actors and during the course of the fighting has taken on a life of its own:

> There had been a continual emergency from 1983 onwards, racial attacks and political killings. The terrorism of the separatist guerrilla groups, who were fighting for a homeland in the north. The insurrection of the insurgents in the south, against the government. The counter-terrorism of the special forces against both of them. The disposal of bodies by fire. The disposal of bodies in rivers or the sea. The hiding and then reburial of corpses.
>
> It was a Hundred Years' War with modern weaponry, and backers on the sidelines in safe countries, a war sponsored by gun- and drug-runners. It became

evident that political enemies were secretly joined in financial arms deals. 'The reason for war was war.' (Ondaatje, 2000: 42–3)

Conflict is a social process in which the original structural tensions are themselves profoundly reshaped by the massive disruptions of war. Wars can mutate and issues that lead to the emergence of large-scale violence are not necessarily those that cause its intractability or longevity. As Tilly argues, 'war is a form of contention which leads to new forms of contention' (cited in Keen, 1998: 6). Root cause analysis may become decreasingly relevant the more protracted the conflict becomes.

Particular structural factors may create the permissive conditions for violent conflict. But such structural and historical conditions, while being significant, are rarely sufficient to trigger armed conflict. Otherwise, as Grenier (1996) notes, one wonders why most countries in Latin America are not permanently disrupted by aggrieved masses. No political outcome can be regarded as inevitable. A wide variety of outcomes is possible and perhaps this applies to a greater extent in unstable, developing countries than in democratic, developed countries where there are institutional mechanisms for dealing with conflict. There is no convincing account of why difficult pre-existing conditions lead to conflict in some places and not in others (Pankhurst, 2003: 155). What transforms structural violence into open violence? Under what conditions are grievances likely to be mobilized for violent ends? To answer this one must also examine contingent factors or conflict triggers, specific policies, individual actors' incentives and interests, and how these factors interact with background conditions to create a particular conflict dynamic.

Rather than following a predictable pattern or cycle, contemporary conflicts are often characterized by multiple cycles of escalation and de-escalation. There may be periods and regions of stability mixed with instability, and the boundaries of a conflict are changeable. Recent thinking on conflict has drawn upon complexity theory and post-Newtonian ideas about change. If, as Duffield (2001) argues, conflict systems are analogous to organisms, then understanding them requires an analysis that emphasizes their interconnections, their mutability and their processes of renewal and self-transformation. Societies appear to be more vulnerable to violent conflict during periods of rapid change or transition. Grenier (1996) describes such moments as 'charismatic periods of history', in which there is an 'explosion of politics' as populations are mobilized by disaffected elites around popular grievances. Within the conflict there may be critical thresholds or turning points when alternative options present themselves; these may include opportunities to build peace as well as the threat of degeneration into renewed hostilities. One may also be able to identify stabilizing points, for instance indigenous institutions within civil society around which a new consensus may emerge. As argued in Chapter 1, there are likely to be continuities between wartime and peacetime conditions. The slate is never wiped clean in the post-conflict moment. The legacies of conflict continue to shape political and economic processes long after the guns fall silent.

A focus on conflict dynamics therefore highlights contingency and agency. It brings the conscious political actor 'back in' (Grenier, 1996: 37). Individuals make choices which in turn influence events and wider structures. Jabri (1996) usefully builds upon Giddens' structuration theory to examine how individuals and structures interact with one another in wartime: 'war as a human action is a product of human decision making within the context of structural social relations... violent conflict is itself structured through the actions of agency situated in the relation to discursive and institutional continuities which both enable war's occurrence and legitimate it as a form of behaviour' (Jabri, 1996: 4). Current research with its focus on economic opportunities underplays the roles of political actors and political opportunities. It also fails to recognize the importance of the emotional economy. Violent struggles often provide a language for other conflicts of a social, communal or personal nature' (Kalyvas, 2000: 18). Wars become a welter of complex struggles and popular support is not a fixed commodity but something that is mutable, which can be won and lost over time (ibid.). Individual leaders, both conflict entrepreneurs and peace entrepreneurs, play a role in diffusing ideas which transform social structures and social relations. 'Social energy' may be something that can be stored and released after the conflict, for instance NGO leaders may be protected or held in 'cold storage', so to speak, during the war years and re-emerge in the post-conflict order. Lederach (1997) highlights the important role played by middle-level leaders who may act as connectors between the grassroots and senior political or military leadership. As mentioned earlier, many people, often the majority, choose not to be part of the conflict. Although one should not idealize or overestimate their role, a focus on greedy warlords risks marginalizing such groups and in so doing misses a potential force for positive peace.

From Theory to Practice

Research findings, as highlighted above, are often confusing and contradictory. Rather than attempt to find an illusory consensus, this chapter finishes by highlighting key themes that are addressed and developed in subsequent chapters.

First, theory matters. Policy and practice are not theory-free zones, they are based on a set of implicit or explicit assumptions about the causes and nature of conflict. Good practice is likely to be based on good theory which is rigorous, coherent and tested empirically. Practitioners who dismiss theory as arcane and irrelevant are likely to be unknowing slaves of someone else's theories—most likely those of their funders. Particular attention will be paid in subsequent chapters to how practitioners and policy-makers analyse violent conflict and the extent to which theory has informed practice and vice versa.

Second, there can be no general theory of war. Research points to a variety of causal paths and a complex interplay of multiple factors. This is a strong argument for a policy of orderly eclecticism in terms of picking and mixing different approaches and theories of conflict. Since there is no uniquely best solution, this means adopting a pluralist approach.

Third, research questions the notion of path dependency, that is, that certain outcomes are pre-ordained because of particular structural conditions. Many conflicts do not exhibit identifiable causes that can be fully understood and for which solutions can be generated. At best, understanding will always be partial, contingencies will play havoc with linear notions of cause and effect, and predictability will be at low levels (Goodhand and Hulme, 1999: 24). Human behaviour is probabilistic (Uphoff, 1992). Similar background conditions can lead to different outcomes in different contexts. This indicates that the probabilities of peace or violent conflict can be influenced through particular policies and interventions. Ideas drawn from complexity theory and an analysis of the institutions that mediate between structures and individuals can usefully inform analysis.

Fourth, as Cliffe and Luckham (1999: 29) argue, the 'political is not an extra dimension of the complexity which has to be analyzed to get practical aid right, it becomes the overriding priority'. This applies not only to the politics of the conflicts themselves but also to the politics of those who analyse and represent them. In the development world, problems are often understood in terms of one's capacity to respond. Hence poverty-focused donors may see conflict as a problem of poverty, while human rights organizations see it as the failure to protect basic and civil rights. Analysis, therefore, is refracted through different political and organizational lenses. For NGOs there may be some positive opportunities in terms of how they understand and represent contemporary wars. The extended notion of security may be seen as a positive trend, as it opens up spaces for non-state actors to engage in areas of high politics traditionally reserved for national security matters. Questions about the environment, livelihoods and social issues are now seen as critical factors in relation to security. NGOs have to an extent benefited from the new mobility between high politics and low politics, reflected in the fact they are increasingly invited to the 'high table' to inform policy debates. While there are concerns that this may lead to co-option, it has also created opportunities to shape debates and to play a role in constructing alternative representations of conflict.

Fifth, a political-economy approach takes us towards an analysis of the state. In recent years mainstream policy has tended to privilege civil society rather than the state, as a cause and a possible solution to violent conflict. The role of the state in relation to violent conflict has been either downplayed or elbowed out of the analysis altogether. And yet research increasingly points to the centrality of the state in terms of how we understand and respond to violent conflict (Cliffe and Luckham, 1999; Milliken and Krause, 2002). This is not to argue that the focus should shift back purely to the high politics of the state. However, it does point us to a closer examination of the institutions, formal and informal, which mediate between state and society and which help forge or undermine the social contract. This means simultaneously seeking to understand the interconnections between the high politics of the state and the deep politics of society.

Sixth, given the multilevelled and dynamic nature of contemporary conflicts, there is a need to think more carefully about levels and linkages. The above analysis has emphasized the international, regional, national and local dimensions of contemporary conflicts. In most conflicts today, therefore, we are not talking about localized introverted wars. We see simultaneously processes of globalization and of localization.[27] In war local considerations may often trump national ones. Developing an analysis of these local considerations to complement an appreciation of the broad regional and global processes is therefore important. Perhaps the biggest gap in current analysis is an understanding of the linkages between the different levels of contemporary conflict systems. Recent work on conflict diamonds has been innovative in this respect and has helped fill in some of the knowledge gaps about the political economy of conflict goods (Smillie, Lansana and Hazleton, 2000). NGOs have played an important role in this process.

Finally, which analysis one chooses depends, to an extent, on political choices. Neoliberal orthodoxies have had a stranglehold over the framework of intervention, which manifests itself in many different ways: from the privatization of peacebuilding initiatives to the focus on greed as the driving force of conflict, to the *cordon sanitaire* approach to drugs and asylum seekers adopted by Western powers.

3

Armed Conflict in Practice

This chapter examines the origins and dynamics of armed conflict with reference to the case study countries. Following the structure of the previous chapter, the origins of the conflicts, in terms of their security, political, economic and social dimensions are examined. The focus then turns to conflict actors and dynamics. A particular emphasis is placed on the institutions that can mitigate, manage and resolve violent conflict.

Conflict Structures

In this section some of the historical and structural antecedents of violent conflict in the case study countries are examined. An exhaustive comparative analysis is beyond the scope of this book, so the focus will be on areas that are of particular relevance to donors and NGOs working in conflict. It is hoped that this will yield insights into the varied nature of armed conflicts and the idiosyncratic challenges that different contexts present to those attempting to build peace.

Table 1.3 provided a summary of the seven cases, in terms of their principal features and key events. These conflicts can be positioned along a bell-curve representing a continuum of peace–war–peace (Richards, 2005), but where they stand on the bell-curve has and is constantly changing. Some have perhaps moved further along the war–peace continuum (Afghanistan, Sri Lanka, Liberia), others have moved in the opposite direction (Nepal), although the remaining cases do not appear to have moved significantly in one direction or the other (Moldova, Armenia-Azerbaijan, Kyrgyzstan). As emphasized in Chapter 1, the distinction between war and peace is a blurred one. For instance in Sri Lanka under the guise of a ceasefire, a brutal shadow war and counter-insurgency operations are being conducted by the LTTE and government forces, in which over 3,000 people have died. With the exception of Armenia-Azerbaijan, these have been intra-state armed conflicts, but with significant external involvement. Evidently the conflicts have different proximate causes, have taken on different forms and have raged at different levels of intensity during their respective life cycles. Although they are dissimilar in many respects, they do not belong to different species. They have a similar 'genetic make-up', in the sense that armed violence constitutes a symptom of a deeper structural crisis, rooted in the nature of the state. These structural factors are explored below.

Security Dimensions

As indicated in Chapter 2, states perform three core functions of providing security, representation and welfare. But mastering violence and providing protection are the heart of the matter. A lack of national security means a loss of legitimacy.

Late statebuilders do not have the luxury of time, resources or the room for manoeuvre of their predecessors, and states emerging from colonialism or communism in the 20th century have had to endure some painful adjustments (Freedman, 2004). In the case studies, states have faced multiple threats from above and below. These can be divided into threats or challenges which emanate from the external and internal security environments.

External security environment. States have historically been protected from the outside by strong international norms (the golden rules of non-intervention and reciprocity), and to an extent these were strengthened during the Cold War period. Because political borders were on the whole viewed as sacrosanct, states had in effect 'certified life insurance' (Sorensen, 2001: 8). Arguably, with the fall of the Berlin wall, inhibitions on intervention have declined, although before 9/11 at least, strategic interests appeared to be less clearly defined and less predictable. The case studies highlight the post–Cold War confusion about 'how to count the costs and benefits of intervention, preparedness and alliance' (Bobbitt, 2002: 7). Particularly in the post-Soviet states like Moldova, Azerbaijan, Armenia and Kyrgyzstan, the patterns of international collaboration and competition are still emerging. Competition in the early 1990s between the US and Russia in Central Asia changed in the late 1990s to a convergence of interests around security and terrorism.

The war against terrorism has arguably imposed a new pattern on international relations, and this is particularly apparent in Central Asia where authoritarian regimes have been recipients of US military and financial support to combat militant Islamic groups. Counter-insurgency operations provide an umbrella for diverse constituencies to pursue their own projects, and may create new spaces for impunity (Keen, 2000). Insecure governments with a poor human rights record, like the royalist regime in Nepal, have been able to attract international military and financial support, partly because of concerns about so-called terrorism.[1] On the one hand, this strengthens the regime's position in relation to the Maoists and parliament, but on the other, it may undermine domestic legitimacy, a similar paradox to the one faced by the Karzai-led government in Afghanistan. But the GWOT interacts with regional and domestic politics in different and sometimes unexpected ways. In the case of Sri Lanka, one could make a strong case for the positive impacts of US and Indian concerns about terrorism on the dynamics of the conflict. Although there are numerous reasons for the initiation of the Sri Lankan peace process, one cannot discount the effects that the post-9/11 environment had on the calculations of the LTTE. Growing pressures on the organization, particularly in terms of its political and fund-raising efforts, helped create the preconditions for peace talks (Saravanamuttu, 2003; Goodhand and Klem, 2005).[2]

One characteristic shared by all the case study countries is their weak, peripheral status, which is defined by their location on a geopolitical faultline and/or next door to a regional hegemon. All suffer from adverse incorporation into the state system. Geopolitical constraints and international actions (and inaction) have had significant impacts on the external security environment, influencing regional power dynamics as well as the domestic security of conflict-affected countries. International policies may have indirect signalling effects, as for instance Kyrgyzstan's admission into the WTO or Romania's pending entry into the European Union (EU), which in turn influence the regional balance of power and conflict dynamics in the Ferghana valley and Transdniestria respectively. The more obvious and direct impacts on security have been the result of interventions (or 'serial abuse' as Freedman (2004) aptly describes foreign adventures in Afghanistan) by external powers or neighbouring states. Afghanistan has been subject to either the wrong kind of international involvement (superpower rivalry in the 1980s) or the lack of involvement (malign neglect in the 1990s). The statebuilding strategies of neighbouring powers, notably Pakistan, have also had a calamitous effect on governance arrangements in the country. In the case of Nagorno-Karabakh, conflict resolution is connected to wider geostrategic factors, notably competition between Russia and the US for strategic influence and control of oil and gas reserves in the southern Caucasus.

The regionalized nature of conflict is striking in all the cases. Although Afghanistan, Nagorno-Karabakh, southern Kyrgyzstan and Liberia are more obviously nodes in a regional conflict formation, all have regional security dimensions.[3] All to an extent are small countries located in 'bad neighbourhoods'. In many of the cases, most notably Afghanistan, Sri Lanka and Armenia-Azerbaijan, regional and international diasporas supported warring groups. Where the outer boundaries of the Caucasus, Central Asian and West African regional conflict systems lie is unclear, since the networks and circuits of exchange are so dynamic and global in their reach. Regional state and non-state actors have played a role in causing conflicts and acting as spoilers in preventing their resolution. Small arms and other conflict goods such as diamonds or opium circulate through regional social solidarity networks. Particularly important in the case of Afghanistan have been Pashtun diaspora communities in Dubai and Karachi with their links to Quetta in west Pakistan and Kandahar in southeast Afghanistan.

Domestic security environment. Classically sovereignty creates a sociopolitical unit with some measure of autonomy or insulation from the outside (Sorensen, 2000: 1). But states are able to do this to varying degrees. A strong state or high-capacity regime has a hard shell which insulates and protects its citizens. A weak or eggshell state cannot perform this function so effectively and at its worst becomes an 'insecurity container' (Herz, cited in Sorensen, 2000: 3). Unlike early statebuilders, countries like Afghanistan developed the means of coercion through external support. They 'acquired their military organization from the outside, without the same internal forging of mutual constraints between rulers and ruled' (Tilly, 1985: 185–6). Their armies faced inwards rather than outwards (Sorensen, 2001). In the Afghan case, despite external support to build up and concentrate the means of coercion, the state lacked either empirical sovereignty or legitimacy.[4] Regimes that have failed to develop a strong and loyal army have been resisted and ultimately overthrown.[5] High-capacity regimes—whether democratic or authoritarian—are better able to contain discontent. Crises may be precipitated when the state proves unable to contain and resolve tensions through either violent or non-violent means. States lose their legitimacy when they fail to ensure the basic security of citizens from human rights abuses, crime and physical violence. Weak states may in fact seek to make life less secure for certain groups and tend to increase conflict by addressing it solely as a security problem rather than engaging with the underlying sources of grievance. In Sri Lanka, there has been a tendency to label the conflict a terrorist problem, leading to a belief in the military solution, which has in turn fuelled ethnically-based grievances. A similar pattern can be detected in Central Asia, where authoritarian states treat Islamic radicals as a terrorist problem (particularly after 9/11), contributing to a spreading and destabilizing militancy. As violence becomes more protracted, there is likely to be a shift in power towards military actors. Security forces may increasingly take on state functions and are only loosely controlled by democratic institutions. In Nepal a state of emergency was declared in 2000 which in effect gave the Royal Nepalese Army powers to come out of their barracks to address the Maoist insurgency. This signified a shift in the political balance of power away from the democratically elected politicians back towards the palace and the army. It has also been a deliberate Maoist strategy to escalate the conflict and militarize the state (ICG, 2005c: 30).

War or the threat of war may provide military elites with political or economic opportunities that do not exist in peacetime. Azerbaijan and Armenia, for instance, have become increasingly militarized states as the security forces on both sides have developed vested interests in the continuation of the no-war, no-peace status quo. In Sri Lanka lucrative arms contracts led to the enrichment of high-level military figures during the 1990s. Non-state military actors also profit from the related processes of weakening states and an increasingly global environment. They are able to link into global markets and operate in the space left by weakened states, with the result that the economic-military nexus becomes increasingly entrenched. As Keen (1998) and others have argued, rather than trying to win a war, non-state entities may be primarily concerned with controlling spheres of influence and providing a stable environment for taxation and the predation of resources. The classic examples of this are the warlord phases of the Afghan and Liberian conflicts. Specialists in violence have proven themselves to be extremely adaptive and innovative. An unstable and unruly peace may provide similar opportunities for self-enrichment. Some warlords in Afghanistan may have a vested interest in a weak central state and ongoing instability, in order to maintain their political and economic spheres of influence, carved out during the war years. Peace in Sri Lanka and Kyrgyzstan has been characterized by chronic insecurity for much of the population. The agents of this insecurity are as likely to be state actors (particularly the army and police force) as non-state or anti-state groups.[6]

The geography of security and insecurity in regional conflict formations deserves to be studied further. One can speculate that borderlands are prone to chronic instability; they are likely to be situated on the periphery of the state in geographically or ecologically marginal areas,[7] and suffer from chronic poverty and political and social exclusion. They may have an insurrectionary tradition, acting as a magnet for dissident groups, while also being well situated to finance themselves through the crossborder shadow economy (see below). Borderlands appear to be 'neuralgia spots' (Pugh and Cooper, 2004: 37) in regional conflict systems, acting as incubators of violent resistance to central government. They may potentially also be strategic nodes for peacebuilding. For instance in Sadakhlo market in Georgia on the border between Azerbaijan and Armenia, Azeri and Armenian traders and businessmen live and work side by side cooperating in small businesses, retail shops and restaurants (ICG, 2005d). Nagorno-Karabakh, southern Kyrgyzstan, the midwest of Nepal, eastern Afghanistan and Transdniestria can all be classified as borderlands that became base areas for rebellion. In fact, Afghanistan and Nepal are themselves borderlands or frontier states, which were historically constituted as buffer states, 'a zone of low administrative intensity outside the centres of empire' (Moraya, 2003: 271). Conflict itself generates new borders, often internal ones. Sri Lanka, for example, has been divided into 'cleared' (government-held) and 'uncleared' (LTTE-held) areas. The grey buffer zones between government and LTTE territory have tended to be the most unstable areas. Villagers inhabiting border areas lived in a climate of impunity and in a sense fell 'below the law' (Keen, 1998), coming under the protection regime of neither the government nor the LTTE. It was the demand for protection that caused many Tamils to support or join militant groups.

Particularly at the subnational level the distinctions between war and peace may be blurred, and the labels attached by external agencies have limited accuracy or relevance. In Kandahar in southern Afghanistan in 2000, for instance, there was relative peace with a thriving economy and evidence of substantial inward investment.[8] But in southern Kyrgyzstan militarized incursions from the Islamic Movement of Uzbekistan and internal displacement exacerbated growing poverty and a sense of disillusionment with the Kyrgyz state. And yet the former was categorized as an emergency and the latter as a development setting by international relief and development agencies.

Similarly, external representations of non-state military actors are often inaccurate. For instance, the narco-mafia type of narrative applied to groups like the IMU and the Taliban may serve to justify certain types of intervention, but it elbows political and social analysis out of the picture entirely. It may also foreclose opportunities to engage with such groups. For instance, in post-Taliban Afghanistan it is important to take into account the different backgrounds, histories, political interests and constituencies of non-state military actors. Some may transform themselves into statesmen, others into economic entrepreneurs, while some may be co-opted or disarmed. Labelling them all greedy warlords is unhelpful. Non-state military actors may be providers of protection and even humanitarian assistance. The response of the LTTE to the Sri Lankan tsunami, for instance, in many respects outmatched that of the government.

Political Dimensions

State formation. Civil wars tend to be rooted in pathologies of the state. Violent conflict is a manifestation of an underlying institutional crisis and wars are often preceded by other forms of violence. Before the Sri Lankan secessionist conflict began in 1983, there were riots, pogroms, political violence, population transfers and a Marxist youth uprising. These were all manifestations of growing grievances which the state was unable to contain or manage. At the root of the so-called ethnic conflict was a crisis of the state, and specifically the way the post-colonial state reinforced exclusive conceptions of political community and citizenship (Goodhand, 2001b).

The case studies point to the need for a careful analysis of the history of state formation and transition. Afghanistan's troubled history can only be understood in relation to its origins as a buffer state between the Russian and British empires. Historical contradictions and tensions both within and outside the country led to challenges to the state. The process of state formation is rarely, if ever, a smooth and linear one. It more commonly occurs in fits and starts, in a trajectory of 'punctuated equilibrium' (Cramer and Goodhand, 2002), in which statebuilding is periodically interrupted by non-violent or violent resistance. A historical analysis of the former Soviet republics of Moldova, Kyrgyzstan, Armenia and Azerbaijan highlights the artificiality of the state, which has a poor fit with nation. Though all states face disjunctures between social and political boundaries, the task of building a coherent political community has been particularly acute for the leaders of post-Soviet states, given the period in which they entered the state system, and the ethnic and language divisions in the new states. Statebuilding has involved layered relationships of the state to different segments of the population, something Migdal (2004) refers to as a 'segmented citizenry'. Core groups are understood as the legitimate owners of the state, although other sections of the citizenry are labelled as dangerous and antithetical to the central goals of state leaders (ibid.: 33). In all the cases, state leaders have selectively hardened inter-group boundaries, in order to exclude certain minorities. The basis for exclusion may be ethnicity (the Tamils in Sri Lanka, the Uzbeks in Kyrgyzstan), language (Russian-speakers in Moldova), religion (Shi'as in Afghanistan), or a combination of these and other markers of identity. Insider and outsider access to material benefits is consequently connected to group identity, and the state becomes associated with particular interests.

Therefore, nation-states are not a given, they have to be created, and the case studies support Howard's (2002: xviii) observation that it is states that create nations rather than vice versa. And to a great extent, the problem of statebuilding remains unsolved; effective states are less common than 'states that have signally failed to create nations and can barely function as states at all' (ibid.).

State crisis. In addition to its role as a security container, the state's political legitimacy is bound up with its ability to provide representation, wealth and welfare. In the case studies, states have varied across time and between one another in their capacity to perform these functions. Legitimacy is intimately connected to the extent to which the state's identity and institutions retain a degree of independence and separation from society. The Afghan state, for instance, was never able to escape its Pashtun and tribal origins. States that have been captured or colonized by particular interest groups lose their legitimacy in the eyes of those excluded. In Kyrgyzstan the state was captured by the *nomenklatura* or old communist elite. In Nepal the practice of *chakri* (in effect a form of institutionalized sycophancy) is an extreme manifestation of patronage politics. The conspicuous consumption of Kathmandu-based politicians has further fuelled the sense of grievance and legitimates violence in the countryside.

In Sri Lanka, violent conflict is a manifestation of a structural crisis in the identity, legitimacy and capacity of the state (Bastian, 1999). These three factors are interrelated; the state's declining capacity undermined its legitimacy. The lack of public service provision to the northeast and the state's close association with a Sinhala Buddhist discourse further undermined its legitimacy with the Tamil population. University entrance requirements, language policy and land colonization programmes all reflected a tendency for public policy to respond to the interests of the Sinhala majority. Even if policies are enacted, they may not be implemented because of the politicization of the bureaucracy.[9]

Weak states are challenged from above (by globalization, transnational commerce and aid donors) and from below (colonization by civil society interest groups and the growth of militant groups). Encouraged by international donors, reform programmes force states to cut back on their social welfare functions, which in turn undermine social contracts. This process has been most abrupt in the post-Soviet countries, to the extent that the public sphere is fast disappearing (Anderson, 2004b: 13). In Kyrgyzstan, as the economy became increasingly informalized, the government's revenue base shrank, while non-state actors such as the IMU were able to thrive and grow by generating resources through the shadow economy.

The case studies point to the destabilizing effects of democratization. Kyrgyzstan, Moldova, Armenia-Azerbaijan, Nepal and Sri Lanka have all, to varying degrees, experienced failed or stalled democratic transitions, leading to a gap between citizens' aspirations and the state's capacity to deliver, which has in turn fed a growing sense of grievance. In Nepal, although democracy was the result of the *Jana Andolan* (people's revolution), it only 'mimicked a revolution' (Brown, 1996: 22), amounting to an elite pact between the palace and the urban middle classes of the Congress Party. In the years following the *Jana Andolan* the chasm between democratic aspirations and democratic practice led to growing dissatisfaction. Although Sri Lanka has a much longer history of democracy, this has not immunized the country from violent conflict. In fact democracy and intolerant nationalism have been organically linked (Snyder, 2000; Spencer, 2004). Sinhalese political elites have historically indulged in a process of ethnic outbidding in which mainstream parties sought to corral the Sinhalese vote by competing with each other on an anti-minority stance. Sinhala nationalism has been hegemonic since the 1950s and this had led to reactive cycles of Tamil nationalist identification (Rampton and Welikala, 2005). In spite of the introduction of the proportional representation system, that enables minorities to get a voice for the first time in mainstream politics, the bargaining process for the formation of a coalition is usually not on the basis of policies, but much more for securing patronage that follows access to state power (Bastian, 2005: 4).

There is a considerable difference between formal procedural democracy and substantive democracy and, to varying degrees, the countries have failed to institutionalize democratic politics. Although Kyrgyzstan had many of the forms of a democratic polity, following independence, the underlying norms were still based on personalized patronage politics. The product of the so-called transition was a hybrid form of governance, which combined elements of the older patrimonialism with the institutions of a modern nation-state. Therefore a formal constitution and laws may be necessary but not sufficient as guarantors of a viable social contract. Ultimately these contradictions and the growing authoritarianism of President Akaev led to the Tulip revolution of 2005, which overthrew the old regime. Periods of transition represent important turning points and the choices made at such times of system change are critical (Bastian and Luckham, 2003). In Nepal, for instance, the introduction of multi-party politics in 1990, rather than representing a break with the past, was a messy compromise. It is too early to tell whether this will be the model of political change for Kyrgyzstan.

The important role of political parties as drivers of change (positive or negative) and as transmission belts between the state and civil society comes out strongly in the case studies. In the former Soviet states and in Nepal the political party system is fragile and embryonic. In Nepal coalition politics has failed to produce effective and stable governance. Even in Sri Lanka, with a long history of democratic politics, the political process is characterized by a dangerous combination of political mobilization alongside institutional decay. Parties tend to have opportunistic and short-term agendas and lack rootedness. This contributes to the lack of citizens' voice and engagement in the political process. As one commentator in Moldova commented: 'We don't have citizens, only inhabitants' (cited in Woodward, 2000). In Nepal, the greatest block to public action for the poor is the weakness of the organized voice of the poor. As recent research on poverty highlights, where the state is weak and fractured the same is likely to apply to civil society (Moore and Putzel, 1999). There was limited evidence from the research to suggest that civil society could by itself resolve or prevent violent conflict. Civil society organizations tended to reflect the wider faultlines and tensions within the state and society at large.

State failure.[10] The delegitimizing processes outlined above may contribute to widespread alienation from the regime, from the political process and ultimately from the state itself. The proximate cause of violence may be the breakdown of elite pacts, as in the case of Nepal (the communists representing elements of the disaffected intelligentsia and rural masses against the palace and the urban middle classes).

War exposes the state—it 'lays open the anatomy of the body politic' (Bobbitt, 2002: 205). Armed conflict may itself be viewed as a form of compressed transition, leading in some cases to progressive outcomes. Arguably in Sri Lanka, Tamils achieved more through military action than they did through several decades of democratic politics to get political elites to take the issue of state reform seriously. War in Afghanistan has advanced the position of the minorities, and their newfound political voice is reflected in the constitution of 2003.

State failure and collapse are exceptional events. Although states may be under stress, they are also remarkably resilient and adaptive. Even when challenged by armed opposition, in most cases states do not collapse, the two exceptions among the case studies being Afghanistan and Liberia, and even then, only during particular phases of the conflict. Moreover, the absence of the state does not simply produce chaos. Alternatives to the state emerge in the form of regional military-political structures, social and religious networks or international humanitarian structures.

In several countries, new and competing sovereignties have emerged and where violent conflict has become entrenched, quasi-governmental structures have developed. As the Communist Party of Nepal—Maoist (CPN-M) and LTTE demonstrate, for significant proportions of the population, legitimacy resides outside the state. Such non-state structures increasingly take on state-like functions by providing security and regimes of taxation (and predation). State failure may therefore be something that is actively striven for rather than just reacted to. Opposition is often a rejection of the state altogether as much as it is a demand for participation (Anderson, 2004b: 11).

Where the state has collapsed and political authority fragments, the conflict resolution challenge becomes far more complex. Competing elites may have only loose control over their constituencies and cannot deliver on promises made at the negotiating table. Weak and militarized states like Moldova, Armenia and Azerbaijan are less inclined or able to compromise and negotiate. Poor-quality governance, which is an underlying cause of conflict, also impedes its resolution. The greater the number of factions the greater the challenge for conflict resolution (Doyle and Sambanis, 2000). To an extent state and non-state military actors appeared to mirror one another, so that a fractured and incoherent state is likely to produce fractured and incoherent non-state military actors. As the case of Liberia testifies, the quality of political authority that emerges from the peace settlement has an important bearing on whether peace is sustainable. Taylor was heavily involved in commerce related to the war in Sierra Leone and followed a strategy of President Mobutu of Zaire, which involved renting out the prerogatives of sovereign power to the highest bidder. The aim was personal gain rather than institution-building.

Economic Dimensions

State legitimacy, as already mentioned, is partly determined by its performance in the economic sphere. In many of the countries, uneven development patterns and a perception of state bias led to the creation of discontented groups. This applies geographically, for example between the north and south in Sri Lanka, Moldova and Kyrgyzstan and between the centre and west in Nepal. It also applies to rural–urban differences, and becomes extremely explosive when economic exclusion coincides with ethnic boundaries, as for example in Sri Lanka. Nepal has the highest Gini coefficient (a measure of inequality) in South Asia, and is a society characterized by extreme inter-regional inequalities (Bray, Lund and Murshed, 2003).

Sri Lanka and Nepal are liberalizing economies, which began to open up and deregulate in the 1970s and 1980s respectively. In both countries deregulation and liberalization led to initial successes in macro-economic stabilization and growth. However, particularly in the case of Nepal growth has slowed down. To an extent declining performance can be attributed to the lack of institutions to sustain growth. In Sri Lanka liberalization has accentuated regional differences.

The enclave economy of the northeast has progressively declined as a result of the conflict. In the south, growth has mainly occurred in the urban, western province, leaving significant pockets of poverty and underdevelopment in the deep south. Growing horizontal inequalities contributed to the JVP uprising in the late 1980s (see below).

The post-Soviet countries are ostensibly undergoing transitions from a command economy to a market economy. Liberalization has opened up fragile economies and increased their vulnerability to external shocks. Kyrgyzstan and Moldova, for example, were badly hit by Moscow's stockmarket collapse in 1998.[11] Both countries are heavily indebted and dependent on multilateral credits from the IMF and the World Bank. The aid dependence of these countries (like Nepal) heightens their economic vulnerability because aid flows are so volatile and unpredictable. All post-communist countries have experienced a devastating decline in economic performance. In Moldova economic growth has been negative in every year since 1990. The Moldovan economy has experienced 'the most devastating peacetime decline in economic performance and living standards of any country in modern times' (Ronnas and Olova, cited in Woodward, 2000: 8). In Kyrgyzstan real incomes dropped by over 73 per cent between 1991 and 1997. A process of deindustrialization has taken place with the privatization of state-owned businesses, which has led to quick asset-stripping and then the closure of many of them, causing widespread unemployment. As Freedman (2004: 254) observes, 'In many societies, the success of the [neo-liberal] reform will not only be measured in terms of the convertible currencies, low inflation, and low debt, but also in terms of whether social systems can cope with the consequences.' In many respects the problem in the post-Soviet countries is less one of there being too much state, than how to strengthen the role of the state in protecting individuals from the overbearing influence of non-state actors, particularly in the economic sphere (Freedman, 2004).

Moldova and Kyrgyzstan were viewed as regional showcases by the multinational lending agencies because of their strict adherence to macro-economic reform programmes. However, in the same way that the political transition has resulted in a hybrid system, the economic system, though it meets many of the reform criteria, is dominated by elite interests. In Kyrgyzstan, for instance, those few sectors of the economy that are profitable have been cornered by the family members of the political elite. In Sri Lanka and Nepal market reforms to protect the poor and vulnerable from the private greed of the affluent are either weak or non-operative (HSC, 1999: 90). The lack of a strong legal framework discourages foreign investment and neither Moldova nor Kyrgyzstan has been able to attract significant amounts of foreign direct investment (FDI).

In Nepal (see Box 3.1) and Sri Lanka there are pockets of deepening poverty. This problem is accentuated by politicized poverty alleviation programmes which have been badly targeted and captured by political elites. In both countries the tendency for donors to withdraw development assistance

Box 3.1 Poverty and Conflict in Nepal

Poverty is central to the discourse and dynamics of conflict in Nepal. The Communist Party of Nepal—Maoist (CPN-M) has mobilized rural support around the issues of social exclusion and poverty. The epicentre of the conflict is in the midwest and west, the areas experiencing the highest levels of poverty and with the least voice in democratic politics. The incidence of poverty is 2.6% higher than in urban areas and is closely linked to other forms of exclusion, including caste, gender and ethnicity. The majority of CPN-M cadres are from low-caste hill tribes and include a high proportion of women.

Poverty and prolonged economic stagnation have undermined the legitimacy of successive governments. Although the government highlighted poverty in its 9th Development Plan of 2000, poverty-focused programmes have failed to trickle down, fuelling rural resentment. The labour force is increasing by 300,000 per year, whereas the estimated number of additional jobs amounts to only 150,000. The underemployment rate is estimated to be as high as 47%.

In addition to mobilizing around grievances, the CPN-M has taken on state-like functions, having organized land reform, community development programmes and law courts.

In Nepal, poverty seems to be both a cause and a consequence of conflict. It has provided a legitimizing discourse for violence, while the conflict itself has led to deepening poverty in heartland areas. It is clearly a significant structural factor which needs to be addressed to prevent further escalation of the conflict.

from conflict-affected areas exacerbates the exclusionary dynamic which feeds the conflict. Poverty and horizontal inequalities may not by themselves lead to violent conflict. Although in Moldova and Kyrgyzstan the figures show growing numbers of people in absolute poverty, this is experienced on an individual level and in many respects contributes to growing passivity. The critical factor which contributed to armed violence in both Nepal and Sri Lanka appeared to be the existence of excluded elites who were able to mobilize discontent and finance military action.

In situations of protracted conflict, three distinct types of economy tend to emerge: a combat economy (in which conflict entrepreneurs generate resources to wage war); a shadow economy (in which profiteers engaged in illicit activities benefit from the lack of a strong state); and a coping economy (which the majority of the population rely upon) (Goodhand, 2004). The official economy may increasingly become peripheral in relation to these other economies. Economic behaviour also becomes increasingly opportunistic in conflict-affected areas owing to the lack of regulatory frameworks and uncertainty about future prospects. Moreover, such economies may persist into the post-conflict period.

In practice there are no clear boundaries between these three economies, and networks have developed with complex overlapping connections. In relation to the poppy economy in Afghanistan, the incentive systems vary at different levels of the commodity chain. For a resource-poor farmer, poppy is part of the coping or survival economy; for the landowner leasing his land or for the opium trader it is part of the shadow economy; and for commanders who tax poppy it is part of the combat economy. The *sarafi* or moneychanger is an important node in this network; his services are used by warlords, profiteers, communities and aid agencies.

In border areas this intermingling and overlapping of various licit and illicit flows—of arms, drugs, smuggled luxury goods along with wheat, watermel-ons and refugees—is most apparent, though not always visible. The Afghan borderlands are areas in which opium is produced, transported, stockpiled and to a limited degree consumed. These borders are places of opportunity and exploitation.[12] Borderlands are also places of constant flux as the geography of the conflict ebbs and flows and the policies of neighbouring countries change. This symbiotic relationship between shadow economies and borderlands is common to many of the cases. For instance at a macro level the Transdniestria shadow economy dwarfs the Moldovan official economy and the de facto state has acted as a duty-free zone and haven for smuggling (Kemp, 2005).[13] At a micro level military checkpoints separating cleared from uncleared areas in Sri Lanka provide opportunities for all sorts of gatekeeper livelihoods related to the taxation of commodities crossing from one protection regime into another. It is also important to note that these economies of wartime are not simply predatory and destructive, and they cannot accurately be described as 'development in reverse', as the World Bank would have it.[14] In many respects war economies contribute to processes of 'actually existing' development in which profits are accumulated and livelihoods are maintained.[15] The example of Kandahar given earlier is illustrative; the drug economy contributed to inward investment and many lives and livelihoods depended upon it.

Conflict resolution approaches tend to assume a clear division between pro-war and pro-peace constituencies or between a criminalized war economy and a licit peace economy. But network war dissolves the conventional distinctions between people, army and government (Duffield, 2001). The networks which support war cannot easily be separated out and criminalized in relation to the networks that characterize peace. Following the fall of the Taliban there were discussions among policy-makers about how to close down the informal money exchange or *hawalla* system. This would have had a catastrophic effect on the livelihoods of the bulk of the population as well as those of the warlords and profiteers.[16]

It is also unhelpful, as mentioned in Chapter 2, to see greed and grievance as binary opposites, given the overlapping and mutually reinforcing motives for political violence. For instance, government corruption (or greed) in 1980s

**Figure 3.1 The Interactions Between
Greed and Grievance in the Ferghana Valley**

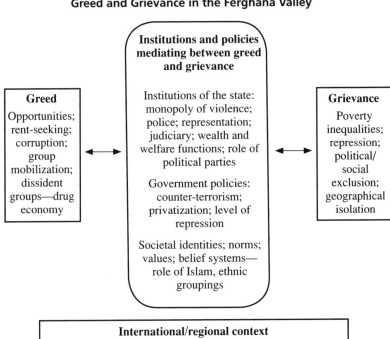

Liberia and 1990s Nepal led to growing dissatisfaction (or grievance), which ultimately exploded into violent conflict. As both cases show, although contemporary research tends to focus on the greed of rebel groups, the rent-seeking behaviour of governments may be equally if not more significant as a cause or catalyst of violence. There is a need to think carefully about the institutional mechanisms, both formal and informal, through which differences are reconciled and resources are distributed. The formal and informal institutions of state and society play a central role. Figure 3.1 highlights the range of contextual and institutional factors that mediate between the dynamics of greed and grievance in the Ferghana Valley of Central Asia.

Social and Cultural Dimensions

A political economy approach tends to emphasize interests and the functionality of conflict. However, as mentioned in Chapter 2, this overlooks the importance of passions (or the emotional economy). As Keen (2002) has noted, violence seems to emerge from a peculiar combination of powerlessness and power. In Sri Lanka, for instance, the conflict cannot be understood without an analysis of the double minority complex of Tamils and Sinhalese, both of whom see themselves as embattled minorities.[17] One of the most important blocks to resolving conflict in Sri Lanka is the lack of a trans-ethnic historical mythology. The mythical histories of Tamils and Sinhalese are reinforced by the media and by an education system that emphasizes ethnic and language boundaries. As Ignatieff (1998) notes, what is important is not how the past dictates to the present, but how the present manipulates the past.

In the case studies, language was a particularly important marker of identity, and a currency used by elites both to mobilize and to exclude certain groups. In Moldova there are tensions over the use of the Romanian and Russian languages, in Kyrgyzstan over the use of Kyrgyz, Russian and Uzbek, in Sri Lanka over Tamil and Sinhala and in Nepal over Nepali and local dialects. English or Russian may have the potential in some of the cases to be a link language which mitigates tensions. However, it can also reinforce exclusion, by being a language of the elite, as has been the case in Sri Lanka.

Militarized violence in the different cases has influenced (and been influenced by) social organizations and relationships in a range of complex and context-specific ways. War economies are not anarchic and do not depend purely on coercion. Trust and social cohesion are critical. In Afghanistan, for instance, counter-intuitively, it may be the absence of a state and predictable social relations which engenders greater trust and solidarity at the local level; people depend upon these networks for their survival.[18] In the former Soviet Union countries the relative dearth of autonomous social organizations at the local level has been important in two respects. First, it has meant communities are more vulnerable to the shocks induced by liberalization, leading to an erosion of human security and increased social friction. Second, it perhaps plays a role in preventing dissatisfaction from turning violent. During the 1990s there was a mood of political exhaustion and disillusionment with reform. This, combined with a 'culture of acceptance' (Lines, 2001: 32), and a tradition equating strength and stability with strong personal rule did, perhaps, limit the potential for political entrepreneurs to whip up animosities. However, the Tulip revolution in Kyrgyzstan suggests that people are no longer so accepting. And the emergence of Islamic groups like Hezb-e Tahir suggests that the shrinking of the public sphere has enlarged the realm of religious commitment, enabling the growth of social organizations and networks which compete with the state.

In Sri Lanka in some respects there has been a depletion of social capital with declining faith in the state and an erosion of bridging social capital between groups. However, one can also discern a tendency to fall back on bonding social capital through the extended family and kinship groups. Leaders have been able to utilize networks of social capital for perverse outcomes. For instance, the LTTE has skilfully mobilized around Tamil identity to fight the war, while attempting to eliminate regional, class and caste-based tensions within the Tamil community.[19] One can hypothesize that there is a relationship between high levels of violence, death and destruction, and deep roots of hostility. Violence is formative—it shapes people's perceptions of who they are and how they interact with their social and physical environment (Feldman, 1991). Conflict entrepreneurs harness faultlines in civil society to wage war.[20] Societies in which armed conflicts have destroyed assets and associated forms of human, financial and environmental capital are likely to have low net capacities for managing and resolving violent conflict. Where economic opportunities beyond the combat and shadow economies are limited and bridging social capital has been eroded, with communities divided into ethnic enclaves, the peacebuilding challenge is likely to be much greater.

Identity and conflict. Findings from the case studies concur with research that questions essentialist, fixed notions of identity. Individuals or groups assume multiple identities, often as part of an elaborate survival strategy. In Sri Lanka, for instance, Tamils in Colombo may wish to emphasize their class identity rather than their ethnicity, as a form of protection. While identity can be a connector which helps populations to survive in crisis, it can also be used by political entrepreneurs to mobilize groups for divisive purposes. In Sri Lanka ethnic scapegoating and the assertion of ethnic chauvinism have been instruments deployed by political and military entrepreneurs to achieve their goals. Although it is beyond the scope of this book to examine the question of identity in depth, Box 3.2 provides a summary of some of the issues raised in the case studies.

In the above section on conflict structures, a range of factors were identified, which together may create the permissive conditions for armed conflict. These are summarized in Box 3.3. Though it is evident that conflicts have multiple causes, it is also important to recognize that they have *different* causes. One of the chief analytical challenges is how one weights the different factors—which of the many causes are more important in each particular case? Clearly some factors have greater significance than others. Second, it is important to think about the linkages and connections between these different factors. It is never possible to narrow things down to a single root cause; it is about which combinations of factors taken together create a combustible cocktail in a particular environment. This moves the analysis into conflict dynamics and actors, which are dealt with next.

Conflict Actors

The critical role of conflict spoilers has been highlighted in other studies.[21] Conflict environments are defined by uncertainty and in such an environment

Box 3.2 Identity and Conflict—Observations from the Case Studies

Ethnicity. Rather than ethnicity causing conflict, hardened identities were primarily a consequence of conflict. In Sri Lanka, for instance, the conflict has become increasingly ethnicized, leading to competing Tamil and Sinhalese nationalisms. Ethnicity has disabled class and caste politics. Although one should not discount ethnicity as a possible source of conflict, the critical factor is perhaps how ethnic cleavages are built and managed by entrepreneurs, i.e. how individuals mobilize identity rather than vice versa.

Gender. Conflict has profound but mixed impacts on gender roles and relationships. Women may increasingly enter the public realm in becoming heads of households or may even play important roles in rebel movements (as in Nepal and Sri Lanka). Despite this, the fundamental values to which males and females are socialized remain largely intact and durable, even in the middle of conflict. After conflict there may also be strong pressures for a return to normality in terms of gender roles.

Religion. Communal identity based on a religious ideology which is of a fundamentalist and exclusivist nature appears to have particular power to capture imaginations and fire conflict. This was most pronounced among the Taliban in Afghanistan, where religion represents a powerful force for mobilizing and radicalizing groups, particularly those excluded from economic and political transitions. Religion in Kyrgyzstan also provided a sense of refuge for those dissenting from authority.

Age. Mainstream analysis of identity conflicts tends to focus on ethnicity or religion, with surprisingly limited attention paid to intergenerational tensions. In Nepal, for example, Maoist recruits are primarily disaffected youths, while in Sri Lanka it was the educated youth who were responsible for the JVP uprising. In spite of the evidence that countries with a high proportion of disaffected youth are likely to experience violent conflict, governments and donor policies tend to pay insufficient attention to the needs and aspirations of young people.

Class. An analysis of class interests is important in terms of understanding conflict in countries such as Nepal. The democratic transition represented an elite pact between the royalists and the urban middle classes of the Congress Party, and did not meet the aspirations of the educated middle and working classes in rural areas. Similarly, the Sinhalization of Sri Lanka was particularly significant because it had the greatest impact on the Tamil middle classes which relied on government employment. This led to growing political activism from the Tamil middle classes and eventually to armed resistance.

Urban-Rural. These tensions often combine with or mask other forms of tension linked to culture, religion or competition for resources. It is striking that in many countries affected by conflict the epicentres of violence are isolated, resource-poor areas suffering from government neglect and chronic poverty. As conflict becomes violent in these areas, government and donor services usually withdraw, thus feeding into the negative dynamic of the conflict.

Source: Adapted from Goodhand (2001a).

Box 3.3 Summary of Structural Sources of Tension and Conflict

Security
- Security forces have limited capacity and are weakly controlled
- Human rights abuses from security forces/armed groups
- High levels of military spending
- Presence of non-state military actors
- Poorly controlled/contested borders
- Unstable regional/international context (e.g. political changes in neighbouring countries)
- Legacy of past conflict
- Proliferation of light weapons

Political
- Weakly institutionalized/ unrepresentative political system
- Lack of independent judiciary
- Lack of independent media and civil society
- Culture of impunity and corruption
- Elite infighting, lack of an elite pact
- Weak political parties, lack of accountability
- Lack of popular participation and gender imbalance in political and governance processes
- Flawed election processes
- Political exploitation of ethnic and religious differences
- Systems for managing conflict weakly developed
- Weak and uncoordinated international engagement
- Destabilizing role of diaspora populations

Economic
- Economic decline: trends in poverty, unemployment, inflation, food security, access to social welfare
- Widening economic disparities: growing Gini coefficient based on regional or ethnic divisions
- Macro-economic instability
- Shift to destabilizing external investment patterns or destabilizing international economic policies
- Increasing competition over shared resources
- Development of war economy

Social
- Social exclusion
- Legacy of unresolved ethnic conflict
- Discourse of victimization/victimhood
- Absence of crosscutting social and civil society organizations
- Tensions over language, religion, ethnicity
- Failure of dispute resolution mechanisms and decreasing legitimacy of authorities

Source: Adapted from Goodhand, Vaux and Walker (2001).

the calculation of the spoilers may be that the benefits of war outweigh the costs of peace. This is not only about an economic calculus—the emotional economy is also significant. Particularly in long-running conflicts, the space for compromise may be quite narrow; war produces accumulated grievances that narrow the psychological space for reconciliation (MacFarlane, 2000). For instance, political elites in Armenia and Azerbaijan are constrained in peace negotiations because of the spoiler role played by extremist political parties. Regional spoilers may be an important destabilizing factor.[22] Furthermore, diasporas in a number of case studies were a significant impediment to conflict resolution.

Table 3.1 maps out some of the sources of insecurity emanating from conflict spoilers in Afghanistan in November 2003 and international efforts to address them.

As noted in Chapter 2, structural analyses of conflict tend to give insufficient weight to the importance of individual agency and leadership. A comprehensive conflict analysis must include questions related to the interests,

Table 3.1 Conflict Spoilers and International Responses in Afghanistan, 2003

Regional actors (e.g., Pakistan, India, Russia, Iran, Uzbekistan)
Interests: Regional powers support proxies to further their security or economic interests. Pakistan, for example, has concerns that a stable Afghanistan will be pro-Indian. Russian support for Fahim to expand its sphere of influence in the north and likewise with Iranian support for Ismael Khan in the west.
Indicators: Border incidents with Pakistan; Russian provision of arms to Fahim.
Types of intervention: Good Neighbourly Relations Agreement; Tripartite Commission on border security.

Neo-Taliban/Al Qaeda/Hekmatyar
Interests: Total spoilers whose common interest is the failure of the peace process and the ending of an international presence.
Indicators: Growing number of terrorist incidents including targeting of aid agencies; night letters; increased presence in southeast.
Types of intervention: Operation Enduring Freedom; Afghan National Army training; border police; counter-narcotics.

Factionalism
Interests: Warlords both inside and outside the government. Differing interests, but all jockeying for power and building up their political and economic power bases.
Indicators: Recent talks between Fahim, Rabbani and Sayyuf; clashes between northern warlords Dostam and Mhd. Atta, and between Ismael Khan and Gul Agha in the south and west.
Types of intervention: Security sector reform (SSR), including Ministry of Defence reforms; DDR; customs and revenue reform; counter-narcotics.

Criminality/banditry
Interests: Opportunistic and survivalist responses to the power vacuum.
Indicators: Growth of narcotics trade; banditry on roads.
Types of intervention: Police reform; judicial and penal reform; counter-narcotics strategy; alternative livelihoods.

Source: Goodhand with Bergne (2003).

incentives, capacities and relationships of the various conflict stakeholders. Box 3.4 provides an example of an analysis of conflict actors in the Ferghana Valley region of Kyrgyzstan.

Evidently, motivations and incentives are complex and multifaceted. As Collier (2000) notes, leaders may generate a loud discourse of grievance to hide economic agendas which may take precedence over political or military factors. Contemporary wars may contain numerous free-wheeling elements that are loosely controlled by military leaders. Some analysts in Nepal, for example, see the head of the CPN-M leadership becoming increasingly detached from the body of the field-based cadres. In such a case, peace negotiations which only involve getting the leadership round a negotiating table are unlikely to lead to sustainable peace. UN-led negotiations in Afghanistan faced similar problems with the fracturing of the resistance parties in the early 1990s. Alliances and counter-alliances changed with bewildering regularity, so that the peace-makers were continually on the back foot. The same applied in Liberia with the civil war being fought by eight factions with limited coherence militarily or ideologically. The more protracted the conflict, the more likely the splintering of military factions as the war begins to take on a life of its own. Even in Sri Lanka, seen by many as a classic 'old war' in the sense of having two clearly defined parties with largely ideological agendas, there has been a decentralization of violence, with numerous semi-autonomous paramilitary groups being used by the government to wage war on the cheap.

The combat, shadow and coping economies schema highlights the importance of looking at individual actors and how incentive systems may work in favour of peace or war. The conflict entrepreneur, for example, may with the right kinds of incentives have an interest in becoming a political entrepreneur or statesman. General Dostam, a northern Afghan warlord, for example, since the fall of the Taliban appears to have political ambitions at the central government level and may be prepared to lay down his arms to achieve this ambition. On the other hand, the primary motivation of extreme spoilers like Gulbadin Hekmatyar appears to be undermining the new political dispensation. Some specialists in violence such as the LTTE leader Velupillai Prabakharan, may have a strong political agenda, while for others, like Charles Taylor, economic interests may be more significant. Motivations also vary at different levels: for the fighter the AK47 may purely be a means of survival. They may have more to gain from peace if alternative livelihoods are created than a mid-level commander who has grown rich by taxing the opium trade. One also needs to look beyond the national level, given the critical role of diaspora communities in supporting violent conflict. Most noticeable examples from the case studies are the roles of the Tamil and Armenian diasporas which have been bankrolling separatist or irredentist movements for a decade or more.

The relationship between leaders and followers is more complex than simply a coercive one; in some respects military leaders may be providers of a public good, such as security or financial support to fighters and their families,

Box 3.4   Local Conflict Actors in the Ferghana Valley, Kyrgyzstan

Post-Soviet Elites. Despite the democratic reforms of the post-Soviet era, officials from that time have been successful in retaining much of their former power and have developed sophisticated mechanisms for using the state apparatus for their own gains. In particular they have been successful in directing the benefits of development projects to their own advantage. Because the process is exclusive there are risks of alienating ethnic minorities as well as creating general grievance in society.

Drug Traders. Although the region is poor, spectacular wealth can be made in the drugs trade from Afghanistan. This acts as a magnet for young men who otherwise have very little hope of employment. The trade results in the spread of weapons and violence. It also leads to an increase in drug addiction and more crime by drug addicts. If outside forces attempted to suppress the trade there could be a violent reaction.

Religious Radicals. There is widespread depression, especially among young men, because of the economic situation. Many are turning to fundamentalist religion. This might act as a safety-valve except that in neighbouring Uzbekistan and widely throughout the region Islamic radicals have been viewed as opposition to state power and potentially dangerous. Russian and US perceptions could lead to the suppression of such groups and this could trigger violent popular reactions.

Military and Police. The huge imbalance between Kyrgyzstan's weak military and Uzbekistan's much larger forces could lead to border incursions. There are already strong tensions over the sharing of resources, notably water and energy. At a more local level, the police offer little help in resolving tensions and often exacerbate them by corrupt practices. Along with a corrupt judiciary, these factors mean that the state has lost its ability to mediate.

General Public. Although conditions may not be much worse than in other poor countries, the people of this region had been used to high levels of employment and very good health and education services until recently. The memory of lost happiness exacerbates the sense of grievance and could become the fuel by which a conflict is created by those with an interest in doing so. Grievance could be directed against the state, or more probably against vulnerable ethnic minorities.

Source: Vaux and Goodhand (2001).

particularly if the state no longer performs such functions. Therefore a form of social contract may emerge between non-state military actors and the populations under their control. The leader–constituency relationship is a dialectical one; to some extent, leaders may be dictated to by their constituency and forced to take a more hardline stance in peace negotiations than they would wish.

In Sri Lanka this has been one of the blocks to successful peace talks. At the same time, political and military entrepreneurs probably have greater agency than would be the case in more rule-bound environments; this is reflected in their ability to relatively quickly mobilize support for their own projects. For instance, nationalist entrepreneurs during the break-up of the former Soviet Union were able to maintain and strengthen their positions by whipping up nationalist sentiments and exploiting the generalized distress engendered by the political transformation.

However, local concerns may trump national, ideological factors. Sometimes what happens on the ground may work against wider military strategy. For example, even during the Taliban blockade of the Hazarajat, the central highlands, trade between Hazaras and Pashtuns continued, defying and thus undermining the military strategy. Interviews with villagers revealed that violent events become a significant part of individual and community memories, which is something that entrepreneurs frequently use to mobilize fighters. However often it may be less about choosing violence than a desperate last resort, a squeezing of options in an environment where few other choices remain. Also many choose not to fight and examples can be found in all cases of peace entrepreneurs, as well as conflict entrepreneurs, as discussed further in Chapter 5.

Conflict Dynamics

It is possible to list the relevant precursors of conflicts or come up with lists of countries at risk, but it is far more difficult to predict the onset of particular conflicts. Identifying what converts disputes into violent conflict and what are the thresholds and triggers for widespread violence is a complex task. Box 3.5 summarizes some of the potential conflict triggers in Moldova in 2000.

Conflicts themselves reshape politics, the economy, social institutions and the state, creating their own dynamics, mutating and changing over time. Dividing conflict into phases divided into the period before, the period during and the period after is therefore too simplistic. In reality there may be several conflicts entwined with one another, often going through their own micro cycles. Causal analysis may become decreasingly relevant, as addressing the original sources of grievance is unlikely to address the conflict dynamic. For instance, the political solutions to the Sri Lankan conflict are likely to be very different from what would have worked 10 years ago. People's expectations of the state have been changed by the experiences of war.

As conflict becomes protracted, violence becomes part of the social experience. Increasingly violence acts as the key arbiter of societal grievance and it becomes routine and normalized. This in itself becomes a major obstacle to the resolution of the conflict. Conflicts may reach an enduring equilibrium or become frozen in a no-war no-peace dynamic, as has been the case in Nagorno-Karabakh and Moldova. Sets of interests at the regional and national levels are

Box 3.5 Possible Conflict Triggers in Moldova in 2000

Elections. Election campaigning tends to throw rational discourse to the wind; the more the economic decline, the higher the stakes of winning political power.

Chechen Refugees. Although their numbers are small (64 case files in February 2000, about 145 known), their presence has already polarized the public on issues of citizenship, refugees, separatism, xenophobic attitudes (towards Chechens and Russians). This could coalesce with a dispute over language rights and discrimination.

Land Privatization. Violence has already erupted locally over land disputes to the point that USAID officials have halted the programme until guarantees are given that the implementation will not create conflicts.

Adoption of Schengen Rules on the Romanian Border. Accession talks with the EU will require conformity with Schengen rules, leading to visas and border closings with Moldova and a possible panic (exacerbated by mass media presentation) and population movements.

Major Corruption Scandal. A scandal that confirms popular suspicions and rumours, pushing frustration at levels of official corruption, penetration of organized crime into the structures of power; and economic deprivation over the level of popular tolerance.

Source: Woodward (2000).

locked into the status quo and it is unlikely that internal solutions will be found in such a context unless the international and regional constellation of actors change their positions. As mentioned in Chapter 2, regional conflict formations appear to be the most difficult types of conflicts to resolve, largely because of the displacement effects; conflicts may be addressed in one area but the problem simply migrates across the border, as has been the case in Sierra Leone and Liberia in recent years. Similarly, if the opium economy were eradicated in Afghanistan in all likelihood it would migrate over the border to Pakistan or Central Asia.

As the case studies demonstrate, war creates its own dynamic. Lives and livelihoods get sucked into the vortex of violent conflict as the combat and shadow economies grow and become the main generators of wealth and a primary source of survival for many. A self-sustaining war economy creates incentives at all levels for the continuation of conflict, particularly where no significant alternatives exist or are placed on the negotiating table. Non-state military actors may be less inclined to sue for peace when they have ready access to resources and recruits.[23] The longer the war continues the more likely the above factors will apply.

As noted in Chapter 2, in all conflicts there are likely to be critical thresholds or moments of change and stabilizing points. At these times there is perhaps the greatest opportunity to influence the trajectory of war. With the benefit of hindsight one can perhaps identify particular moments of change when intervention might have made a difference. For example, the period when the Afghan war mutated from a cold war proxy conflict into a regionalized civil war was perhaps a period when with the right international backing the conflict might have been resolved. In Sri Lanka there have been five periods of peace talks when again there was the opportunity to address the roots of the conflict.

Institutions for Managing and Generating Armed Conflict

As argued in Chapter 2, structural tensions[24] do not by themselves lead to armed conflict—rather it is the interaction of several factors, including the following.

- A society's *structural vulnerability* to armed conflict, in terms of political tensions, intergroup conflicts and economic inequalities, which together undermine human security. This chapter has highlighted the centrality of the state, arguing that violent conflict is likely to be a surface manifestation of a deeper crisis of governance. Furthermore, institutional crises commonly have deep historical roots. The transition from politics to violence is rarely a bolt out of the blue. Societies vulnerable to conflict are characterized by high levels of structural violence, and armed conflict is often preceded by other forms of physical violence. In contexts so fragile one could perhaps describe this as 'latent war' (Debiel, 2002: 1). Furthermore, marginalized groups commonly choose violence only after repeated attempts to pursue their goals through political means. Violence may therefore be a last resort rather than an instrument of choice.
- A society's *capacity to manage or resolve conflict*. Weak states or low-capacity regimes lack the resources to contain or manage conflict and are less likely to compromise or address the grievances of disaffected groups. Institutions that might play a mediating role lack the requisite legitimacy and capacity, and may deliberately marginalize certain groups.
- The *opportunity to profit from instability and violence* by elite groups. This includes the political benefits as well as the pursuit of economic agendas or greed. In unstable and unruly settings, political elites may have greater agency than would be the case in more stable, rule-bound contexts. Often the proximate cause for the outbreak of armed conflict is the breakdown of an elite pact, leading to a re-ordering of the political and coercive forces within a society.
- Particular *contingent events* or external shocks (such as a famine, a natural disaster or stockmarket crash) may act as conflict triggers. High-

capacity regimes are better able to cope with such shocks. But their effects are likely to be much greater and more deadly in contexts where there is already a structural vulnerability to conflict.

Perhaps the most critical factor which comes out from the case studies and lies at the nexus of the four variables outlined above is the role of institutions. This, in many respects, is the key to understanding the causes, dynamics and possible solutions to violent conflict. Mediating institutions play a critical role in terms of predicting or responding to violent conflict by containing opportunities for greed and responding to grievance. The formal and informal institutions of state and society in the security, political, economic and social spheres play a central role in shaping the incentives, preferences, norms and ideas of groups and individuals. It should also be recognized that institutions, like the state, were themselves forged through violence and are a reflection of wider power arrangements. They mirror asymmetries of power between different groups and are the product of coalition building, bargaining and conflict (Srivastava, 2003). Institutions generate power and legitimacy, though clearly some are more powerful and more legitimate than others. The failure to generate raw power or to gain wider legitimacy is likely to signal conflict. Rapid transition and violent conflict (itself a form of compressed transition) place institutions under extreme stress. However, as already mentioned, war, even when it leads to state breakdown, never creates an institutional vacuum. War itself creates new institutions, and alternative economic and sociopolitical arrangements emerge. The political elites of the LTTE, Nagorno-Karabakh and Transdniestria arguably think and act like states, and have created state-like institutions to address the interrelated challenges of security and legitimacy.

There is clearly no ideal set of institutional arrangements that can inoculate a society against violent conflict. What constitutes a 'good' institution is highly specific to a country's circumstances and its particular task. However it is fairly clear from the case studies that an effective social contract—including the rule of law, political voice and redistributive mechanisms—is fundamental to avoiding war or building peace. Based on the evidence of the case studies, exogenous factors play an important role in impeding or supporting the development of effective and legitimate institutions. International interventions in the areas of economic and political reforms, for example, can play a role in dismantling institutional arrangements (Putzel, 2004).

Conclusion

The focus of this chapter, like the previous one, has been on the causes, dynamics and effects of armed conflict. NGOs have not been part of the picture so far, the reason for this being that informed judgements about their roles and impacts are not possible without a robust understanding of the conflict-affected environments in which they operate. It is hoped that this chapter, with its focus on the empirical evidence from the case studies, complements the more theoretical treatment of conflict in the previous chapter, and thus prepares the ground for the analysis of international intervention and the role of NGOs.

A number of key points can be highlighted. First, like the previous chapter, the analysis has focused on the role of the state. A state-centred (rather than state-centric) approach was adopted because the evidence from the case studies suggests that the processes of state formation, crisis and failure are central to understanding why people turn from politics to armed violence. Although questions of causation remain unclear—weak states and underdevelopment may be both a cause and a consequence of armed conflict—how institutions manage contending political, social and economic forces within society appears to be critical in terms of understanding and responding to violent conflict. Although the focus of this chapter has been on institutions under stress, it is also important to emphasize that the state is a remarkably resilient institution and it is rare for it to collapse entirely. In fact, based on the evidence of the cases, the more common problem is one of authoritarian or repressive states. Even democratically elected governments in Sri Lanka and Nepal aggravated conflict by pursuing policies which excluded marginalized groups.

Second, as the case studies show, contemporary conflicts share a number of common features, which are themselves surface manifestations of a deeper institutional crisis. The most challenging and difficult environments for NGOs and peacebuilders are those which combine in extreme form many of the defining characteristics of contemporary conflicts, including: protracted duration; a history of failed peace agreements; regional and international meddling; significant diaspora involvement; a failing or failed state; multiple warring groups with access to a thriving combat and shadow economy; widespread humanitarian distress and destruction; a polarized civil society; and few mediating institutions connecting society with the state. Such conflicts appear to be stuck in a negative equilibrium and even the onset of 'peace'—as in Sri Lanka or Afghanistan—may have a limited effect on levels of human security in the country, due to the 'baleful legacies' of conflict (Luckham, 2004: 488).

Third, though they share similarities, each conflict is different with its own unique combination of structures, actors and dynamics. These conflicts are not all of the same cloth. They are evidently different in terms of their particular phases and their ripeness for resolution. But they also have different histories, and states have adopted different strategies to the challenges of security and the constitutional order. As Luckham (2004: 490) persuasively argues: 'conflicts are best understood not as the product of individual causes, or even as the outcome of particular patterns of governance and non-governance, but rather in terms of the varying historical trajectories that create and sustain violent conflict'. The picture also becomes even more variegated at the subnational (and transnational) level. The critical role of borderlands comes out strongly in the case studies, both as reservoirs of violent resistance and potentially as incubators of peace. As Pugh and Cooper (2004) note, contemporary conflicts need to be placed more firmly within a regional context.

Fourth, states rarely fail purely because of endogenous pressures. Bad governance is usually the result of a combination of international and domestic factors. External pressures on weak peripheral states have grown during the 1990s and their room for manoeuvre is much less than was the case in earlier phases of statebuilding. How the GWOT has influenced the level of empirical sovereignty of such states it is probably too early to judge, but the evidence suggests that much depends on the geostrategic importance of such states and the regional balance of power. The following chapter examines the question of international intervention in greater depth.

4

Understanding Responses to Conflict: International Intervention and Aid

In this chapter some of the key academic and policy debates on conflict, aid and NGOs are examined. The role of NGOs is explored in a context of growing international interventionism in countries affected by instability. Close attention is paid to the critique of humanitarianism that developed in the 1990s, and the donors' and NGOs' responses to this critique. Finally, in the light of the changed international environment, some of the principal challenges faced by NGOs attempting to work in or on conflict are highlighted.

NGOs, Peacebuilding and the New Security Terrain

The last decade has seen the dramatic rise of NGOs. They have become significant players at a global level in terms of numbers, resources and influence.[1] According to Lewis (2002: 373), this increased significance has been associated with three interrelated trends, of which the first is the disillusionment in the 1980s of international donors with the ability of governments to tackle development problems. Second, NGOs became ideologically attractive at a time of privatization policies linked to structural adjustment programmes imposed on Southern governments by Northern donors. Third, there was renewed interest in civil society generated by popular resistance to eastern European totalitarian states and to Latin American military dictatorships. NGOs were viewed as part of the third sector which had the potential to strengthen democratic processes, widen citizen participation in civic life and contribute to the formation of social capital (Putman, Leonard and Nanett, 1993). A fourth factor, not mentioned by Lewis, but one that has evidently contributed to the growth of NGOs, has been the rash of small wars at the beginning of the 1990s. In contrast to the Cold War period when they operated on the fringes of conflict (Macrae and Zwi, 1994; Prendergast, 1996; Duffield, 1997), NGOs in the 1990s found themselves playing a significant and sometimes central role in a succession of multilateral peace operations and humanitarian experiments (Macrae, 1999a). Many of the major international NGOs that originated in the aftermath of the First or Second World Wars expanded their operations as a result of the growing funding and humanitarian needs created by the armed conflicts of the 1990s.

This chapter focuses on the international response to war and its role in shaping NGO strategies and approaches. In the last decade the fields of peace-making/security, development and humanitarianism have converged. It can be illustrated diagrammatically as three (increasingly) overlapping circles (Figure 4.1).

The conceptual models, institutional arrangements and policies associated with peace and security, development and relief that were distinct and separate during the Cold War years have increasingly merged in the 1990s. Conceptually, ideas have coalesced around the framework of human security. Institutionally this is reflected in the growth of multi-mandate peace operations bringing together military, diplomatic, development and humanitarian actors. Programmatically it has been articulated through the idea of three-way programming, which involves combining peacebuilding, development and humanitarian objectives under the same umbrella (Goodhand and Hulme, 1997).

Views about this convergence are divided. Liberals tend to take a benign view of the trend towards more expansive, multi-levelled approaches. NGO interventions, it is argued, can contribute to peacebuilding efforts by comple-menting and reinforcing other tools and instruments. Others argue that the basic thrust of Western interventionism has been to protect liberalism from unruly parts of the world. Duffield (2001) characterizes this attempt to quarantine war (Richards, 2005: 3) as the imposition of a 'liberal peace', a term which

Figure 4.1 The Relationships Between Relief, Development and Security

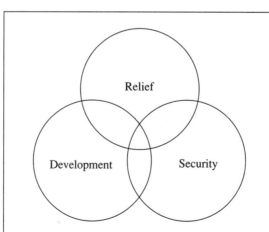

is meant to capture the ideological mix of libertarian concepts of democracy, market sovereignty and conflict resolution (Pugh and Cooper, 2004).[2] NGOs are viewed as the agents of the liberal peace, since it is difficult to separate their development and humanitarian activities from the pervasive logic of the North's new security regime (Duffield, 2001: 16). The tensions between these two positions have become even more acute as a result of the GWOT, as explored further below.

NGOs and Peacemaking

Growing Interventionism

Conflict resolution and peacebuilding have become a new growth area for NGOs, though these fields have a long pedigree.[3] NGOs' increased involvement in this area[4] has led to growing concerns about their role and effectiveness in the 'late Westphalian' environment, as more complex roles are ascribed to them (Richmond, 2003: 2).

One of the principal differences between the Cold War and post–Cold War period has been a redefinition of the notion of national sovereignty. In 1992 the *Agenda for Peace* of the newly appointed UN secretary-general, Boutros Boutros-Ghali, declared the 'time for absolute and exclusive sovereignty has passed'. The progressive incorporation of human rights and humanitarian values into the international political and normative structure were arguably symptomatic of a shift in the centre of gravity of international relations away from states towards individuals (Yannis, 2002: 824). NGOs played a role in this process. In the subsequent UN report of 1994, *Agenda for Development,* three areas were identified in which NGOs could build peace: preventative diplomacy, humanitarian provision and post-conflict peacebuilding. States and intergovernmental organizations have provided or been pressured to provide avenues of participation for NGOs, and they in turn have endeavoured to constrain states in whether and how they use force against other states and against their own people (Richmond, 2003: 2). NGOs, it is suggested, are relatively unencumbered by sovereign concerns, which enables them to work in normative frameworks untainted by official, state and systemic interests (ibid.: 5).[5]

The end of the Cold War and the triumph of liberal capitalism seemingly opened up a new space for multilateralism. The *Agenda for Peace* (UN, 1992) outlined an expanded role for the UN, declaring its right to intervene under Chapter VII in the name of citizens' rights. The UN, it was argued, should be involved in preventative diplomacy, peacekeeping, peacemaking and post-conflict peacebuilding, its role stretching from the earliest stage of conflict prevention through to the final stages of post-conflict reconstruction. Peacebuilding was therefore increasingly associated with multi-track or system-wide responses linking different official and unofficial conflict resolution tracks.[6] With this came a growing focus on coherence and coordination arrangements, because, in the words of the Carnegie Commission (1997: xiv): 'the prevention of deadly conflict is, over the long term too hard—intellectually, technically and politically—to be the responsibility of any single institution or government, no matter how powerful. Strengths must be pooled, burdens shared, and labour divided among actors.' An important role was ascribed to civil society actors, with their potential to 'deepen and widen islands of civility that have endured in war conditions' (Kaldor, 1999: 111).[7] This new agenda for peace entails deep intervention in aspects of governance, humanitarian aid and development (Richmond, 2003).

While the idea of sovereign inviolability may never have been as sacrosanct as conventional wisdom assumed, the 1990s have seen the emergence of increasingly robust interventionary strategies, from Kosovo to East Timor to Afghanistan.[8] UN peacemaking activities have increased nearly fourfold from four in 1992 to 15 in 2002 (HSC, 2005: 153). The UN peacekeeping budget increased from $230 million to US$3.6 billion between 1994 and 1997 (Ottunu and Doyle, 1998: 299).[9] Four different types of international mandated peacebuilding operations can be identified, running along a continuum from consent-based/limited engagement at one end to coercive, multidimensional engagements at the other (Doyle and Sambanis, 2000):

1. Monitoring or observer missions;
2. Traditional, consent based peacekeeping, under Chapter VI of the UN;
3. Multi-dimensional peacekeeping;
4. Peace enforcement under Chapter VII of the UN.

Interventionism in its most extreme version has taken the form of international trusteeship, with the UNSC acting as the alternative custodian of sovereignty.

Most accounts of the activism of the 1990s focus on its multilateral character, rather than the domestic politics of Western powers. But the growth of interventionism and an associated human rights discourse can also be understood as part of a search for an external source of legitimacy by Western leaders following the end of the Cold War. A discourse (and a reality) of failing states and humanitarian crises created a new justification for intervention. According to Chandler (2003: 303) a so-called ethical foreign policy was a 'strong card for western governments, under pressure to consolidate their standing and authority at home'. This moral mission in the international sphere could be contrasted with the uncertainties of domestic policy-making, at a time when the old left/right political framework appeared to have collapsed. An ethical foreign policy helped buttress the moral authority of governments, although it involved very little pressure to account for final policy outcomes (ibid.: 310). It is therefore as well to remember that global governance and the UN have not escaped state power, even though during the 1990s, collectively, 'conflict prevention, humanitarian interventions and post-conflict peacebuilding became parts of an activist international agenda' (Tschirgi, 2004: 4). The normative framework underpinning liberal internationalism (Paris, 2004) was captured in a report published in 2001 by the independent International Commission on Intervention and State Sovereignty (ICISS), entitled *The Responsibility to Protect*. First, like the *Agenda for Peace*, it questioned absolute sovereignty, and second, it presented a case for intervention based not on realpolitik but on morality.[10] Essentially this involved prioritizing human security over national interests and setting out thresholds for intervention on this basis. Some optimistically felt that this signified the emergence of a Kantian democratic consciousness, based upon cosmopolitan frameworks. It has been argued that 9/11 and the consequent US commitment to unilateral activism fundamentally undermined the normative framework for liberal peacebuilding. But in some respects it intensified the pre-existing trends of international activism, the militarization of peacebuilding and the blurring of the boundaries between conflict prevention, peacekeeping and peacebuilding (Tschirgi, 2004). If there has been a shift, it has been in the underlying rationale for intervention, with the focus of the debate moving from human security to homeland security. Arguably peacebuilding is now about protecting 'our' people, rather than protecting 'other' people. Peacebuilding has therefore become increasingly associated with a discourse and set of institutional arrangements related to nation-building, regime change and counter-insurgency. In the post-Iraq world, it is likely to be more difficult to build consensus around the idea that intervention may be a force for good.[11] For NGOs, there are fears that the US shift towards unilateralism is being associated with efforts to shut civil society out of development issues, as the government moves to grant more contracts to private companies instead of non-profit organizations (Soederberg, 2005: 291).

The Effectiveness of Peace Operations

What has been the track record of international attempts to enforce or build peace? Evidence and opinions are mixed. According to Wallensteen (2002), of the 110 armed conflicts between 1989 and 1999, 75 had terminated by the end of 1999. Out of these there had been 21 peace agreements and 22 outright victories. The largest category out of the 110 is continued conflict. However, according to the authors, one-quarter of all conflicts end in negotiated settlement sooner or later. Wallensteen (2002: 31) argues that peacemaking has become a global enterprise and in its absence the number of wars would probably increase significantly. Studies by the University of Maryland (Marshall and Gurr, 2005) together with the *Human Security Report* (HSC, 2005) provide an even more positive prognosis, drawing a direct link between the decline in civil conflicts in the 1990s and the upsurge of activism by the international community in the areas of conflict prevention, peacemaking and peacebuilding (ibid.: 155).

Others draw more sceptical conclusions from the empirical data. Stedman

(2001), for instance, found that between 1900 and 1980 85 per cent of civil wars were decided by one side winning. Only 15 per cent ended as a result of a negotiated settlement. Similarly Licklider (1995), who analysed civil conflicts between 1945 and 1989, found that 58 out of 93 conflicts were settled, but out of these only 14, or 24 per cent, were solved through negotiation. Fighting resumed in seven of the 14, meaning only 12 per cent were resolved through negotiation. Peace settlements may have perverse outcomes. Two massive outbreaks of violence in the 1990s—Angola in 1993 and Rwanda in 1994—followed the failure of peace agreements to end these wars, leading to death tolls of 350,000 and 800,000 respectively. As Stedman (2001) notes, far more people died in the aftermath of peace implementation in these two cases than had died from the preceding years of civil war.

Where warring parties have access to resources and a vested interest in the continuation of fighting, consent-based models may have severe limitations. In the case of Sierra Leone, for instance, it was ultimately the use of force through the deployment of the private security company, Executive Outcomes, that changed the balance of power in favour of negotiations (Shearer, 1997). What clearly does not work is peacebuilding on the cheap, variously referred to as a 'bargain basement' model (Ottaway, 2002) or 'nation building lite' (Ignatieff, 2003). There is rarely a correlation between the ambitions of the international community and their willingness to invest time and resources. In Sierra Leone, for instance, the set of prescriptions for state reconstruction was so exhaustive that it could not possibly be followed in practice (Ottaway, 2002: 1009). 'The bargain basement option has the virtue of being relatively cheap, it soothes the international conscience because something is being done. It is based on international principles of democracy and human rights. Unfortunately it does not appear to work.' (ibid.: 1022)

In a study of peacekeeping operations (PKOs), Doyle and Sambanis (2000) found a strong correlation between the difficulty of the context and the robustness of the international response. Without a peace treaty the likelihood of success of a PKO drops substantially. But multilateral UN peace operations were found to make a positive difference, particularly in the case of missions with extensive civilian functions, including economic reconstruction, institutional reform and elections oversight.

Different analyses and interpretations of the shortcomings outlined above lead to different prescriptions. One is to argue for less intervention, as neo-realists like Luttwak (1999) do. In an article entitled 'Give war a chance', he states: 'an unpleasant truth often overlooked is that although war is a great evil, it does have a great virtue: it can resolve political conflicts and lead to peace' (ibid.: 36). This may be a cheap option in the short run and it may ultimately lead to the emergence of an internal solution to the problem. However, international neglect may also have blowback effects.[12] An alternative option is that of 'liddism' (Rogers, 1999), or the containment of disorder, since the West cannot garrison every failed state (Hirst, 2005: 47). This can be characterized as a conservative multilateralism, which involves 'providing the minimum of force necessary to sustain the current liberal international economic system and prevailing interstate order' (Hirst, 2005: 47). The *Report of the Panel on United Nations Peace Operations* of August 2000 (otherwise known as the Brahimi report) argues for a more activist multilateralism. It found major deficiencies at the political and institutional levels, noting that 'for peace-keeping to accomplish its mission... no amount of good intentions can substitute for the fundamental ability to project credible force' (UN, 2001: viii). Arguably, this approach gained ascendancy in the late 1990s, but has since been added to, or even usurped by, the unilateral activism of the US in Afghanistan and Iraq. These different variants of peacebuilding co-exist alongside one another, even though one may be hegemonic at a given point in time. To an extent none is empirically grounded, but Northern policy-makers find them attractive because they resonate with particular sets of ideological presuppositions (Richards, 2005: 6).

The empirical evidence suggests that NGOs' impacts on conflict resolution are likely to be ephemeral and have a limited effect on wider political processes unless there is a credible and robust Track One process (Ramsbotham and Woodhouse 1996; Miall, Ramsbotham and Woodhouse, 1999; Goodhand with Atkinson, 2001). The profile and scope of NGOs' conflict resolution efforts appear to be inversely related to the geostrategic importance of a particular conflict. For instance, it would have been unthinkable for International Alert to have played the same kind of role in the former Yugoslavia as they did in Sierra Leone, where they were involved in Track One negotiations (Sorbe, Macrae and Wohigemuth, 1997). Therefore, NGOs' role may be residual rather than complementary in the world's discretionary conflicts where there is limited or arm's-length international engagement. An evaluation of International Alert, for instance, concluded that NGOs alone cannot 'compensate for the failure of governmental and inter-governmental bodies to effectively confront the problem of international war' (ibid.: 75). In contexts like Kosovo, where the objective is explicitly to construct neo-liberal democratic entities, this raises serious questions for NGOs about their roles, objectives and relationship with militaries, states and other non-state actors (Richmond, 2003: 1). These questions are brought into even sharper relief in the context of the GWOT and NGOs' associations with an occupying power.

Neo-Kantianism or Neo-Imperialism?

Debates on the ethics and efficacy of international engagement are therefore marked by wide divisions. Liberals tend to take a benign view of intervention, based on the belief that the international system is falteringly moving towards the doctrine outlined in the *Agenda for Peace*. NGOs are seen to complement the role of governmental and intergovernmental agencies, primarily by strengthening people's voice and participation in peace processes (Woodhouse, 1999; Lederach, 1997; Miall, Ramsbotham and Woodhouse, 1999). Critics of the liberal position argue that Western powers are not disinterested parties. Peacemaking and peacekeeping within the Westphalian system tends to replicate the flaws of that system (Richmond, 2003). In the absence of a centralized international system that can authoritatively articulate, interpret and enforce the common interests and values of the international community, peace enforcement approaches risk being perverted and becoming an arm of the foreign policy of dominant states (Yannis, 2002: 830). NGOs, it is argued, have contributed to the privatization of peacebuilding, which paradoxically undermines the overall goal of peace and stability by eroding the authority and legitimacy of states. Furthermore, like other organizations attempting to regulate conflict, NGOs take it upon themselves to adjudicate over internal processes of social and political transformation, even though they lack a political and ethical framework capable of distinguishing between just or unjust claims (Voutira and Brown, 1995; Duffield, 1997).[13]

The tension between these two positions, that might be characterized as Kantian or Clausewitzian, manifests itself in different ways, for instance, in the European focus on soft security and the US focus on hard security (Duffield, 2001), or the tension between the UN as 'we the member states' and the UN as 'we the people', in other words, between the UNSC with its foundational principles of member states' sovereignty (which usually means privileging the sovereignty of Western powers) and the UN as the General Assembly with its responsibility towards the protection of the welfare of people within states and the laws of the UN, Geneva Conventions and human rights treaties (Donini, 2003b).

NGOs, Development Aid and War

Development Aid and Conflict in the Cold War

The increased involvement of NGOs in peace operations can be attributed partly to the growing significance of specialist conflict resolution agencies involved in Track Two activities. However, also important—and perhaps more so in funding terms—has been the mandate expansion of development NGOs[14] into Track Three work.

The development enterprise has until recently been largely agnostic towards matters of conflict and insecurity (Uvin, 2002: 5). In Rwanda, for example, between the late 1980s and the early 1990s the annual flow of aid to the Rwandan government rose by 50 per cent, notwithstanding the regime's complicity in inciting violence by Hutu extremists against the Tutsi minority (Boyce, 2002c: 1032). Even in countries with fresh memories of civil war, such as El Salvador, aid donors were criticized for being conflict-blind. In the period immediately following the peace agreement the IMF pushed ahead with its economic reform package, failing to coordinate with, or make concessions to, the fragile

UN-led peace process (Boyce, 1996). In many parts of the world, concerns about conflict were less pressing than the need to support Cold War allies. For instance, a World Bank study found that between 1970 and 1993 aid allocations by bilateral and multilateral donors were dominated by politics, both the international politics of the Cold War and the internal politics of aid agencies (cited in Boyce, 2002b: 62). Though development NGOs were less constrained by the Cold War straitjacket, an analysis of Oxfam's response to the Ethiopian famine of 1984 highlighted their blindness to the links between emergencies, conflict and development (Vaux, 2001).

The Post–Cold War Radicalization of Development

The end of the Cold War removed the rationale for nurturing a complex web of political allegiances through military and development aid. Arguably this opened the political space for aid donors to make funding decisions based primarily on development criteria such as needs, effectiveness or impact.[15] NGOs gave them the flexibility to do so. They became a central part of the new aid paradigm (Duffield, 1998), filling the gaps created by the withdrawal of governmental control under pressure of neoliberal reforms (Hulme and Edwards, 1997; Van Roy, 1999). Aid donors became increasingly involved in the internal politics and economics of recipient countries. By the 1990s donors had added political reforms to the economic template of structural adjustment. This was associated with a radical shift in thinking. It involved moving from the realization that certain political and economic preconditions were required for development aid to work, to the belief that aid itself could create these preconditions (Macrae, 2001). The end result was a level of intrusion and social engineering that would not have been countenanced by earlier generations of aid donors.

During the last decade significant resources have been invested in areas threatened, affected or emerging from violent conflict.[16] A third generation of aid conditionality emerged as awareness grew about the links between conflict and development. Peace was added to economic and political reforms as a further condition to be placed on aid. Peace conditionality, the use of formal performance criteria and informal policy dialogue to encourage the implementation of peace accords and the consolidation of peace, has increasingly been applied to aid in conflict-affected countries (Boyce, 2002a: 1025).[17] In practice peace conditionalities involve a series of mini-bargains with leaders and communities and the judicious application of 'carrots' in the form of aid and 'sticks' in the form of sanctions or the withdrawal of assistance.

The reinvention of development as a strategic tool for conflict management and peacebuilding has been described by Duffield (2001) as the securitization of aid. In a sense aid and politics have been reunited, although in a different fashion from the Cold War period. Whereas development and security were interstate affairs during the Cold War, the locus of security has become the nature and quality of domestic relations (Duffield, 2002: 1066). This is seen to be the natural domain of NGOs, who have been encouraged to reconceptualize their development activities as peacebuilding programmes, reflecting earlier ideas of NGO comparative advantages: they are closer to the grassroots, better informed, can more easily build trust, are flexible and so on (Duffield, 1997: 88). Development and security concerns have coalesced around the issue of civil society, in spite of the absence of any consensus regarding what civil society is or how it works (Voutira and Brown, 1995; Stubbs, 1995; Duffield, 1997). At best it is an ill-defined space 'of uncoerced human association' (Hopgood, 2000: 1) between family and the state.[18]

Conflict is seen as the result of internal development malaise and the prescription is to build human security through a range of economic and social policies, including poverty eradication, tackling corruption, protecting human rights and supporting popular participation—and also new more sensitive areas such as reform of the security sector and the judiciary (Uvin, 1999). Somewhat perversely, as ambitions increased and the conditions placed on aid grew, there was a decline of aid in real terms from $63 billion in 1992 to $55 billion in 2000.[19] However, aid flows were increasing prior to 9/11 and in 2002 reached a record high. Paradoxically, although development actors have never had it so good in terms of funding levels and political profile, there is a deep unease among donor agencies. This stems from concerns that with growing funding has come diminished autonomy. Development actors feel increased pressure to align themselves behind security objectives related to the GWOT rather than the Millennium Development Goals. Although it is too early to come to firm conclusions, the changed pattern of funding appears to confirm these fears. Mirroring the subordination of development programmes to foreign policy in the Cold War period, the distribution of funding is beginning to reflect the new division of the world into rogues and allies. Therefore, Pakistan, a key ally in the GWOT, was the highest recipient of aid in 2002. In 2003, the US pledged US$20 billion for reconstruction in Iraq, equal to one and a half times the US's annual development aid budget (Cosgrave, 2003: 1). Moreover, in the same year the US created the Millennium Challenge Account, a development fund of $5 billion per year, the qualifying grounds being largely political (Soederberg, 2005).

Therefore, during the 1990s there has been a merging of development and security and this process appears to have intensified since 9/11. Arguably, in the 1990s development and security were viewed as different but equal, in the sense that development assistance was largely shaped by and implemented according to development criteria. The GWOT has meant that security has risen to a position of determinacy (Duffield and Waddell, 2004). The recalibration of aid appears to involve a new quid pro quo: it is about providing 'them' with development, in return for 'our' security. For many aid agencies the hardening of the security agenda has reversed the progress of the 1990s in relation to human rights, arms sales and poverty reduction (ibid.: 3).

Peacebuilding and Institutional Reform

The radicalization of development is reflected in corresponding changes in donors' strategies, approaches and institutional arrangements. The fact that conflict prevention is currently accorded a priority by the World Bank, the UN, OECD/DAC and the G8 would have been inconceivable even five years ago (Mack, 2002).[20] New organizations have been created such as the World Bank's Post Conflict Unit,[21] the US Office for Transition Initiatives (OTI) or DFID's Conflict and Humanitarian Affairs Department (CHAD), and new coordination arrangements have been developed.[22]

NGOs are only one set of actors in a multilevel, networked system involving different contracting arrangements and partnerships with a range of state and non-state, commercial and not-for-profit actors. However, the extent to which this radical new agenda is implemented in practice can be questioned. Donor behaviour appears to be much more variable—between individual donors and from country to country—than many commentators seem to allow. Uvin (2002), for instance, maps out a continuum of donor approaches to conflict and peacebuilding, ranging from minimal adaptation ('rhetorical re-packaging') to a fundamental reorientation of strategies ('global system reform'). The former tends to involve feel-good changes such as tinkering with projects and the development reflex of arguing that development by definition promotes peace. The latter involves a more radical rethinking of the development business, necessitating a global vision which 'redirects the spotlight back onto the rich countries and the global international political economy where their corporations and citizens occupy such a privileged position' (Uvin, 2002: 20). The obstacles to effective peacebuilding assistance lie not only on the recipient side, but also, as Boyce (2002a) argues, on the policies and practices of aid donors and operational agencies. For instance, the Utstein evaluation study of peacebuilding (GTZ, 2003) by Norway, the Netherlands, Germany and the UK found that none of the countries was able to articulate an agreed policy or doctrine on peacebuilding.

NGOs, Humanitarianism and War

The Growth of Humanitarianism

> In the West, the term humanitarian has become elastic. It can be a straight synonym for 'compassionate'; or it can embrace a wide spectrum of aid based on commitment to shared humanity; or it can refer more specifically to the technical delivery of relief in zones of disaster or conflict. (Bentham, 2002: 28)

Humanitarianism is rooted in 17th-century enlightenment and 18th-century philanthropy, but its emergence as a component of the international response to war is a more recent phenomenon. For much of the 20th century emergencies have been treated as aberrant phenomena to be treated with relief. Many of today's major NGOs were formed in response to emergencies or war: the Red Cross as a result of the wars of Italian unification, Save the Children at the end of the First World War and Oxfam in response to the Greek famine of 1943 (Smillie, 1995). Up until the 1980s, humanitarian aid was confined to the periphery of conflict, to safe government areas and refugee camps in neighbouring or neutral countries. However, with the thawing of Cold War relations, gaining access to the victims of conflict was increasingly articulated as a humanitarian right. International intervention in several war-torn countries was seen as evidence of humanity trumping sovereignty. NGOs linked to rebel movements, as in Tigray and Afghanistan, delivered humanitarian assistance without the consent of the Ethiopian and Afghan governments respectively. Operation Lifeline Sudan, established in 1989, was the first attempt to institutionalize a framework to secure access to civilians on both sides of the conflict (Macrae, 1999a: xiv).

During the 1990s NGOs became significant players in a number of humanitarian experiments conducted under the umbrella of the UN, which sought to develop new approaches to conflict-related disasters. In non-strategic conflicts humanitarian action has tended to be the primary if not the only form of international engagement. In high-profile emergencies, however, NGOs have had to contend with a complex set of agendas and relationships with non-aid actors, many of whom claim to be acting under the banner of humanitarianism. Kosovo was after all declared a 'humanitarian war' by the British prime minister, Tony Blair. In such conflicts there has often been deliberate blurring of the lines between the military and the humanitarian. The visibility of humanitarian aid was important in legitimizing military and political interventions both to the domestic public in Western democracies and internationally (Macrae et al., 2002: 12).

These experiments were made possible by the rapid expansion of the aid system. By 1999 some 40–50 million people were direct beneficiaries of humanitarian assistance. Between 1990 and 2000 the volume of official humanitarian assistance almost tripled from $2 billion to $5.9 billion. It also increased as a proportion of ODA from 5.83 per cent to 10.5 per cent (Macrae, 2002: 11). By 2000 one-half of the UN aid budget was devoted to relief (Forman and Patrick, 2000: 2). Successive emergencies have had a ratchet effect and have served to lever up the overall volume of humanitarian assistance. This has been in the context of declining global ODA, leading to concerns that development funds have been cut at the expense of emergency funding.

NGOs have been one of the chief beneficiaries of this expansion. They have been instrumental in extending the reach of the humanitarian system, as donors increasingly directed resources through them based on a belief in their comparative advantages over governments and multilateral agencies. In 1980 there were 37 NGOs on the Thai border; in 1995 there were 200 in Goma and in 1996 the number had grown to 240 in Bosnia (Natsios, 1995, cited in Cooley and Ron, 2002: 10). There has been a trend away from multilateral methods of disbursing humanitarian assistance towards direct support for NGOs. By the late 1990s most OECD countries were disbursing at least 25 per cent of emergency assistance through NGOs and by 1998 over 60 per cent of the European Commission Humanitarian Aid Office was being spent through NGOs (Reindorp, 2001). The 1980s and 1990s have seen the growth of a number of super-NGOs or transnational NGOs, such as CARE, Plan International, Save the Children and Oxfam, who in many conflicts rival or surpass the UN in terms of operational capacity. There are six or seven major NGOs who manage $2.5–3 billion, amounting to 45–55 per cent of global humanitarian assistance (Smillie and Minear, 2004: 195).

Humanitarianism in Crisis?

In the eyes of many people, humanitarian aid has lost much of its moral currency. Once an undisputed symbol of solidarity with those struck down by misfortune and adversity, humanitarian assistance is now vilified by many as part of the problem, feeding fighters, strengthening perpetrators of genocide, creating new war economies, fuelling conflicts and perpetrating crises. (Clare Short, former Secretary of State for DFID, cited in MacFarlane, 2001: ix)

During the 1990s the aid system came under increased scrutiny. This was related to the growing role and public profile of humanitarianism and the introduction of public management reforms in Western governments. Both led to an increased focus on NGO performance, value for money, accountability and impacts. For humanitarian NGOs a number of defining events including Somalia, Rwanda and Kosovo focused attention on the dark side of aid and its potential to have unintended impacts. Somewhat perversely, emergency assistance has never been subject to so much external scrutiny and internal reflection, while the demand for such assistance has never been greater. The critique of humanitarianism has many different strands, but it can broadly be divided into three areas: first, aid has become politicized and is manipulated by non-humanitarian actors; second, aid has perverse effects; third, aid actors are unaccountable, unregulated and ineffective. Whereas the first two focus on the relationship between intervention and the wider context, the third is concerned with the internal deficiencies of the aid system.

The politicization of aid. Humanitarianism is not a political project. It has the modest but vitally important ambition of ensuring the most vulnerable are not sacrificed in times of conflict and crisis (De Torrente, 2004: 28). This reflects the hardwon practical wisdom of organizations like ICRC and MSF. But actually existing humanitarianism rarely maintains such a distinct and independent position in relation to politics. Humanitarian intervention always involves considerations that are non-humanitarian. As Smillie and Minear (2004: 23) note: 'No government's humanitarian policies are free-standing—they flow from a country's foreign and domestic policies and projects.' In practice they have tended to mirror global politics, so that more robust and concerted programmes have been conducted in areas of strategic interest like Kosovo, in contrast to those of less immediate importance like the DRC or Sudan. This is the argument of humanitarianism instead of politics, in other words the idea of aid as a fig-leaf for Western inaction.[23] A variance of this analysis is the more radical idea of politics through humanitarianism or, to put it differently, humanitarianism as the continuation of politics by other means. Simply by applying the label 'humanitarian' the normal rules of sovereignty are suspended. Whereas economic and political conditionalities have to be negotiated and require the consent of the governments exposed to such measures, 'humanitarian intervention can take place without such consent. In other words, humanitarian intervention involves setting aside the protective barriers of international norms, the defence device which allowed the post-colonial state elite a free rein in domestic affairs.' (Sorensen, 2000: 6)

As Ignatieff argues in relation to Kosovo, humanitarianism is essentially an imperial enterprise 'because it requires imperial means: garrisons of troops and foreign civilian administrators, and because it serves imperial interests: the creation of long-term political stability in the south Balkans, the containment of refugee flows into Western Europe, and the control of crime, drugs and human trafficking... Humanitarianism is in the service of long-term state interests of the rich nations on the Security Council' (Ignatieff, 2003: 60). On the whole Ignatieff appears to be supportive of this development, though in his view imperial power should project itself more robustly and consistently. Sovereignty, it is argued, should be treated instrumentally, not as a shibboleth (Keohane, 2003: 10), and the sins of omission, like Rwanda, are more serious than the sins of commission. Others are less comfortable with 'state-led humanitarianism' (Rieff, 2002), as through its incorporation into a wider conditional aid package it loses its unconditional and universal value (Duffield, 2002).

An analysis of funding trends illustrates how responses to conflict are highly selective and bear little relationship to humanitarian needs. Comparatively generous donations tend to flow to emergencies in the media spotlight: virtually 100 per cent for former Yugoslavia from 1993 to 1995, though falling to 69 per cent while the area was out of the news in 1996. Other crises, with perhaps just as much need, are largely ignored. In 1999, for instance, a refugee in Kosovo could expect to receive $207 per year in international aid, while an Afghan would receive on average $23 per year. The UN Consolidated Appeals Process (CAP) is the nearest thing to a global assessment of need. Figures from the CAP for 2000 show great variation in appeals per head, ranging from less than $10 per head in Uganda and Tajikistan to $185 per head for southeastern Europe (Macrae, 2002: 14). In 2002 global funding for humanitarian assistance was $4.7 billion, of which 83 per cent was spent in Iraq, though few agencies have identified a humanitarian crisis there (Duffield and Waddell, 2004).

It has been argued that there is now a closer relationship than ever between the assertion of national interests and the provision of humanitarian assistance because of the trend towards the bilateralization of aid. Bilateralization is understood as donors reducing the share of their aid channelled through multilateral institutions in order to exert influence more directly (Macrae et al., 2002: 10). Between 1996 and 1999 the volume of assistance channelled multilaterally increased by 32 per cent compared with the previous decade, while bilaterally managed expenditure increased by 150 per cent. A very small group of donors account for the bulk of humanitarian spending. The US dominates, providing about one-third of spending in 1998–2000. The US and eight other bilaterals account for 93 per cent of official humanitarian aid (ibid.: 3).

Aid fuels conflict and undermines local capacities. The links between humanitarian aid and conflict are very old,[24] though discussion on this topic is comparatively recent (MacFarlane, 2001). One can identify a range of unintended effects, direct and indirect, on conflict structures and dynamics, as follows.

• Assistance may have perverse *political* effects: NGOs which set up parallel systems of service provision may undermine the social contract between governments and their citizens (Hanlon, 1991; de Waal, 1997). Because of the overriding imperative to gain access, NGOs can inadvertently legitimize unrepresentative groups (Anderson, 1999) and remain silent in the face of widespread human rights abuses (Keen, 1998).
• Aid may have a range of *economic* effects, which can fuel war economies: Le Billon (2000) identifies a number of ways in which relief is either directly manipulated by armed groups (e.g. taxation or diversion, manipulation of populations or humanitarian space, purchasing of protection) or has unintended effects on the war economy (e.g. substituting or distorting effects). These impacts appear to be greater in instances where there are few other valued resources (MacFarlane, 2001: 64).
• Aid has important *social* effects: particularly in camp situations it has been argued that the manner in which aid is delivered can undermine community coping strategies and create dependency (Harrell-Bond, 1986). Aid interacts with the emotional economy as well as the political economy of war and it may have symbolic value for either pro-war or pro-peace groups.

Aid actors are unaccountable, unregulated and ineffective. The humanitarian system tends to improvise a new response for each successive crisis (Forman and Patrick, 2000). The NGO sector, as Smillie (1995) notes, is a haven for 'wheel inventors'. The multi-donor evaluation of the Rwandan crisis, for example, could not locate one-third of the 170 NGOs registered and $120 million of funding went unaccounted for (Bryans, Jones and Stein, 1999: 14). The evaluation also noted the waste and duplication of efforts in the aid community, due to a lack of strategic co-ordination.

Emergencies attract a multiplicity of actors with diverse mandates, who all claim to be humanitarian but have very different and often contradictory approaches. In such settings the accumulated lessons of best practice gained in development contexts are either ignored or viewed as irrelevant. As noted by Pottier (1996: 57): 'Emergencies are internationally interpreted as occasions for swift action, not as opportunities for critical reflection. In emergencies therefore, it has become legitimate to ignore clients' views of problems and solutions. This leads to top-down approaches to crisis management.' Part of the difficulty lies in the fact that short-term thinking, short-term mandates and short-term funding are being used to confront entrenched and long-term problems and needs. As Edwards (1999) argues in relation to humanitarian intervention in the former Yugoslavia, too many resources were wasted on poorly designed technocratic quick fixes and not enough on slower, longer-term initiatives. Also important has been the increased marketization of aid (Cooley and Ron, 2002). According to de Waal, one of the most strident critics of humanitarianism, in a situation of unregulated NGO activity, a form of humanitarian Gresham's Law[25] takes over, whereby 'debased' humanitarianism drives out the authentic version (de Waal, 1997: 138). The capacity to learn has no marketing appeal and openly questioning the success of the aid project means putting future funding at risk (Schloms, 2003). In spite of the veritable cottage industry that has developed around humanitarian research, evaluation and lesson learning, there is limited evidence of fundamental change in the humanitarian system: 'the international system appears to have an extraordinary capacity to absorb criticism, not reform itself and yet emerge strengthened' (de Waal, 1997: vi).

Responses to the Critique

Broadly there have been two reformist responses to the humanitarian critique. One argues for a maximalist approach, which involves broadening the humanitarian mandate to include development and peacebuilding objectives. The other argues for a minimalist approach involving a return to the narrower and more tightly defined classical humanitarianism. Some of the key features of these two approaches are summarized in Table 4.1.

Beyond relief? Broadening humanitarian responses. One response to the humanitarian critique has been for NGOs to adopt a more expansive approach to humanitarianism, which has involved the collapsing of old distinctions between politics and aid, relief and development, aid and human rights (Macrae et al., 2002). There has been a lateral movement into 'non-copyright'[26] areas (Smillie and Minear, 2004) as donors have encouraged NGOs to think beyond relief and to conceptualize their interventions along a relief–development continuum, so that relief activities contribute to development as peace returns. Agencies are increasingly invoked to do no harm (Anderson, 1999) and a growing number of NGOs have become involved in conflict prevention and conflict resolution activities.[27] In practice, these distinctions mean little to those living through violent conflict and it is argued that NGOs should aim to achieve the optimum mix of activities, matching them to the needs of individual contexts (White and Cliffe, 2000; Roche, 1994). Multi-mandate organizations may be best placed to exploit the synergies between such activities, whether they are categorized as relief, development or peacebuilding.

Associated with these changes has been a shift from duty-based ethics, in which simply attempting to do good was seen to be sufficient, towards conse-quentialist ethics, in which agencies need to consider the possible effects of their interventions and whether they do good or do harm. This has involved harnessing humanitarianism to higher goals such as justice and peace. Copyright humanitarianism, on the other hand, which places neutrality as its highest value, fails to engage with what is right or wrong in a conflict (Anderson, 2004a: 70). That humanitarian NGOs have a role to play in peacebuilding was officially recognized in 1999 when MSF was awarded the Nobel peace prize.

Back to basics: reaffirming humanitarian values. Aid workers have been drawn to ideas about peace and rights because of frustrations over the limitations of what humanitarianism can achieve on its own in a political vacuum (Rieff, 2002). But to what extent has this frustration led to unrealistic expectations of

Table 4.1 Maximalist and Minimalist Responses to the Humanitarian Crisis

Maximalist	Minimalist
Strategic issues	Strategic issues
• NGOs should become more accountable for their direct or indirect impacts on conflict.	• Peacebuilding is a fundamentally political task. Humanitarianism should be kept as a sepa-rate and distinct area of policy and intervention.
• More reflective, conflict-sensitive ap-proaches are required given aid's track record of exacerbating conflicts.	• The potential impact of aid on the dynamics of conflict and peace (positive and negative) should not be overstated.
• Developing coherence between relief, development and peace objectives, including building institutional and political links with non-aid actors.	• Politicization corrupts humanitarian princi-ples. Return to the fundamentals of universality and the humanitarian imperative.
Operational issues	Operational issues
• Move beyond a palliative approach and seek to sustain livelihoods as well as save lives.	• Strictly maintain neutrality and impartiality. This will help maintain humanitarian space and staff safety.
• Develop synergies between relief, develop-ment and peace programming.	• Keep a clear relief focus.
• A more explicit focus on peace so that op-portunities can be grasped when they arise.	• Improve the management, delivery and ac-countability of humanitarian assistance, e.g. SPHERE, Humanitarian Accountability Project, Code of Conduct.
• Greater emphasis placed on building local capacities and supporting constituencies for peace.	• Strengthen political analysis to ensure assist-ance does no harm.

humanitarianism? As Macrae (2002: 7) says, 'The 1990s saw the concept of humanitarianism transformed from a distinctive but narrow framework designed to mitigate the impact of war into an organizing principle for international relations, led largely by the West.' With aid being increasingly politicized, the humanitarian imperative and principles of neutrality and impartiality are at risk.

The overall thrust of the minimalists' reform agenda is that humanitarianism should go back to its roots, in the sense of reaffirming the core beliefs and principles of humanitarianism. It is about recovering and safeguarding the original meaning of humanitarianism from the well-meaning but dangerous reformers (Barnett, 2003: 412). This position is based on a number of assumptions and assertions: first, that humanitarian intervention is driven by the humanitarian imperative, in other words saving lives comes first; second, that the key frameworks and tools for achieving this are the principles of neutrality and impartiality and international humanitarian law.[28] Humanitarian neutrality in essence involves a morally justified suspension of judgement (De Torrente, 2004), which in turn creates a suspended space or humanitarian no-man's-land for those giving and receiving aid. Third, although it is recognized that there is a need to ensure aid does not fuel or prolong conflict, it is not part of its mandate to try to resolve conflict. Ethically there is no justification why future benefits derived from achieving peace or development should outweigh the immediate rights of victims to receive life-saving aid (ibid.). Nor, it is argued, should aid become more developmental. Development assistance depends on bilateral relations with a recognized and legitimate state, something that is usually absent in today's wars (Macrae, 2001). Extending the logic of development assistance in peacetime to humanitarian assistance in war is to misunderstand the specificity and relevance of humanitarianism to the victims of war (De Torrente, 2004). Therefore, minimalists are concerned with fidelity to the humanitarian imperative, developing accountability and improving standards for relief delivery and protection. Iraq and Afghanistan, it is argued, highlight the dangers for NGOs of extending their mandates and thus exposing themselves more directly to the influence of state interests.

Minimalism and Maximalism: A Polarized Debate

Is minimalism a nostalgic and naïve call for political virginity (O'Brien, 2004)? Or is it a vigorous defence of the specificity and relevance of independent humanitarianism? The debate between the minimalists and maximalists has become unnecessarily polarized (Jackson and Walker, 1999). Its quasi-religious tone and the 'with us or against us' polarity strangely mirrors the language of the GWOT. One is reminded of Ignatieff's (1998) 'narcissism of minor difference', such is the anger and passion generated between the different humanitarian 'tribes'. The passion is understandable, but it tends to lead to oversimplistic arguments, postures and defensive reactions. As Jackson and Walker note, the debate has generated more heat than light.[29] There is insufficient understanding of the impacts of aid on the dynamics of conflict and peace and there is a lack of tools to measure and calibrate them. The maximalists probably overestimate the impact that aid can have on political processes, as in the majority of conflict-affected countries aid flows are limited in relation to other economic inputs, and consequently have little political leverage. So far maximalism has remained largely aspirational and there is limited empirical evidence of humanitarian actors building peace from below. There are fears that it may lead to unrealistic expectations of what NGOs can achieve and be held accountable for in areas of conflict.

In some respects debates have moved on and the key point now is less about aid's leverage over conflict than its legitimizing effects on international political and military interventions, as Macrae suggests (2002: 8). However, the minimalists appear to abdicate any responsibility for engaging with the wider political context. The thrust of their argument is about what not to do; and essentially it is concerned with damage control through minimalist inputs of food and medicine (Christoplos, 1998: 1). It is also an extremely Northern-led debate, with humanitarianism being seen as 'our' problem.

Both sides of the debate overstate the newness of contemporary wars and the consequent need for new approaches. NGO workers who cut their teeth in Biafra would recognize many of the political and operational challenges faced by contemporary NGOs in the DRC or Liberia: from the politicization of aid, to dealing with non-state actors, to the denial of access, to the charges that aid prolonged conflict. Overstating the novelty of the post–Cold War landscape limits the important lessons that earlier experience can teach. As Minear (2002: 6) states, there is a need to situate humanitarianism within its broadest possible historical context: 'to have expected the Cold War years to have been followed by an era of principled multilateralism and a new sense of humanity seems historically naïve'.

In practice there is probably a lot more middle ground than the purists on either side would care to admit. One of the few studies on the connection between conflict and aid, for example, concluded that: 'relatively small-scale and contextually sensitive efforts to adjust humanitarian programming in active conflicts may have a positive effect in mitigating the impacts of war. Moreover, carefully delivered transitional assistance may assist in building sustainable peace' MacFarlane (2001: 62). Aid agencies are not usually faced with the simple choice of providing or not providing aid; it is normally about how much to provide, of what types, to whom and with what conditions attached (Boyce, 2002a). Boyce says that conditionality does not require a threat to cut off all aid and can be applied selectively to the subset of aid of greatest benefit to political leaders and least benefit to at-risk populations.[30] The idea of doing no harm is perhaps less useful than benefit-harm (O'Brien, 2001) analysis, since the latter recognizes the inevitably negative effects of aid and the need in many situations to choose the least-worst option.

At the heart of the minimalist-maximalist debate is the question of which objectives should be elevated. Should conflict prevention and peacebuilding have the same value as saving lives and sustaining livelihoods? Should peace be prioritized over justice? Does this mean that agencies should be judged on their ability to prevent violent conflict and build peace? In practice it forces agencies to confront deep ethical questions about the ends their aid is meant to serve. However, such questions cannot be addressed without reference to individual contexts and agency mandates. What has often been lacking in such debates is substantive analysis of particular contexts at particular times with reference to different types of NGOs.

Conclusion

> However diverse and pluralistic the world may seem to Western eyes, to non-Western eyes it can appear to be dominated by a group of victorious powers that seek to impose an ideological hegemony of their own and that do not tolerate opposition. (Freedman, 2004: 253)

Debates on NGOs and peacebuilding suffer from being too aid-centric. To appreciate the potential and limitations of NGOs in peacebuilding it is necessary to look beyond aid, at the wider political framework in which NGOs operate. This chapter has outlined some of the key features of the political and institutional landscape which set the basic parameters for NGO operations in areas of conflict. This was complemented by an analysis of some of the key trends and debates within the NGO sector in relation to aid, conflict and peacebuilding. A number of conclusions can be drawn from this analysis.

First, globally there has been a growth of interventionism and militarized peacebuilding. Although international intervention has been selective and often half-hearted, a defining feature of the post–Cold War period has been the widening and deepening of the international community's engagement with war. Following Somalia, there was a temporary reluctance to get involved in military adventures. But overall, there has been a trend towards more coercive forms of intervention and a greater commitment to engagement in the post-conflict context. Interventions have become more ambitious, wide-ranging and trusteeship-like. The humanitarian experiments of the 1990s and the humanitarian wars at the turn of the century have been justified in terms of universalistic and legal ethics. But in the absence of credible and effective mechanisms of global governance, the rhetorical commitment to universalism has been undermined by the assertion of national interests.

Second, how one understands peacebuilding depends on one's interpretation of these trends. Critical analysts argue that peacebuilding has become a liberal and increasingly imperial project, and is essentially a means of pacifying unstable regions which threaten the core interests of dominant powers. 'Peacebuilding is in effect an enormous social experiment in social engineering—an experiment that involves transplanting Western models of social, political and economic organization into war-shattered states in order to control civil conflict: in other words, pacification through political and economic liberalization' (Paris, 1997: 56). The liberal view, on the other hand, is that peacebuilding, underpinned by an expanded notion of human security and soft power, is a progressive and benign attempt to operationalize the Agenda for Peace doctrine. After 9/11, this position is more difficult to sustain, as arguably concerns about homeland security and counter-insurgency have led to a recalibration of peacebuilding, resulting in an increasingly illiberal peace. Looking again at Figure 4.1, perhaps a more accurate representation now would be for 'security' to encircle both 'humanitarianism' and 'development'. However, neither of these views fits neatly with the empirical evidence; the discourses may appear to be monolithic but the practice is certainly not. A variable approach to the issue of weak and failing states has emerged and it may be more accurate to talk about different variants of the liberal peace being applied in different contexts (Richmond, 2005). It is difficult, for example, to explain interventions in East Timor or Sierra Leone purely in terms of the assertion of liberal (or imperial) interests, though Kosovo, Afghanistan and Iraq fit more obviously into this framework.

However one interprets these trends, it is clear that a model of third-party intervention based upon the assumption of neutral or benign outsider interests is unrealistic. It is not possible to separate out international action as though it were an independent and neutral variable in relation to conflict. Interventions are likely to have an influence on the underlying causes and dynamics of conflict, as well as shaping what emerges afterwards. War may be seen as a point of leverage for the international community, particularly in the post-conflict moment, when sweeping reforms will meet limited resistance. The motivations and incentives of those who make peace are just as mixed and complex as those who make war. Just as the discourse around war cannot only be taken at face value, the same applies to the discourse around peace. Humanitarian intervention has become an important mobilizing idea, which according to Chandler (2003) and Rieff (2002) is now part of the West's conception of itself. War is legitimized through a particular kind of emotional economy. Peace pursued through foreign intervention similarly requires a strong sense of mission and moral certitude, which serves to mask the divergent interests of the peacemakers. The concept and practice of peacebuilding expanded in the 1990s partly in order to accommodate the growing number of actors and interests involved. It has become a mobilizing metaphor, like participation or good governance, 'whose vagueness and ambiguity are required to conceal ideological differences, to allow compromises, to enrol different interests and to multiply criteria of success' (Mosse, 2004: 663).[31]

Third, in terms of achieving stated goals, neither hard power nor soft power appears to be working very well. Institutional reform has not kept pace with the changing political-military landscape. There is a poor fit between the determinants and dynamics of state collapse and the external solutions offered. We do not have sufficient knowledge of the causes of state collapse or the mechanisms for reconstructing failed states. But we do know that though conflicts are complex and variegated, the international response tends to be formulaic and off the peg. It is characterized by Ottaway (2002) as the Procrustean model, meaning the model is given and then the country is pushed and pulled to fit it. There is also a mismatch between the expectations of the international community and the time and resources they are prepared to commit. The fiscal policy to pay for peace that was so central to the success of the Marshall Plan has been absent in most contemporary peacebuilding efforts. It is therefore important to keep external efforts to engineer peace in perspective. Development and humanitarian aid are relatively tiny proportions of global wealth. One should be modest about their potential peacebuilding role in countering the effects of much more powerful military, economic and political interests in intra-state conflicts. Aid is rather a small part of the story of conflict (MacFarlane, 2001).

Fourth, in the last decade there has been a reworking of the relationship between aid, politics and security. Development aid and to an extent humanitarian assistance are seen as strategic tools for the promotion of security. Peace conditionalities have been added to economic and political conditionalities to effect changes in recipient countries. All forms of assistance, it is argued, have to be coordinated and made coherent with the underlying goal of building peace. Aid policy finds itself subordinated to political calculation: 'when the crunch comes, politics nearly always trumps universal principles' (Donini, 2003a: 4). To a great extent the key issue is not the impact of aid on conflict but how its legitimating effects are used by other international actors. But again these trends can be interpreted differently. The relationship between politics and humanitarianism is ambivalent and two-directional. Though politics clearly intrudes upon humanitarianism, some would argue politics is being humanitarianized: humanitarian concerns have forced their way up the political chain and are now aired and discussed at the highest levels (Minear, 2002).

Fifth, NGOs have had to adapt to these changes and increasingly find themselves working in intensified political engagements involving new demands and new pressures. This has involved developing an understanding of the political economy of the response as well as the political economy of war. NGOs have been encouraged by donors to reconceptualize their humanitarian programmes in areas of conflict by moving beyond relief into developmental and peacebuilding activities. There are concerns that more expansive approaches will lead to the distortion of humanitarian principles and prevent aid agencies from achieving their primary goal of saving lives. Although there is some agreement that agencies should develop their capacities to work in conflict more effectively, the idea that they should have an explicit focus on peacebuilding is more contentious.

There has been limited systematic research to support the argument of the maximalists or the minimalists.

Finally, it is important to take the long view on these issues and debates. Wars are not new and neither are the debates about the politicization of aid or the links between aid and conflict. It is important to take a historical perspective on these questions. Moreover, the debates tend to extrapolate and generalize to such an extent that they lose sight of the variability of individual contexts. Actually existing practice is messy, contingent and unpredictable. The debates tend to be shaped more by the concerns of the interveners than the particular challenges of individual contexts and the experiences of people living in them.

5

NGOs and the Dynamics of Conflict and Peacebuilding

This chapter explores the interface between NGOs' activities and conflict and peace dynamics. It examines the direction, nature and magnitude of these interactions: first, how conflict has an impact upon NGOs and their activities; second, how NGO programmes affect violent conflict; and third, how NGO interventions influence peacebuilding processes. The chapter provides an empirical grounding to contemporary debates on NGOs' relationship with warmaking and peacebuilding. It finds that NGOs' impacts are relatively modest and much depends on the precise nature of the context, the NGO itself and the timing of the intervention.

Introduction

The focus here is on the question of how NGO interventions interact with violent conflict and peacebuilding processes. Debates on NGOs and peacebuilding are based on limited empirical evidence. Both the minimalist and maximalist positions draw heavily on anecdotes, usually building up arguments on the basis of either worst- or best-case scenarios. Generalized assertions are made about aid having positive or negative impacts, rarely with any disaggregation in terms of types of contexts, NGOs or activities. It is equally rare for underlying assumptions about the model of change, the agents of change or the level of impact to be specified. NGOs (and researchers) have therefore been quite poor at systematically comparing and analysing over time the interactions between their activities and the dynamics of conflict and peace.

The aid–conflict interaction is a two-way process and this chapter explores how conflict affects NGOs' behaviour and programming as well as how their activities have an impact on the dynamics of conflict and peace. This is done through a synthesis of key findings across the seven cases. The focus here is on domestic conflict and peacebuilding. Chapter 6 explores the interactions between NGOs and the international dynamics of warmaking and peacebuilding.

The different cases represent a patchwork of operational environments, and similarly there is a great deal of variation between the NGO sectors in the different countries, as summarized in Table 1.3. Some have a long history and are relatively embedded (Sri Lanka, Nepal), and others are a fairly recent phenomenon, the product of international engagement due to war (Afghanistan, Liberia) or post-Soviet transition (Moldova, Armenia-Azerbaijan, Kyrgyzstan). The study also covers a range of different categories of international and local NGOs, including niche conflict prevention and peacebuilding organizations (e.g. Tolerance International, Kyrgyzstan; National Peace Council, Sri Lanka; MICOM, Moldova), classical Dunantist NGOs (e.g. MSF) which focus on humanitarian relief and protection, and multi-mandate NGOs which cover a range of activities including relief, development and (sometimes) peacebuilding (e.g. Oxfam, SCF–UK, CARE International). Some are on-site operational NGOs which deliver services in situ and others are off-site, lobbying and advocacy NGOs which focus on specific issues like human rights or constitutional change, unencumbered by projects on the ground.

The Challenge of Assessing Peacebuilding Interventions

The term 'impact' can be defined as: 'the positive and negative, primary and secondary, long-term effects produced by development intervention, directly or indirectly, intended or unintended (OECD/DAC, 2002: 24).[1] According to Hulme (2000), there are three main elements in a conceptual framework for impact assessment: a model of the impact chain, the specification of the unit or level of analysis and the types of impacts to be assessed. But the initial and most fundamental question in relation to peacebuilding is not the technical one of how it is measured but the political one of how it is defined. What constitutes a negative or a positive impact depends on one's normative and political framework. Different measures of success may be used, from the minimalist one of re-establishing a monopoly of force (negative peace) to the more ambitious criteria of popular participation in political processes, rule of law, etc. (positive peace). Clearly definitions are contested and consequently so are measures of success and failure. Who is doing the assessing is also important. There may be a considerable discrepancy between agencies' perceptions of performance and the perceptions of the affected population (Hallam, 1998).

How can negative or positive changes be attributed to a particular intervention without counterfactual or reliable data? Peacebuilding, like capacity building or advocacy, has a long impact chain and is therefore particularly difficult to measure. To what extent are unintended (positive and negative externalities) as well as intended effects considered? Should the focus of enquiry be the effects on the short-term dynamics of conflict (shallow peacebuilding) or the long-term structural causes (deep peacebuilding)? These problems are compounded by a lack of reliable data, particularly in areas of long-term conflict. The absence of comparative data, baselines and indicators about effects and effectiveness is a generic problem in the humanitarian system, providing decision-makers (and researchers) with little guidance.

Another significant challenge is that of time frames. When the measurement is done may make a significant difference to the findings. Impacts may not be felt until several years after the original intervention. There is also the question of the unit of analysis. Are impacts being assessed at the individual, household, community, sectoral or national level? Aid agencies' activities may have positive impacts at the micro level but relatively limited impact at the structural level. If interventions are assessed purely in terms of their impacts on peace writ large, most would be judged as failures. Therefore criteria to measure impact should be proportional to a particular initiative's performance potential, taking into account its scale and scope (Lund, 2000). Impacts at the institutional or macro level are usually the result of joint efforts by a range of organizations, in which case it becomes difficult to attribute impacts to a particular agency or intervention and to judge the aggregated impact on conflict as a whole.

Although it is clearly a complex task, there is a need to explore the question of impact in a systematic way using the available evidence, while keeping in mind that at best one can talk about increasing or decreasing the probabilities of peace or conflict.[2] Precise cause-and-effect chains relating to discrete projects may be desirable for accountability purposes, but they do not exist in this field.

In spite of the difficulties, for the purposes of this study an initial model is put forward to explore interactions between NGOs and conflict or peace. Broadly one can identify three types of interactions between NGO interventions and the dynamics of conflict and peace. It is also possible to characterize NGOs' efforts to either mitigate or amplify these interactions. These can be summarized as follows:

- impact of conflict on aid policies/programmes/projects (conflict proofing);
- impact of policies/programmes/projects on the dynamics of conflict (do no harm);
- impact of policies/programmes/projects on the dynamics of peace (peacebuilding).

These are illustrated in Figure 5.1.

Although this may provide a useful shorthand for aid–conflict interactions and NGO responses, one should keep in mind that peace and conflict are rarely binary opposites. As highlighted earlier, conflict is not necessarily a negative phenomenon, and the presence of conflict in a given context does not exclude peace on a wider level. Inevitably one cannot reduce such a complex problem to the question of whether interventions either do harm or build peace. In practice,

Figure 5.1 Interactions Between NGOs and Conflict or Peace

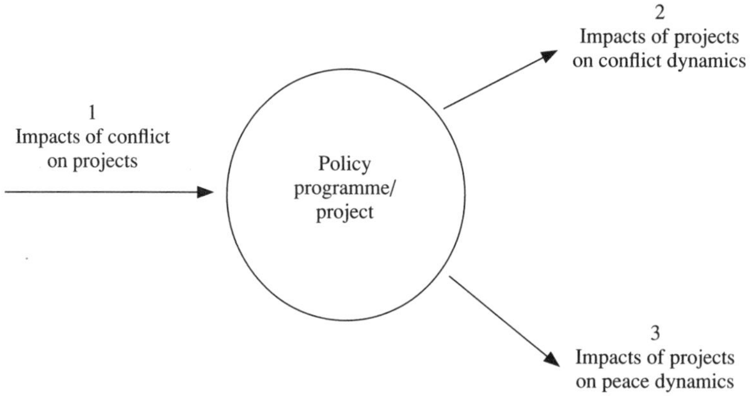

one is making judgements about overall net benefits and the general direction of change. Therefore while impact is itself a vexing question, it is particularly problematic in relation to fields of conflict and peacebuilding. Although impacts cannot be established scientifically or precisely (i.e. they cannot be measured), a systematic comparison of cases reveals common patterns of interactions.

The Interactions Between NGOs' Activities and Conflict and Peace Dynamics

The Impacts of Armed Conflict on NGOs and Their Programmes

Security threats to NGOs varied according to the intensity and nature of the conflict. In three cases (Afghanistan, Sri Lanka and Liberia), during specific phases of the conflict, NGOs operated in a security vacuum engendered both by the emergency itself and the unwillingness of internationally sanctioned forces to address the need for security. In Afghanistan and Liberia, direct threats to the security of aid agency staff were greatest, though in Sri Lanka and Nepal staff were also killed or injured as a result of direct targeting or being caught in the crossfire. To a limited degree, protection was provided to NGO operations by international or regional peacekeepers (Afghanistan and Liberia), government forces (Nepal, Sri Lanka) or non-state military actors (Afghanistan, Liberia and Sri Lanka). However, too close an association may lead to a blurring of the lines between military and humanitarian actors and a perceived loss of neutrality. Afghan solidarity NGOs in the 1980s arguably abandoned neutrality altogether by aligning themselves so closely with mujahideen groups. For the most part, NGOs have attempted to maintain humanitarian space by asserting neutrality and securing the consent of all parties, but in spite of this, they were rarely viewed as neutral by warring groups. NGOs' activities had identifiable consequences (see below), which affected the agendas of military groups. Consequently NGOs were subject to continual efforts to control access or manipulate assistance, one example being the political control of aid to Afghan refugees in Pakistan and another being the Sri Lankan government's economic blockade of northeastern Sri Lanka.

Compared with governmental and intergovernmental agencies, NGOs were more adaptable and adept at working in high-risk environments. Furthermore, LNGOs tended to have a higher tolerance of risk than INGOs. For example, EHED and ADA, in Sri Lanka and Afghanistan respectively, on occasion maintained a field presence after INGOs had withdrawn or suspended operations due to fighting. In contested borderland areas, often beyond the control of the state, like parts of midwestern Nepal, NGOs became important, if not the primary, providers of public services due to the withdrawal of government services and of UN and bilateral donor agencies. In Afghanistan during the 1980s, NGOs were the vehicles of choice for crossborder relief and rehabilitation projects in mujahideen-controlled areas. Therefore NGOs in the case studies demonstrated a level of agility and adaptability in relation to security threats uncharacteristic of other operational agencies.

While framework agreements between warring groups and NGOs have been developed elsewhere,[3] in the case study countries NGOs tended to go it alone and develop their own informal bilateral relations with non-state military groups. The overriding approach for dealing with the likes of the Maoists, the LTTE or the Taliban was one of arm's-length engagement. NGO autonomy and security varied over time and from place to place, depending on a range of factors including their political or symbolic value, the magnitude of their assistance, the nature of their activities and the attitude of state or non-state actors. NGOs serving large populations and delivering significant resources into a resource-scarce environment were more likely to be vulnerable to security threats and political manipulation. The same was likely to apply to those engaged in politically sensitive activities such as conflict resolution and peacebuilding.[4] Paradoxically, a signifier of NGO success in conflictual environments may be attempts by state or non-state actors to influence or intimidate them.[5] Being left alone may be a sign of irrelevance. Conflict-related threats are not unique to war zones—intimidation and the threat of violence were common across the cases[6]—and working in areas of chronic political instability by definition involves learning to cope with insecurity.

NGOs deploy a range of humanitarian tactics to reduce their exposure to conflict-related risks. Table 5.1, based on experiences in Nepal, identifies different categories of risks and associated mitigation or conflict-proofing strategies.

Conflict-proofing tactics in Nepal included: tightening staff safety procedures; improving information sharing and coordination mechanisms; withdrawal

Table 5.1   The Impacts of Armed Conflict on NGO Programmes in Nepal

Sector	Impacts of the conflict on aid programmes	Possible strategies to mitigate impacts
Security	• Threats to staff from Maoists, police and army. • Targeting of NGO offices. • Threats to government implementing partners. • Inability of donors to conduct monitoring.	• Developing security guidelines. • Training for staff in security procedures. • Working through local partners.
Political	• Declining political and humanitarian space—agencies working in heartland areas seen as Maoist sympathizers.	• Negotiating ground rules with de facto authorities in conflict-affected areas.
Economic	• Retraction of government services and targeting of banks in conflict-affected areas, affecting sustainability of projects. • Maoist demands for percentage of staff salaries and project budgets.	• Avoiding bulky assets. • Adapting banking and finance procedures.
Social	• Displacement of communities, migration of men and erosion of social capital, and social mobilization activities.	• Adopting low-key approaches. • Focusing on poverty alleviation and social support programmes.

Source: Goodhand (2000).

or 'hibernation'; working more closely with local NGO partners; and changing the content and style of programming, for instance avoiding large-scale infrastructure projects involving lumpy assets and shifting towards low-profile, community-based approaches in sectors such as health and water and sanitation. NGOs working in Liberia through the JPO and PPHO initiatives established general principles and ground rules for delivering aid in response to widespread looting in the mid-1990s. This included suspending high-profile, high-input relief programmes. On a more prosaic level, conflict may force agencies to adapt their log frames (particularly the assumptions column) and change their budgets. In Nepal, for example, the growing costs of delivering assistance and local taxation of the Maoists increased project costs by over 10 per cent (Goodhand, 2000). The geographical pattern of aid delivery may reflect the shifting distribution of the fighting. In Afghanistan, for example, the pattern of aid distribution was as much a reflection of ease of access, security and political affiliations as absolute humanitarian need. In the 1980s the lion's share of crossborder humanitarian assistance went to the eastern and southern provinces because of proximity to the Pakistani border towns of Peshawar and Quetta.

Withdrawal may be a last resort, and in most cases is a tactical decision in relation to actual or apprehended violence directed at staff, or physical destruction of infrastructure. In 1996, for example, some NGOs were forced to withdraw from Liberia as humanitarian programmes were targeted by military entrepreneurs. Following US missile strikes on Afghanistan in 1998, most aid agencies chose to temporarily evacuate to Pakistan, fearing reprisal attacks from the Taliban and other Islamic radicals. For the most part, the do-nothing option has been invoked as a reactive and often ad hoc measure and was rarely the result of a gradual and phased response to a deteriorating security environment. It was also rare to find unanimity among NGOs on security questions and policies. Bottom lines were applied differently by different NGOs and inconsistently by the same organizations over time. As one aid worker in Kabul in 1997, commenting on policies in relation to the Taliban stated: 'Our bottom line is constantly changing... who'd have thought a year ago we'd be doing what we're doing today?' Even though most NGOs chose to withdraw from Afghanistan in 1998, a significant minority continued working in the country.

Although conflict-proofing and 'do no harm' are interrelated, they are not the same thing. NGOs frequently conflated humanitarian space with the more pragmatic and self-interested notion of agency space. The case studies highlight the fine balance between prioritizing the security of staff and programmes and the security of communities.[7] As a general rule, NGOs best equipped to deal with security threats were those which:

• had a strong analysis of the context;
• had clear security guidelines and procedures;
• empowered staff working at the 'coal face' to make decisions on security matters;
• developed close relationships with the communities they worked with, which ultimately was the best form of insurance for NGOs operating in a security vacuum.[8]

The GWOT has in some contexts intensified the security dilemmas faced by NGOs, as shown by MSF's withdrawal from Afghanistan in 2004. MSF cited security risks, related to the unacceptable blurring of lines between humanitarian and military concerns, as the reason for departure from a country in which it had been working for more than two decades.[9] A detailed examination of how the GWOT has affected the operating environment for NGOs is beyond the scope of this study. But the limited evidence from the case study countries suggests that the effects have been extremely mixed and uneven, and one should be wary of drawing blanket conclusions from extreme cases or outliers like Afghanistan and Iraq. Evidently the discourse and practice of the war on terror plays itself out differently in different contexts, and counter-intuitively it may open up as well as close down spaces for NGOs. Arguably, for example in Sri

Lanka, international re-engagement with the country, due in part to concerns about terrorism, re-energized the peace process and opened spaces for NGOs working on peace-related issues.

In the hyperpoliticized conflicts like Afghanistan and Iraq, it may make little difference whether NGOs take a minimalist or maximalist stance, since they are targeted more for what they represent than what they actually do. However, as Slim (2004: 7) notes, the dynamics of terror and counter-terror do not dominate every setting in which NGOs work. It would be ironic if the GWOT which Western politicians have used to divert attention away from problems at home has a similar effect on NGOs. The resentment, even hostility, towards NGOs in many of the countries studied cannot only be attributed to tensions generated by the GWOT. This has longer-term roots, and is related to the often invasive, top-down nature of humanitarianism: 'Resentment against humanitarians and their organizations continues as a cumulative threat wherever humanitarian action is excessively colonial and invasive in its style or felt to be arrogant, ignorant, disempowering and culturally insensitive' (Slim, 2004: 8).

The Impacts of NGOs' Activities on Violent Conflict and Peace

Although NGO programmes are rarely central to the dynamics of conflict or peace, the case studies do show common patterns of aid–conflict interactions. These can be divided into political, economic and social effects. An analysis of impacts involves modelling and making judgements about the processes of political and socio-economic change. Underlying assumptions are as follows:

   • peacebuilding is not about bringing social harmony, but involves negotiating processes of change, which are always conflictual and intensely political;
   • processes of change are contingent, discontinuous and unpredictable; conflict is likely to intensify and accelerate pre-existing political and socio-economic processes;
   • no outcomes are preordained because of structural conditions;
   • in violent, 'unruly' environments individuals and organizations are more likely to be agents of change with the capacity to shape wider structural conditions than would be the case in more stable and rule-bound environments;
   • behaviour in wartime cannot be understood solely through an individual rational actor model, which examines incentives (for war or peace) in isolation from the political and socio-economic context. War is 'something that is made through social action and something that can be moderated through social action' (Richards, 2005: 3);
   • it is assumed that NGO interventions, which either strengthen or undermine human security at the micro level, have impacts further up the conflict chain; bottom-up and top-down violence interact with one another; therefore, though

the intervention may be targeted at the local level, its ripple effects may extend far beyond this.

Table 5.2 provides illustrative examples of the types of interactions between NGO activities and the dynamics of conflict and peace drawn from the case studies. The model presented in Figure 5.1 is taken a stage further in an attempt to examine systematically the second and third interactions. An in-between category of impact is added which has been called a holding operation. In this scenario interventions play a role in maintaining peacebuilding space that might otherwise be destroyed by conflict dynamics. It is important to note that the presumed agents of change, that is, NGOs, do not themselves share a common goal of building peace. Unlike the niche peacebuilding NGOs, which have the explicit objective of managing or transforming conflict (though their definitions of this may differ), for most multi-mandates it is not their primary objective. Instead it may be an unintended and indirect impact of their work. The operational challenge for them is more complex than simply weighing up benefits and harms; it also involves balancing these negative or positive externalities with other primary objectives related to relief, protection or development.

Fuelling Violent Conflict

First, the case studies show that development policies which preceded conflict had a far more significant impact at the structural level than humanitarian programmes delivered by NGOs once the violence had started. The findings of this research suggest that although NGOs can improve the way they do business, the space for peacebuilding is largely determined by bigger actors.[10] This is explored further in Chapter 6.

Political effects. The focus here is on how NGOs' activities have an impact upon the various levels of domestic governance. Earlier studies on the aid–conflict connection have tended to focus on economic effects and less on the political impacts of NGO programmes.[11] As previously mentioned, situations of chronic political instability are essentially crises of the state, and international policies may contribute to the origins and continuation of these crises. NGOs working in conflict have an ambiguous relationship with the state. Their default setting is to avoid the state. In Afghanistan, NGOs were to an extent the conscious agents of state collapse, through their backing of mujahideen groups. By working closely with regional power-holders, NGO strategies tended to mirror the growing fragmentation and regionalization of Afghanistan (Goodhand, 2002). Although NGOs' resources were limited in relation to superpower military-financial support, they played an important role in legitimizing the Afghan resistance in the 1980s. Political parties in Peshawar and commanders in Afghanistan accrued

Table 5.2 The Interactions Between NGO Programmes and Conflict and Peace Dynamics

	Political	Economic	Social
Fuelling violent conflict	• International and domestic actors using the legitimizing effects of NGOs; inaction of international actors in Afghanistan, Sri Lanka government/LTTE exploiting NGO presence in northeast Sri Lanka. • Silence on human rights abuses, e.g. NGOs in Afghanistan about mujahideen abuses. • Parallel systems of aid delivery, undermining local institutions.	• Taxation and/or looting of relief supplies in Liberia, Afghanistan, Sri Lanka, Nepal. • Relief heightens distributional tensions, e.g. between refugees and settled populations in northeast Sri Lanka, Azerbaijan, Peshawar and Kabul. • Distortionary effects of NGO activities on prices and labour markets. • Dependency-inducing effects of NGO programmes in Peshawar, Kabul, Azerbaijan.	• Legitimizing effects of NGOs being too closely associated with one particular group, e.g. colonization of solidarity NGOs in Afghanistan. • Aid agencies' predisposition to use the language and currency of the conflict, e.g. 'cleared' and 'uncleared' in Sri Lanka or pro-war textbooks in Afghanistan.
Holding operation	• ICRC's protection and dissemination activities. • Humanitarian diplomacy of ICRC, e.g. north Sri Lanka. • Strategic lobbying on aid-related issues, e.g. humanitarian access to Sri Lanka. • UNHCR Open Relief Centres, Sri Lanka.	• EHED's IRDP and Christian Aid's credit programme in eastern Sri Lanka. • SCF/Oxfam—LTD/R, Sri Lanka. • Community development activities of AAD and CARE (Afghanistan) and Oxfam (Sri Lanka).	• NGOs playing a witnessing role in northeast Sri Lanka, midwest Nepal. • Support for civic organizations, e.g. rural development committees in Sri Lanka, *shuras* in Afghanistan.
Peace-building	• Colombo policy and campaigning NGOs' work on constitutional reform. • NPC's peace advocacy, public campaigning. • NGO election monitoring, Sri Lanka, Kyrgyzstan. • ICES, Marga Institute, NPC research on public opinion on the peace process, the costs of conflict, etc, Sri Lanka. • Human rights NGOs' mediation between Maoists and government in Nepal.	• EHED's border village projects, Sri Lanka • Oxfam's support for business leaders alliance for peace, Sri Lanka. • ADA micro-hydro power project, Uruzgen, Afghanistan. • NGO income generation and poverty-focused programmes in southern Kyrgyzstan. • NGO de-mining programmes in Afghanistan. • NGO-supported demobilization and reintegration programmes, Liberia.	• Children's zones of peace, Sri Lanka. • NGO-organized intercommunity exchanges in Sri Lanka. • CPAU, Afghanistan support for local community-based reconciliation. • NGO involvement with BBC's 'New Home-New Life' soap opera. • QPS's confidence-building work, east Sri Lanka. • SEDEC's support for visits by the Buddhist monks to northeast Sri Lanka. • Psychosocial work—demilitarizing the mind, e.g. Butterfly Gardens in Batticaloa, Sri Lanka. • Regional business and media initiatives, Armenia-Azerbaijan.

political capital as well as economic resources through collaboration with NGOs. Some NGOs became deeply infiltrated by resistance party agents. The refugee camps in Pakistan became humanitarian and military sanctuaries.[12] As Terry (2002: 217) notes, 'the legitimacy derived from refugees and the control mechanisms provided by refugee camp structures were the most consistently advantageous aspects of refugee camps to combatants.'

The issue of capacity-building is central to the question of the political effects of NGOs. Tensions between INGOs and LNGOs come out in much sharper relief in conflict settings, where funding and profile tend to be dominated by the large multi-mandate international agencies.[13] A minimalist position of simply avoiding capacity-building (because it risks compromising neutrality), which was adopted by a number of INGOs, should not be seen as a passive stance, as neglect ultimately has the effect of undermining local governmental or nongovernmental structures. In such cases the minimalist remedy may be worse than the disease (Christoplos, 1998). But naïve developmentalism could have perverse effects. Poorly designed attempts at social engineering frequently exacerbated underlying tensions, as illustrated in Box 5.1.

NGOs and the aid regime of which they are part tend to create shadow networks of governance, which can undermine or potentially impede the development of more home-grown forms of governance with local legitimacy.[14] Examples of this included some NGO-created shuras in rural Afghanistan and food distributions in Kabul that strengthened corrupt wakil[15]-dominated structures and donor-created briefcase NGOs. In fact, NGOs and the wider aid system may itself become a form of shadow governance. In Afghanistan after the Taliban donors, at least initially, preferred to use NGOs and the UN as delivery mechanisms for reconstruction, which undermined the government's efforts to build its capacity and legitimacy.

In more stable settings such as the Ferghana Valley, Moldova and Armenia-Azerbaijan, arguably the wrong kind of capacity-building increased structural vulnerability to conflict or hampered its resolution. In Kyrgyzstan, for example, donors such as USAID as a point of principle funded NGOs rather than the state. The privatization of welfare services played into the dynamics of rising conflict in the Ferghana Valley. By undermining the credibility and capacity of the state, this policy contributed to the failure of an embryonic state to forge a new social contract with its citizens. A similar dynamic can be identified in Moldova and Armenia-Azerbaijan, where NGOs were encouraged to set up parallel systems of welfare and service provision. This erosion of state capacity and credibility has a direct effect on the peace processes in the two regions: weak, incoherent states may be less willing and less able to develop a long-term strategy and make the compromises necessary to forge a peace agreement.[16]

Economic effects. The case studies show familiar patterns of aid manipulation by warring groups and distortionary effects on the local economy. The most

Box 5.1 Mullipottanai, Sri Lanka—
Three-way Programming in Practice?

Mullipottanai is a resettled village in the Trincomalee District. Sinhalese, Tamils and Muslims live in the village, but there are strong underlying tensions between the groups, particularly towards Muslims who are perceived to be encroaching on Tamil and Sinhalese land, and who tend to dominate the business sector. Oxfam funded relief and rehabilitation activities, and supported a community group.

Though in a 'cleared' (government-controlled) area, it can be described as a grey zone, with regular incursions from the home guards, army and the LTTE. There is little sense of community, with few village organizations spanning the three ethnic groups. This is related to the social history of the village as a colonization scheme that has experienced repeated displacements. The relations in the village between the ethnic groups have always been weaker than the links outside the village with each group's place of origin. This still continues and when there was displacement the villagers went back to their original home areas. Movement out of the village is mostly to markets and back to visit family in places of origin.

It is an extremely complex operating environment which necessitates a fine-grained analysis of the subtle links between the history and geography of the village, the security situation, the complex social relationships and the levels of ethnic tension. The villagers' perceptions of what constitutes the village were quite different from Oxfam's. Moreover, Oxfam's choice of local partners was at variance with the villagers' perception of who were the local leaders with authority and legitimacy. Although the intentions and objectives behind the programme design had the laudable intention of helping build closer relationships and community cohesion by trying to encourage people to work together on common projects, the effect may have been to heighten pre-existing tensions.

The key learning from Mullipottanai is that attempts at social engineering and peacebuilding that are not based upon a thorough conflict analysis and an understanding of social fabric and relationships can do more harm than good. There is also the vital question of timing. Perhaps, at the beginning of the resettlement process, the communities might have been more open to crosscutting programmes and they might have been fully integrated into the process from the start, ensuring greater local ownership.

Source: Goodhand, Hulme and Lewer (2000).

egregious cases of aid directly fuelling the combat economy were to be found in Liberia and Afghanistan. The magnitude of these impacts varied according to the value of the assistance, the availability of other resources and the phase of the conflict.[17] In Afghanistan, donors were prepared to accept wastage levels of

---

**Box 5.2 The Mixed Economic Effects of
NGO Programmes in Afghanistan**

Pre-war aid contributed to the development of a rentier state and the structural tensions which led to the outbreak of war. During the 1980s, humanitarian assistance was the non-lethal component of support to the mujahideen and much of it fed directly into the combat economy. Aid has also been a significant factor in the coping and survival economy, as the second largest sector of the licit economy after agriculture. Before 11 September 2001 about 25,000 Afghans were employed with aid agencies and the Swedish Committee for Afghanistan, an international solidarity NGO, which was the largest single employer in the country. In urban areas, particularly Kabul, where there is a large aid-dependent population, humanitarian assistance has been critical to survival. Finally, aid interacts with the shadow economy, particularly in the post-Taliban context with relatively large injections of resources into Kabul creating a parasitic bubble economy. The US dollar increasingly dominates the money exchanges in the cities, whereas the countryside remains in the Afghani or Pakistani rupee zone. There is an obvious danger of history repeating itself, with international assistance exacerbating the underlying tensions and disparities between countryside and city.

---

up to 40 per cent (Nicholds and Borton, 1994) and in Liberia people-farming by warlords to attract food aid was reported (Atkinson and Leader, 2000). Although a fully fledged war economy has yet to develop in Nepal, NGOs working in Maoist-controlled areas are subjected to revolutionary taxes, while offices have been robbed and vehicles stolen. A significant proportion of all resources going into northeast Sri Lanka went into the hands of the LTTE and aid delivered through NGOs was no different in this respect. Although other resource flows (such as oil in Azerbaijan or opium and smuggling in Afghanistan) may be more significant than the aid brought in by NGOs, it was clearly a factor that entered into the calculations of local warlords or power-brokers and helped sustain the local war economy. One of its comparative advantages from the perspective of a rent-seeking rebel is its predictability. As Slim (2004: 12) notes, most humanitarian programming is easily read, anticipated and obstructed by its opponents. Going back to the schema introduced in Chapter 4 of the combat, shadow and coping economies, one can identify a number of ways in which aid and NGO programmes interact with these economies. In Box 5.2 examples of these interactions are given with reference to Afghanistan.

NGO projects may also have a range of indirect effects. They may achieve their immediate objectives but have negative externalities. For instance, food aid in certain parts of Afghanistan had the effect of depressing wheat prices and thus increasing the incentives for farmers to grow poppy.[18] Aid is also fungible and frees up resources to wage war. In Sri Lanka, for instance, total annual aid flows were roughly equivalent to government annual expenditure on the war effort. Arguably in Azerbaijan, the willingness of aid agencies to take on the primary burden of supporting the IDP population reduced the pressure on the Azeri government to take responsibility for the group and freed up public finances for military expenditure.

Overall there was limited evidence to support the idea that NGO programmes induce dependency.[19] In the main, this exaggerates the importance of aid to poor people's coping and survival. But the cases do support the commonly observed phenomenon of aid intensifying distributional conflicts. Examples of this were conflicts between Tamil and Muslim communities in eastern Sri Lanka or between refugee and resident populations in Pakistan.[20] In post-Taliban Afghanistan, aid delivered by NGOs risks providing an incentive to fight rather than a stimulus to peace (Surkhe, Strand and Harpviken, 2002).[21] These distributional effects apply both to developmental and conflictual settings, though in the case of the latter such tensions are more likely to become violent and to have contagion effects.

Comparison across cases demonstrates that aid–conflict interactions are far more complex and variegated than the caricature of an aid-fuelled war economy suggests. First, war economies and peace economies are not diametrically opposed, they merge into one another. The coping and shadow economies in Kyrgyzstan and Afghanistan share many common features, and the challenges for NGOs of preventing or mitigating perverse effects are not dissimilar. Second, the combat economy intersects with the shadow and coping economies and cannot be separated out or ringfenced; many people's lives and livelihoods are tied up with these economies. Therefore turning off the aid tap in order to do no harm or in the belief one can strangle such economies is misconceived and likely to undercut the survival strategies of the poorest. Though there is accumulated evidence of aid doing harm, this does not necessarily mean that less aid (or even no aid) will do less harm. For instance, in Kabul in 1997 Oxfam suspended its water and sanitation programme, based on the analysis that Taliban restrictions on access to women prevented them from operating in a principled way. It has subsequently been argued that the overall effect of this was to further punish an already destitute population (Vaux, 2001).[22] A similar kind of logic informed the decision of an NGO in northeast Afghanistan to stop providing funds to repair a village's irrigation system once it became clear that villagers were growing poppy, though in many respects this was contributing to the food security of the village, and by taking this action the NGO would have a negative effect on livelihood strategies. Therefore, as the above cases suggest, NGOs are rarely faced with simple, black-and-white decisions about benefits and harms. Projects have multiple, cascading and mixed effects on a whole range of variables, many of which cannot be predicted and do not become visible until a long time after the intervention. However, being sensitive to conflict dynamics should encourage practitioners to look beyond the project log frame and focus more explicitly on externalities, in other words, the second- and third-order effects of interventions.

Social effects. NGOs also affect the emotional economy of conflict. Perceptions may sometimes be more important than actual events. For instance, in Sri Lanka the perception among the Sinhalese that NGOs provided more support to the northeast than to the south (though the opposite was the case) fuelled a sense of grievance that was skilfully exploited by political entrepreneurs. In Afghanistan during the 1980s solidarity NGOs promoted a pro-war agenda. A notorious manifestation of this was the printing of primary-school textbooks by NGOs, which had children learning literacy and numeracy by counting AK47s and dead Russian soldiers.

Building Peace

In theory NGOs have a number of comparative advantages which equip them to support civil society–led peacebuilding processes: they are mid-level actors with linkages upwards to political leadership and downwards to communities; they have the potential to play a bridging role between identity groups in contexts characterized by extreme horizontal inequalities; they have the ability to work across lines and gain access to communities living on the wrong side of a conflict; they have relatively high comfort levels and can work in high-risk environments; and at their best they can be flexible, adaptive and innovative. NGOs may not always live up to these comparative advantages (in part due to donor pressures); however, evidence from the agency studies suggests that when they do, they can have a positive impact on peacebuilding processes.

Political effects. The resource profile of explicit peacebuilding interventions is small compared with mainstream relief and development funding. However, the political impact of peacebuilding programmes may be out of proportion to their size, particularly where NGOs are perceived to be an important part of the political landscape. In several cases NGOs achieved significant peacebuilding outcomes when they engaged with, rather than avoided, political processes. The space for such approaches varies according to the type and phase of conflict and the profile, positioning and strategy of the NGO. In Sri Lanka, for instance, specialist NGOs that focused on public policy, constitutional reform, human rights and the peace process had significant effects at the macro level, to the extent that NGOs during the 1994–5 peace process were asked by the government to contribute to the drafting of constitutional proposals and they were directly involved in Track One and Track Two peace talks.[23]

However, the ability of niche conflict resolution NGOs to have a significant or lasting impact on peacebuilding dynamics varied from case to case. A DFID Strategic Conflict Assessment in Moldova in 2000 made the following observation about a Track Two diplomacy programme, which involved exchange visits and workshops in Northern Ireland, organized by a UK-based NGO working with a Moldovan partner:

> One can take participants out of the country and perhaps even dispel some of their personal distrust during the workshop, but they return to an unchanged situation. The project does nothing to alter the political and economic structures that led to violence and that make its re-occurrence possible... The field visit suggests that little public knowledge exists at all about the activities of [the NGOs] particularly in Moldova proper where popular attitudes also need to change. (Woodward, 2000: 21)

This is not to negate the work of such organizations—officials interviewed who were involved in the Track One process were convinced of its importance—but their role should be kept in perspective. Similarly in Armenia-Azerbaijan, peacebuilding interventions by NGOs were criticized for being too short-term and involving transitory encounters between civil society groups on both sides, rather than developing long-term, strategic links (Vaux and Goodhand, 2002). In order to address the issues of coherence and sustained involvement in Moldova and Armenia-Azerbaijan, DFID introduced new funding arrangements in the form of what were called peacebuilding frameworks. These involved the provision of longer-term funding for a consortium of NGOs to work in a more strategic way, and at a range of levels, on peacebuilding issues.

A common factor limiting the scope and influence of such interventions was the lack of strategic linkages between Track One and Track Two initiatives. As discussed further in Chapter 6, domestic and international peacemakers tended to exclude civil society actors or keep them at arm's-length, thus limiting their impacts on the negotiation process. Similarly there was often a restricted interface between Track Two and Track Three initiatives. Multi-mandate NGOs kept a strategic distance from niche peacebuilding NGOs, because of concerns about neutrality and political exposure. Furthermore, the approach of some conflict resolution NGOs increased the gulf between the two sets of actors. A social harmony model, which tended to separate out and reify conflict, as though it could be treated in isolation from wider social and political processes, was at odds with a developmental approach involving socio-economic change and empowerment. These tensions came out in the case of a Kyrgyz NGO and a Tajik NGO, which attempted to combine conflict resolution with development objectives in their programmes on the Kyrgyz–Tajik border, as illustrated in Box 5.3.

The impacts of either niche or multi-mandate NGOs depends to a great extent on the context, and where there is either no state (as was the case at certain times in Afghanistan and Liberia) or 'too much' state (as for instance with the increasingly authoritarian regimes of Kyrgyzstan and Azerbaijan), NGOs were at best engaged in a holding operation. NGOs may provide support to stabilizing points in civil society, which can re-emerge once the fighting is over. What

---

Box 5.3   Early Warning and Conflict Management in Kyrgyzstan

The Swiss Development Cooperation (SDC) in Central Asia has funded a Kyrgyz–Tajik Conflict Prevention Project (KTP), implemented in collaboration with two NGOs, the Foundation for Tolerance International (FTI) in Kyrgyzstan and Ittifok (Tajikistan), which run in tandem with the Rehabilitation of Social Infrastructure Project (RSIP) implemented by UNOPS. Both aim to contribute to the peaceful coexistence of different ethnic groups and citizens of Tajikistan and Kyrgyzstan. The programme targets border areas which are thought to be vulnerable to violent conflict due to tensions over resources, disputed borders and intergroup competition. A range of activities are implemented: the KTP focuses on conflict monitoring, education on inter-ethnic tolerance, community mediation and public awareness, and the RSIP rehabilitates social infrastructure.

A complex mix of factors contributes to tensions in the Ferghana Valley region and the area's vulnerability to violent conflict appears to be increasing due to weakening states, growing exclusion and the erosion of structures that could mitigate or manage violent conflict.

An evaluation of the programme in 2000 identified tensions related to its dual objectives of conflict prevention and development. It was found that rather than being mutually reinforcing the twin objectives may work against one another. The conflict prevention component (which involved training in conflict analysis and early warning) tended in practice to focus on elites, 'freezing' society, maintaining the status quo, working towards functional harmony and maintaining a position of neutrality. The development projects were about challenging local elites and transforming social relations, in actual fact causing conflict and often taking sides or expressing solidarity with excluded groups.

The evaluation recommended that the programme either integrate these two components more coherently or separate them out and run them independently of one another.

---

is often lost in over-structuralist analyses of conflict is the role that individuals play in peacebuilding processes. The sources of change in society are often highly motivated, atypical individuals who break the mould (Goodhand and Lewer, 1999). An important but underrecognized impact of NGOs was their role in both supporting community-level leadership and holding in cold storage civic leaders within their own organizations, in an environment where there were few other employment options for the educated. In Afghanistan NGOs stemmed human capital flight and nurtured a cadre of workers who now play a central role in the reconstruction process. In 2003 there were at least three ministers in the Afghan Transitional Administration who came from an NGO background.[24] A similar trajectory might be predicted for Tamil NGO workers in Sri Lanka who, if the peace process survives, could be absorbed into a new political and administrative structure for the northeast.[25] In Kyrgyzstan, one of the effects of the Tulip revolution may be to galvanize NGO leaders into entering party politics. The transition from social entrepreneur to political entrepreneur has been noted elsewhere, particularly in Latin America (Garilao, 1987). Such individuals who have the capacity to link the small politics of society with the big politics of the state may be strategically important actors in peacebuilding processes. The case studies therefore question the notion that NGO proliferation necessarily weakens political voice by providing the middle classes with alternatives to mainstream politics. Certainly, there is the potential for voice to become more diffuse and more distant from the levers of power. But in many of the cases, NGOs (particularly LNGOs) have probably had the effect of keeping a larger proportion of the middle classes engaged with politics than would otherwise have been the case.[26]

At the local level NGO programmes played a role in consolidating local forms of governance, which could become alternative centres of power to warring groups. Arguably, NGO-supported community participation processes in Afghanistan have helped prepare the ground for more democratic forms of governance to emerge after the conflict. Box 5.4 provides an example of micro level peacebuilding involving an Afghan NGO called the Afghan Development Association (ADA).

The key to ADA's approach was sensitivity to, and long-term support for, local capacities, defined by staff in terms of institutions, norms and values. Protracted conflict at the national level had undermined local capacities to resolve internal disputes. Symptomatic of this process was the erosion of relations of trust between Hazaras and Pashtuns (or bridging social capital). Trust was rebuilt by addressing the concrete problems and needs affecting both groups and by working through local institutions—the *shura* or council.

Community-level peacebuilding may have a disproportionate impact in borderland areas such as the Ferghana Valley that have become a focus for grievance and violent insurgency. NGOs have a comparative advantage in being able to access borderland areas and address questions of poverty and insecurity that drive the dynamics of borderland conflicts. Furthermore, because NGOs are likely to be less constrained by sovereignty issues than government agencies, they have the potential to work across borders and address conflicts from a regional perspective. To an extent this has happened in the Ferghana Valley where NGOs have supported conflict prevention programmes linking civil society groups in Uzbekistan, Tajikistan and Kyrgyzstan.

Therefore, the peacebuilding impacts of relief and development programmes go beyond the provision of material needs. Although multi-mandate NGOs were found to place a greater emphasis on service delivery than on protection, community interviews revealed the value of agencies just being there to witness, report and on occasion moderate abuses. On-site NGOs which have developed close relationships with communities can be effective recorders and advocates.

Box 5.4   Peacebuilding from Below?
ADA in Khas Uruzgen, Afghanistan

In 1992 ADA started working in Khas Uruzgen in Uruzgen province of southern Afghanistan. ADA selected this area because of its geographical isolation, the lack of other NGOs working in the area and the fact that it is situated on an ethnic faultline and has on occasion experienced open conflict between the Hazara and Pashtun ethnic groups.

ADA made a conscious decision to work with both Hazaras and Pashtuns in the district, bringing them together on issues of common interest. Though they had no illusions that they could solve the wider conflict, there was a conscious policy of building relationships at the local level to reduce the likelihood of mobilization along ethnic lines in the future. Afghan communities have been very sensitive to attempts at social engineering, and programmes with social objectives have to be extremely low-key and sensitive. Communities were brought together on concrete issues that affected them both. ADA's programmes included the construction and support of schools and micro-hydropower stations, the provision of improved seeds and the development of fruit-tree nurseries. In terms of their rehabilitation and development objectives these programmes were extremely successful. There were tangible signs of recovery and improvement in the district; a number of villages now had electricity, schools had been up and running for the first time for several years,[28] there were many new orchards and agricultural production in the region had increased. Less visible and less easy to evaluate was the broader goal of peacebuilding. ADA pointed to the fact that Hazara and Pashtun students and teachers went to the same schools as each other and both communities continued to work together on common projects. They claimed that this in itself was an achievement when in some other parts of the country the two communities were in open conflict with one another. To get to this stage required a long-term commitment on the part of ADA, combined with a sophisticated and fine-grained analysis of community structures and relations. Project staff had a nuanced understanding of local leadership, tribal and ethnic structures and the incentives systems for cooperative (and noncooperative) action.

ADA never talked openly to the communities about building relationships between Hazaras and Pashtuns. However, both groups worked together on concrete tasks, for example, constructing a school, maintaining a micro-hydropower station or cleaning an irrigation ditch. The primary motivation for working together was economic need and the common ownership of resources. People recognized the need to cooperate out of basic self-interest: 'We have seen the costs of conflict and it has made us poorer.' ADA perhaps decreased the probability of conflict in the future, since both communities had made investments in that future. The people themselves recognized that relationships had improved: 'When ADA came to the area relations between the two communities became softer.' However, it is also important to see the limitations of such an approach. It is about building probabilities rather than certainties. If wider political and military events take a turn for the worse, then the low-key, micro-level work done by ADA may be undermined very quickly. One staff member compared it with planting tree saplings in a nursery, which could be swept away at any minute by a flood. However, one could argue that because of the work done by ADA it would be more difficult for outside events to trigger such a conflict in the future.

**Box 5.5 Listening to the Displaced/Returned (LTD/R)
Oxfam/SCF, Sri Lanka, 1998**

The objectives of LTD/R in the Wanni area in northern Sri Lanka included identifying people's coping mechanisms and capacities to better target future interventions; give a broader and lasting voice to displaced people themselves; and, to identify and prioritize needs with displaced communities within the context of matching short-term relief initiatives with longer-term interventions. From LTD/R the agencies aimed to understand people's preparations, expectations and support systems on their return to Jaffna, to lobby for programmes that would have a beneficial impact on people's lives and to identify people's views on potential interventions. From their findings, SCF and Oxfam listed Key Messages (KM) from the people.

KM 1 Peace and freedom: we want to live in peace and enjoy basic rights and freedoms.
KM 2 Self-reliance: we want to be self-sufficient; this means having access to employment opportunities, agricultural and other inputs, capital and markets.
KM 3 Relief distribution: we don't want to rely on relief, but where relief is provided, we want items which help us towards self-reliance (tools and equipment), and we want them to be distributed in a fair and transparent manner.
KM 4 Water, land and sanitation: we want more access to better-quality land and water.
KM 5 Education and health: we want increased access to reasonable levels of education and health services.

The people interviewed said that peace was their main need, and without this there could be little long-term improvement in their lives. As a result of the surveys, SCF stated that it would revise its relief strategy to actively involve beneficiaries, especially women and children, in the identification, choice and process of distributing items which encourage self-reliance.

Source: Goodhand, Hulme and Lewer (2000).

One example of NGOs providing voice is the Listening to the Displaced/Returned (LTD/R) study conducted annually by Oxfam and Save the Children in Sri Lanka, as described in Box 5.5.

Humanitarian advocacy (and diplomacy[27]) is one thing, but whether NGOs should be more politically involved in supporting forms of resistance, rather than simply helping communities cope with conflict, is a contentious question. There are ethical concerns in encouraging alternative centres of power to warring groups. In Taliban-controlled Afghanistan community-level peacebuilding projects were tolerated by the Taliban so long as they were small and inconsequential. Agencies straddled a fine line between supporting constituencies for peace and fomenting political opposition. In contexts where there is no longer high-intensity conflict as in the former Soviet Union cases, human rights NGOs played a valuable protection and advocacy role, particularly in relation to vulnerable groups and minorities.[29]

Economic effects. NGO programmes may have an indirect (and often unforeseen) impact on the underlying causes or dynamics of violent conflict, by addressing the sources of human insecurity. A range of positive outcomes from NGO activities at the local level can be identified. These include: reducing mortality and morbidity, relieving a subsistence crisis, reducing resource competition, creating alternative livelihoods and providing employment opportunities. Such interventions may counter the bottom-up incentives for violence.[30] By building resilience and in particular the capacity to cope with external shocks NGO programmes may play a role in conflict-proofing communities.

Positive outcomes were achieved through practical interventions, which integrated people across markets and trading networks or common property resources such as irrigation or grazing regimes. These outcomes are likely to be the result of conflict-sensitive approaches to relief or development rather than stand-alone peace projects. In Liberia, for example, the distribution of food aid by NGOs led to the emergence of neighbourhood committees. In Nepal NGO projects in Maoist-controlled areas, as well as meeting practical needs, addressed some of the underlying grievances about lack of basic rights, that led to the outbreak of the 'People's War'. Afghan NGO mine-clearance programmes have had an immediate economic knock-on effect by bringing agricultural land back into use or clearing access roads (Surkhe, Strand and Harpviken, 2002). Such projects play an important role in peace consolidation. This point is underlined by the targeting of NGO staff by remnants of Taliban and Al Qaeda networks, aiming to disrupt the fragile transition from war to peace.

However, the case studies show that the economic assistance provided through NGO programmes is usually supplementary rather than central to coping and survival. The community studies challenge notions of societal breakdown and dependent populations. They show that villagers were not just passive recipients; they actively negotiated with aid agencies, and appropriated interventions by redefining meanings and redistributing the benefits. They also show that humanitarianism is not a Western preserve and the charity of the extended family was usually more central to coping and survival than aid. This charity, which might be described as a form of shadow humanitarianism, took different forms in different contexts. In many cases it had a strong transnational dimension, as for instance in the case of Islamic solidarity networks in Kyrgyzstan and Afghanistan, or the Tamil and Armenian diasporas.[31]

Social effects. As highlighted in Chapter 1, NGOs are expressive organizations. They not only seek to get things done, they embody a particular set of values

or way of thinking about the world. Therefore, just as material resources interact with the political economy of conflict, NGOs' values and ways of thinking
interact with ideational and discursive aspects of war and peace. Individual
peace entrepreneurs were found to play an important role in the diffusion of
ideas and the generation of social energy that can transform social structures
and social relations. In northeast Sri Lanka women have increasingly entered
the public realm as leaders and entrepreneurs due to changing political and
social mores, but also aided by sensitive NGO support (Goodhand, Hulme and
Lewer, 2000). During the rule of the Taliban one of the few employment avenues
open to women in Afghanistan was to work with aid agencies.

NGOs like ADA in Afghanistan helped rebuild trust at the community
level. Such localized peacebuilding ecologies were not about equilibrium but
about dynamic 'adhocracy'. Social capital is a resource whose supply increases
through use and which becomes depleted if not used (Putman, Leonard and
Nanett (1993: 169). It may emerge in unexpected places, mobilized through
the ever-changing activities of entrepreneurial individuals endowed with social
energy (Hirschman, 1984; Christoplos, 1998). As shown elsewhere, successes
are often not sustainable but may appear in different forms around the same
individuals (Christoplos, 1998).

Although NGOs lacked the political and economic purchase to bring peace,
there was evidence that aid, when applied judiciously and at the right time, could
tilt the balance towards cooperation on the ground. Such an approach may go
beyond mere survival or coping, to supporting forms of resistance, resonating
with James Scott's (1976) ideas about the weapons of the weak. The proliferation of secret home schools in Taliban-controlled Afghanistan, run by Afghan
women in defiance of the ban on girl's education, is a potent example of such
resistance, something that was sensitively supported by NGOs.[32] NGOs may
play a role in supporting alternative discourses, whether they are operational
or off-site organizations which develop transnational solidarities with people
living in war zones.[33]

Some activities may have a multiplier effect by creating an enabling environment for peacebuilding. An example of this, common to many of the cases
including Afghanistan, Sri Lanka and Liberia, is the use of the media to broadcast
messages of peace and reconciliation and to counteract pro-war propaganda. Aid
interventions may therefore have an important impact on the emotional economy
by influencing ideas, relationships, social energy and individual leadership. In
Afghanistan the BBC education programme and series, 'New Home, New Life',
is a positive example of how aid may engage in the battle for ideas.[34]

In spite of the above findings, the case studies point to the limits of social
engineering. NGOs were on the whole involved in shallow rather than deep
peacebuilding, having transitory impacts on the local dynamics of conflict and
rarely effecting lasting changes on the wider context. Bottom-up approaches
have their limitations. Local conflict resolution mechanisms may have developed

in response to a very different set of problems from the ones posed by contemporary conflicts. Those advocating grassroots approaches tend to overestimate the capacity of civil society to have an influence on an unaccountable leadership which came to power with the gun rather than through consent. Just as NGOs may romanticize the 'good' players in civil society, they tend to demonize and keep at arm's-length the 'bad' elements. This failure to engage with the unlike-minded or spoilers in a peace process can be costly. Sinhalese nationalists, for example, have been highly effective in mobilizing a constituency for war, using channels such as the vernacular media. NGO efforts to build peace constituencies have in comparison been far more timid, marked by a reluctance to either compete with or engage in dialogue with such nationalist groups.

Where the institutional environment is more promising, NGOs may have higher-order impacts, but even then, it is about following or amplifying existing trends, rather than creating them. It is therefore evident from the case studies that NGOs are rarely the main drivers of change, since in war zones these tend to be an array of state and non-state actors, including warlords, government officials, political parties, social movements and diasporic communities. NGOs working in intensified political engagements who seek to punch above their weight in peacebuilding terms face a constant dilemma, of on the one hand maintaining their neutrality and keeping a distance from the fray, and on the other hand being sufficiently embedded to understand and influence the key agents of change.

Conclusion

The case studies suggest that NGO programmes are unlikely to be a leading edge in moving towards or consolidating peace, but when judiciously implemented they can play a vital support role. The cases also highlight the fact that the interactions between aid and conflict are rarely simple and unidirectional. They are usually complex, mixed and context-specific. This finding should deter the analyst and policy-maker from the belief that one can somehow find universal rules on aid–conflict interactions that can be stripped away from context. What it should do is to encourage practitioners to be less project- or aid-centric, and to make a more careful assessment of the potential unintended impacts of policies and projects—in other words, the negative and positive externalities. Adaptation can then be made to mitigate the negative and amplify the positive. In either case, however, we are talking about increasing or decreasing probabilities rather than creating certainties.

The main message coming out of this chapter is that NGOs and their activities are only a small part of the story of conflict. At best they complement Track One processes, which are themselves often flawed. Therefore one needs to go beyond the policy choices of NGOs or indeed of aid agencies to understand why interventions do, or do not, work. The role of aid has been exaggerated partly as a result of the criticism that aid fuels conflict. As Shearer (2000) argues, stories about aid doing harm tend to universalize from specific situations. They use extreme cases as a starting point to build up an inflated position about the role of aid. Elevating the importance of aid serves a coalition of interests in the diplomatic and aid community. For the diplomats and donors, NGOs provide a humanitarian gloss on interventions and act as a substitute for political action. They represent an arm's-length approach for skittish national governments whose taste for direct political and military action is limited. Aid agencies enjoy 'the attention and insinuated importance far beyond their ability to really influence' (Shearer, 2000: 190). Increased competition for funding and profile between NGOs leads to increasingly exaggerated claims.[35]

The research findings perhaps provide a corrective to more optimistic accounts of NGO peacebuilding efforts. But neither does the evidence support the argument of humanitarian minimalists that peacebuilding is best left to political actors. The case studies show that in contemporary conflicts peace cannot solely be engineered or imposed from the top down through conventional diplomacy or military engagement. Peacebuilding must go beyond the aggregate or national level and address the local dimensions of conflict. This is where NGOs potentially have a comparative advantage.

6

Armed Conflict and the International Political and Policy Landscape

This chapter focuses on the world beyond NGOs, in order to examine the external determinants of NGO performance. It is posited that two facets of international engagement play a crucial role in creating or limiting the space for NGO peacebuilding: first, international efforts to support peacemaking and peace implementation; and second, the policies, practices and behaviour of international aid donors. The variations across the cases are explored in relation to these two variables in order to highlight what makes some contexts more or less difficult in peacebuilding terms. The chapter concludes by examining whether NGOs can themselves influence international politics and so play a role in constructing, or even expanding, the peacebuilding space within which they operate.

Introduction

Many of the most interesting and important issues confronting NGOs in the humanitarian system are located not within it, but around it (Macrae, 1999b: 46). Since NGOs control few of the parameters within which they work, one must examine the world beyond NGOs to understand why, in peacebuilding terms, interventions succeed or fail. Therefore this chapter is largely concerned with a comparative analysis of the contextual factors across the seven cases which influence the impacts and effectiveness of NGOs. Particular attention is paid to: first, peacemaking and peace implementation, which are interpreted here as the activities immediately preceding and following a peace agreement that seek to address the short-term dynamics of armed conflict (primarily in the diplomatic and military spheres); second, international donor assistance which is concerned both with addressing the short-term consequences of armed conflict and its longer-term structural dimensions. These three sets of actors (military,

125

diplomatic and aid) shape the security, policy and funding environments in which NGOs operate. By avoiding an NGO-centric perspective, it is hoped that one can arrive at a more realistic assessment of their potential and limitations. Although aid agencies are clearly accountable for their actions, they also share responsibility for failure (and occasional successes) with states, politicians and other key actors (Minear, 2002: 119).

Contextualizing Peacebuilding

According to Doyle and Sambanis (1999, 2000) the political space for peace-building varies according to the root causes and/or sources of hostility, local capacities for establishing peace and international commitment to assisting change. These are conceptualized in Figure 6.1 as three points on a peacebuilding triangle, which interact with one another, increasing or diminishing the space for peacebuilding.

This provides a useful framework for analysing the case studies. For instance, the scope for peacebuilding may be greater in a context where the roots of violence are fairly shallow, there are robust institutions for dealing with it and there are relatively high levels of social capital and wealth. Moreover, each dimension interacts with the others. For example, if the sources of conflict are deep and complex and the constituencies for peace are weak, the external intervention component may have to be correspondingly greater. Intervention may

Figure 6.1 The Peacebuilding Triangle

International capacities

Root causes

Local capacities

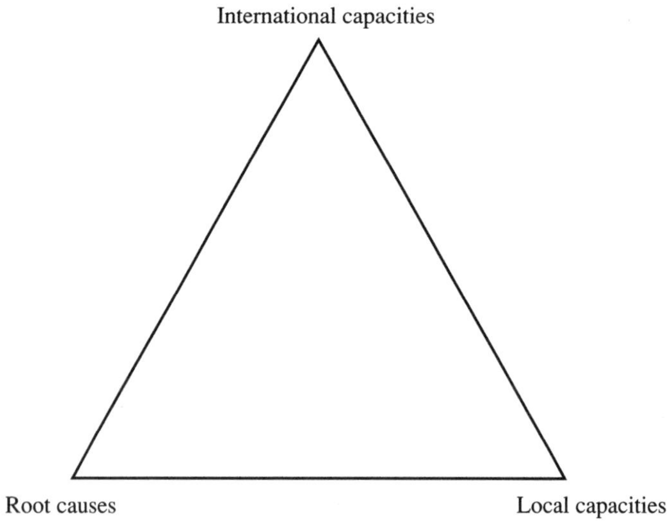

in turn have an impact on the other two dimensions, by diminishing hostilities and nurturing capacities for peace. Variations and interactions between these three dimensions will have an important influence on the scope and impact of NGOs' peacebuilding interventions.

In Sri Lanka an analysis of the changing balance and interplay between these three factors helps explain the relative success of the latest round of peace talks when previous efforts had failed. First, events on the battlefield had led to a hurting stalemate. Both sides had experienced heavy losses and neither could expect to reach their goals militarily. In the north and the south there was a growing war-weariness. This expressed itself in the south through the electoral victory of the UNP on a platform of direct negotiations with the LTTE. This signified an important shift in the local capacities for change. The international climate after 11 September 2001 also had an impact on the desire for peace. The US-led GWOT impressed on the LTTE the importance of being, and appearing to be, on the right side of the global ideological and military divide (Saravanamuttu, 2003: 132). Furthermore, the acceptance by both sides of Norway as a third-party mediator was a significant factor, given the government of Sri Lanka's previous reluctance to accept international mediation. Finally, international donors led by Japan pledged \$4.5 billion of reconstruction aid to support the economic transition from war to peace. Therefore shifts in all three factors in the peacebuilding triangle translated into a broadly supported peace process.[1]

This model can be contrasted with the case of Afghanistan, in which internal factors have been less important than the sudden and dramatic change in international policy towards the country. Whereas years of UN-led mediation failed to break the deadlock, the US-led coalition in a matter of months transformed the military and political landscape. The Bonn Agreement of December 2001, although not a peace settlement, provided a road map for peace which involved the appointment of an Afghan Transitional Administration, the drafting of a new constitution and the holding of presidential and parliamentary elections. Although each of these milestones had been reached by September 2005, the situation remained fragile because there had been limited change in relation to the local sources of hostility and domestic capacities for conflict resolution.

The peacebuilding triangle therefore highlights the nexus between context, resources and strategies. What works in one context may not work in another. A consent-based, light-footprint approach may be appropriate for a particular stage of the Sri Lankan conflict, where there is a functioning state and two clearly defined parties with explicitly political agendas and strong command and control over their troops.[2] However, this kind of a strategy never stood a chance in Afghanistan in the 1990s in a context of multiple, freewheeling parties, a regionalized war economy, significant interference from neighbouring countries and limited interest from the great powers. Clearly some contexts are inherently more demanding than others, which needs to be reflected in the strategies and resources that are brought to the table by international

Table 6.1 Policy Objectives and Instruments of International Actors Involved in Peacemaking and Peacebuilding

	Security	Diplomatic	Trade	Immigration	Aid
Interests and concerns	• Global/regional stability. • Prevention of terrorism. • Homeland security. • Control of illicit flows of drugs, arms, etc.	• Supporting peace processes. • Managing diplomatic relations.	• Access to markets. • Open trading relationships and security of investments. • Membership of global and regional trade organizations.	• Migration control. • Preventing refugee outflows. • Promoting repatriation, right to return.	• Building security. • Promoting economic liberalization and good governance. • Support for human rights and humanitarian needs.
Examples of policies	• ISAF in Afghanistan. • Indian intervention in Sri Lanka. • ECOWAS peacekeeping force in Liberia. • US and UK governments' proscription of LTTE as terrorists.	• OSCE diplomacy in Kyrgyzstan and Moldova. • UNSC sanctions towards Afghanistan. • Norwegian support for Sri Lanka peace process.	• Trade agreements. • Foreign direct investment. • Provision of military equipment.	• Tightening of border control regimes. • Bilateral agreements with individual countries. • Prevention of human trafficking.	• Provision of credit and grants for liberalization, good governance and poverty alleviation. • Provision of humanitarian relief.
Common shortcomings	• Focus on containment rather than sustainable resolution. • Regulation regimes voluntaristic at the global level. • Insufficient sensitivity to interests of regional powers.	• Peacemaking efforts insufficiently informed by an understanding of incentives. • Disconnects between diplomatic and other policy instruments. • Sanctions poorly targeted.	• Unequal terms of trade. • Lack of regulatory mechanisms for TNCs. • Exposing fragile economies to global competition too early, e.g. Kyrgyzstan's entry into the WTO. • Tensions between deregulation and stability.	• Focus on right to return has led to erosion of right of asylum and repatriation to unsafe areas. • Protection mandate of UNHCR weakened.	• Lack of adaptation of policy responses to local context. • Short-term time frames and project-based approaches. • Focus on liberalization may undercut other objectives such as poverty alleviation and stability.

interveners. This in turn shapes the opportunities and constraints for NGOs attempting to work in or on conflict.

Governmental and intergovernmental actors involved in peacemaking and peacebuilding pursue different policy objectives through a range of instruments and interventions, which may have direct or indirect impacts upon the structures and dynamics of armed conflict. Some of these are illustrated in Table 6.1.

The table illustrates the fact that state and intergovernmental actors that engage in peacemaking are not disinterested parties; they have their own agendas and interests, which shape interventions as much as, if not more than, humanitarian concerns. There are sufficient similarities between cases to support in broad terms Duffield's liberal peace thesis. Responses on the whole reflect an emerging consensus among Western powers concerning their core security, political and economic interests, though a hardening of the security agenda has become more evident following 9/11. On the other hand, the liberal peace analytical lens tends to gloss over the significant differences between, and even within, states in terms of their responses to conflict. As argued earlier, one can detect different variants of the liberal peace, with thick versions in frontline states like Afghanistan and thin versions in non-strategic countries like Nepal or Moldova. The research findings indicate that the policies of the interveners varied from country to country and over time. Much depends on the specific interests and capacities of both the exporters and importers of the liberal peace in individual contexts, as outlined further below. The Indian approach to peacemaking in Sri Lanka, for instance, was very different from the Norwegian approach. Furthermore, India's position today has shifted significantly from the time of the Indo–Sri Lankan Accord of 1987. Even within the same intervening country there may be competing interests: the military, diplomatic and development establishments may have different perspectives leading to divergent and sometimes contradictory polices.[3] Although the table separates out interventions from conflict dynamics, as argued in Chapters 3 and 4, international policies and interventions are likely to be an intrinsic part of the conflict. Armed conflicts may be the product of previous interventions, or they may mutate as a result of current ones. Peace processes affect the dynamics of conflict by influencing the capacities and calculations of the players. It is not useful, therefore, to see peace mediators or implementers as somehow standing above the fray, neutrally influencing events from a distance. Intervention in all its forms is part and parcel of the conflict.

International Peacemaking

The following section focuses on top-down efforts at peacemaking and peace implementation. A comprehensive analysis of peace processes and peace settlements is beyond the scope of this study.[4] The intention here is to highlight some of the key lessons about peace operations from the case studies that have a bearing on the potential for NGOs to build peace.

An Overview of the Cases

In complex, multifaceted peace operations the very concept of success and failure is ambiguous. What criteria or standards are used and when are they applied? Success may be defined in terms of achievement of mandate, but this begs the questions of who sets the criteria and how demanding their measures are. Are pragmatic criteria to be used, for instance, a reduction of existing levels of violence, or a modicum of a stable centralizing government? Or are more demanding measures to be employed, such as democratization, the rule of law, and social and economic development? If the bar is raised too high, then we are faced with a world of undifferentiated failure. It may perhaps be more useful to discriminate between the unmitigated failures and the flawed successes (Downs and Stedman, 2002: 49).

What is defined as successful depends also on when the assessment is done. The Abuja II Agreement in Liberia, for instance, was viewed at the time as a partial success, but seven years later the conflict reignited. The problems of time frames and attribution are difficult to overcome. As more time elapses after the ceasefire or peace agreement, it becomes more difficult to attribute impacts, since other extraneous factors come into play.

Most fundamentally, when is a peace process a peace process? Those who wage war may view it as a process designed to lead to peace. Similarly, belligerents may wage peace in order to further their wartime objectives. In eastern Sri Lanka, for example, under the shadow of a ceasefire and faltering peace process there has been an intensification of inter- and intra-group violence, as each side attempts to strengthen its bargaining position. Externally imposed frameworks are often highly subjective and suppress power, politics and history (Kriger, 2003: 20). They may be more a reflection of the agendas of external agencies than the political realities and needs of the affected countries. In Afghanistan in the winter of 2001, peace was defined by the US-led coalition in terms of ensuring the country no longer harboured terrorists. In the war over Nagorno-Karabakh, Armenia would like to call the status quo peace, while Azerbaijan takes the opposite view (Vaux and Goodhand, 2002: 27). Therefore, how one defines success is fraught with methodological and political difficulties.

In the case study countries a range of policy instruments and interventions were employed by a variety of international actors to address conflict at its different phases. Examples of these are outlined in Box 6.1.

The case studies point to the limited and frequently perverse effects of international peacemakers in protracted conflicts. In Afghanistan, two decades of UN attempts to broker a settlement failed (Fielden and Goodhand, 2001). In Sri Lanka, fragile ceasefires were the precursors of intensified fighting. Attempts by both the warring parties themselves and third parties, such as India, failed to deliver sustainable peace. A Norwegian-brokered ceasefire has survived since February 2002, but talks between the government and LTTE broke down in April 2003 and have yet to be resumed. In Liberia, peace of a kind was achieved through buying out the warlords. Whether in the long run engineering peace from above will lead to long-term structural stability can be questioned. Warlords signed 13 separate peace agreements before Abuja II. Those who argued at the time that the warlord peace failed to address underlying grievances and would

---

Box 6.1   Interventions to Address Violent Conflict

• Early warning and prediction, e.g. Swiss Development Cooperation, UNDP Ferghana Valley Preventative Development Programme and OSCE conflict monitoring, Kyrgyzstan.

• Preventative diplomacy, e.g. OSCE, Kyrgyzstan.

• Official diplomacy (Track One), e.g. OSCE, Moldova; Minsk Group, Armenia-Azerbaijan; Norwegians, Sri Lanka; UNSMA Afghanistan.

• Unofficial diplomacy (Track Two), e.g. MICOM, Moldova; Quakers and International Alert, Sri Lanka; human rights NGOs, Nepal.

• Peace agreements, e.g. Indo-Lanka Peace Accord, 1987, Sri Lanka; Abuja II, 1996, Liberia.

• Peace enforcement, e.g. IPKF, Sri Lanka; ECOMOG, Liberia.

• Peacekeeping/ceasefire monitoring, e.g. international peacekeeping forces, Moldova-Transdniestria and Azerbaijan-Armenia; ISAF, Afghanistan; SLMM, Sri Lanka.

• Peace implementation/post-conflict peacebuilding, e.g. EU, Liberia; UNAMA, Afghanistan.

---

lead to further violence were perhaps proved right by events in 2003. Liberia highlights the difficulty of dealing with the unlike-minded and the miscalculation by the international community of the real power base of Charles Taylor and his ability to win elections and continue pursuing predatory strategies. In Liberia peace brought into power a regime which practised the corrupt patrimonial politics of the past.

In Moldova and Armenia-Azerbaijan international mediation and peacekeeping prevented the escalation of violence. And yet perversely it played a role in freezing the conflict and maintaining a no-war no-peace status quo (Lynch, 2004). This serves the interests of politico-military elites on both sides but undermines the long-term development prospects of the affected countries and the wider region. In Kyrgyzstan international actors have invested in early warning and conflict prevention in a context of rising tensions, but these efforts are undermined by interventions in other spheres. Military support for repressive regimes in the region and a growing focus on counter-terrorism may undercut other stated goals, such as the promotion of human rights and good governance. In Nepal, international efforts to mediate between the government and Maoists have been resisted, the government fearing its sovereignty is threatened by internationalizing the conflict. International actors' primary source of leverage in relation to the conflict has therefore been through their development assistance programmes.

During the research period 1997–2001, whether one employs modest or more ambitious evaluative criteria, international efforts to bring peace had mixed effects. The scorecard could be summarized as follows: modest achievements in managing or preventing the escalation of conflict (Kyrgyzstan, Moldova and Armenia-Azerbaijan); a flawed success in Liberia in the form of Abuja II and subsequently the Comprehensive Peace Agreement of 2003; and repeated failures to negotiate peace agreements in Nepal, Sri Lanka and Afghanistan. However, by 2005 external interventions had transformed the ground situation in two of the case study countries. In Sri Lanka and Afghanistan heavily internationalized peace processes had changed the domestic constellation of power in the two countries. Whether these interventions will lead to sustained peacebuilding outcomes remains to be seen.

Therefore, in the case studies, a negotiated settlement was the exception rather than the norm. A victor's peace (Liberia in 1997 and Afghanistan in 2001), a frozen peace (Moldova, Nagorno-Karabakh) or continuing warfare were more common. As the Sri Lanka case shows, peace processes themselves are conflict-producing, because they represent a key moment of change when the new rules of the game are decided. In this case, negotiations acted as a lightning rod for wider societal tensions, leading to political fragmentation in the northeast and the south. Moreover, across the cases a history of broken and non-implemented agreements undermined the confidence and trust of the various parties, which itself impeded the search for a solution.

Who Intervenes?

The case studies reinforce the point made in Chapter 4 that in contemporary wars there has been a proliferation of actors involved in managing or resolving violent conflict. In each conflict it is possible to map out a range of actors working on different conflict-related tracks at different levels of the conflict. This is illustrated in relation to Nagorno-Karabakh in Table 6.2.

The performance of mediators and implementers affect the quality and outcome of civil war termination (Stedman, Rothchild and Cousens, 2002: 9). In theory, third parties can play a role in creating the security that is a prerequisite for reaching and implementing a peace settlement.[5] Whether this happens in practice depends to a great extent on the knowledge, legitimacy and credibility of the third parties as honest brokers. These third parties varied from case to case including multilateral (UN, OSCE), regional (IPKF and ECOMOG) and bilateral (Norway, India) actors.

In Afghanistan the primary responsibility for peacemaking was assigned to the UN, but internal deficiencies, including the performance of successive UN secretary-generals, undermined its role (Maley, 1998). However, most important was the lack of superpower backing in the early 1990s, followed by one-sided re-engagement after 1996 involving sanctions and missile diplomacy, which

Table 6.2   International Actors Working in or on the Nagorno-Karabakh Conflict

Conflict resolution track	Activities	Organizations
Track One Preserve ceasefire arrangements and pursue settlement of the conflict through official channels.	• Official negotiations among representatives of Armenia, Azerbaijan and NK.	• OSCE Minsk group. • EU Troika. • Council of Europe. • Bilateral intergovernmental talks, e.g. Russia or US.
Track Two Develop unofficial contacts between parties to the conflict and build up public support for a settlement.	• Workshops and study trips for decision-makers. • Civil society support, e.g. journalists, business people, academic exchanges, support for war veterans. • Prisoner exchange.	• Foreign embassies. • INGOs, e.g. Soros, Eurasia Foundation, International Alert. • Individuals including business people, academics, journalists.
Track Three Provide development assistance which addresses the wider context of the conflict through supporting regional integration, good governance, civil society support or poverty eradication.	• Infrastructure development linking the countries of the southern Caucasus; development projects, humanitarian assistance for the displaced. • Demining and rehabilitation in NK.	• EU, multilateral donors—World Bank, UNDP. • Bilaterals, e.g. USAID. • INGOs, e.g. Save the Children. • Oxfam. • ICRC. • Oil companies.

undermined the neutrality of the UN. Therefore, though the UN mouths the principles of global society it continues to follow the dictates of states (Stedman, Rothchild and Cousens, 2002: 19). Regional actors may have the virtue of being more committed since they are the most directly affected by the instability on their doorsteps. But they are also likely to have their own agendas. For instance ECOMOG's political masters, ECOWAS, were hopelessly divided over the intervention in Liberia (Adebajo, 2002: 599). Some members where opposed to intervention, while others supported various anti-NPFL factions. In Sri Lanka, India played the role of a 'blundering regional hegemon' (Bose, 2002: 632) in its misguided and unsuccessful intervention between 1987 and 1990. Similarly, Russia has simultaneously played the role of peacemaker and troublemaker in relation to Nagorno-Karabakh. It has been instrumental in securing a ceasefire and plays an active role as co-chair of the Minsk Group. But Russia has always acted in the belief that it has historical claims to be the predominant voice in the affairs of the region. Policy towards the conflict is shaped by concerns over Chechnya and access to natural gas and oil, undermining confidence in its role as a neutral mediator. Norway is perhaps the most successful example of a third-party mediator, though it is too early to say whether this will ultimately be judged a success. Important factors appear to be that both sides accepted Norway as a neutral party;[6] Norway's role has been low-key and responsive, with the two main parties being in the driving seat; the mediators have support at the highest levels, both from the Norwegian government and other international actors; and they have long involvement with the country and have the requisite knowledge and credibility and consequently the trust of both parties.

Political Engagement

The lack of concerted, long-term engagement, sometimes referred to as political will,[7] from international actors can be highlighted across the cases. As mentioned earlier, international actors practise a kind of triage, which distinguishes between more and less 'deserving' conflicts (Gurr, Marshall and Khosla, 2001). In Afghanistan, Sri Lanka and Liberia[8] during the 1990s the primary thrust of international engagement was one of strategic containment.

Conflict resolution processes were rarely supported in a sustained way. States tended to shy away from long-term entanglements, influenced by domestic actors, the short-term exigencies of electoral politics or targeted pressure groups. Strategies were rarely shaped by the unfolding needs of the conflict-affected countries. US policy towards the Armenia-Azerbaijan conflict, for example, has been strongly influenced by the Armenian lobby in Washington. Section 907 of the Freedom Support Act is one manifestation of this influence. This ruling allowed some US humanitarian spending in Azerbaijan but prohibited any flows of aid through the government. Armenia received three times as much aid per head from the US as Azerbaijan. This undermined Azeri confidence in the internationally supported peace process and the US co-chair in particular (Vaux and Goodhand, 2002: 30). Similarly, Indian involvement in Sri Lanka was motivated by domestic concerns and the need for the Congress Party to shore up flagging popularity and deflect public attention from various scandals and failures through a foreign policy triumph (Bose, 2002: 654). In 2004 there were concerns that the pace of US-dominated reconstruction efforts in Afghanistan were dictated more by the upcoming US presidential elections than the needs on the ground.[9] The half-hearted nature of externally supported conflict resolution is manifest in the weak international mandate of OSCE and the limited political involvement of the EU in Moldova, Armenia-Azerbaijan and Kyrgyzstan.

The case studies suggest that without a robust Track One process other policy instruments such as development and humanitarian aid can have limited impact. In fact they are likely to become a substitute or alibi for the lack of meaningful political engagement. In the main, interventions correspond to Ottoway's (2002) 'bargain basement model' mentioned in Chapter 4. International actors set ambitious goals but lack the corresponding commitment and resources to carry them through. The costs of not engaging are well illustrated in Afghanistan, where the vacuum left by superpower withdrawal was filled by neighbouring countries and radical Islamic groups. Borderlands clearly cannot be left in an 'isolation ward', as they tend to export their insecurity to the region and beyond.

As already mentioned, the findings from the case studies suggest that the overall picture is more complex and varied than the liberal peace thesis implies. On the one hand, some of the cases (Afghanistan and Sri Lanka after 9/11) support the view that changes in international thinking and policy are reflected in more interventionary responses to weak and failing states. On the other hand, there are wide differences in approaches from one case to another. International interest has waxed and waned, highlighting the fact that there is no political consensus on criteria for intervention or consistent upholding of international law. The idea that the liberal peace is being foisted on the world as part of the apparatus of international hegemony may be too simplistic. First, the empirical evidence suggests that even if this were the intention, how it is implemented in practice varies across cases. Second, liberal norms enjoy wider legitimacy in the international system and in developing countries themselves (Luckham, 2004: 484). NGOs may themselves play a role in propagating these norms. Therefore the liberal peace thesis perhaps places too much emphasis upon its exporters and not enough on the importers. For instance, the Sri Lankan prime minister, Ranil Wickramasinghe, was the main driving force behind the heavy internationalization of the Sri Lankan peace process in 2002. Third, the case studies demonstrate that domestic actors have greater agency than is commonly perceived to be the case. Though interventions may indeed be top-down and neo-colonial, this does not necessarily prevent domestic actors from instrumentalizing or even colonizing international engagement in order to pursue their political projects. Sri Lankan nationalists, for instance, demanded increased Indian intervention to act as a counterbalance to Western influence and to undermine the position of the LTTE. A critical factor in the success or otherwise of liberal peacebuilding appears to be the complex triangular relationship between the exporters, importers and broader societal actors. Where the importers have a limited constituency and rely too heavily on the exporters for their power and legitimacy, the foundations for peacebuilding are likely to be shaky. To a great extent this contributed to the downfall of Wickramasinghe, and Karzai similarly faces a crisis of legitimacy because of his perceived reliance on international backers.

Consent or Coercion?

The cases reveal a recurring tension between the use of hard power (coercive approaches) and soft power (consent-based approaches). Table 6.3 provides examples of various forms of international intervention, dividing them into unilateral and multilateral, coercive and non-coercive approaches.

The more difficult the conflict environment, the greater the need for more coercive and multidimensional approaches (Doyle and Sambanis, 2000; Stedman, 2001). However, aside from ECOMOG and the US-led coalition in Afghanistan in 2001, multilateral coercive approaches such as those employed in Kosovo and East Timor were not supported. Third-party military engagement through regional powers took place in three cases—the Indian Peacekeeping Force (IPKF), ECOMOG (Nigeria) and the 14th Soviet Army (Moldova)—but none

Table 6.3 Approaches to Peacemaking and Peacekeeping

	Unilateral	Multilateral
Coercive	• IPKF, Sri Lanka, 1987–90. • Russian military intervention, Nagorno-Karabakh, 1991.	• ECOMOG and UNMIL Liberia. • International peacekeepers, Armenia-Azerbaijan and Moldova. • US-led coalition, Afghanistan, 2001 to present.
Non-coercive	• Norwegian third-party mediation, Sri Lanka. • Indo-Sri Lanka Peace Accord. • Track Two initiatives, e.g. MICOM, Moldova, International Alert, Sri Lanka. • Russian-brokered ceasefire, Armenia-Azerbaijan, 1994.	• OSCE Minsk Group, Armenia-Azerbaijan. • Abuja II, 1996. • UNSMA-supported peace talks, Afghanistan. • SLMM ceasefire monitors, Sri Lanka.

of the interventions led to sustainable peace. They were seen to be partisan and lacked the capacity to transform the military balance of power. In contrast, the US-led coalition in Afghanistan, the security guarantees provided by the US and India to the government of Sri Lanka and the 15,000 UNMIL troops in Liberia are examples of how either the use or the threat of coercion can transform the security environment and potentially open up spaces for peacebuilding.

The questions of domestic coercive capabilities and military power-sharing arrangements are crucial. As shown elsewhere, sustainable peace depends upon the demilitarization of politics (Stedman, 2001). Peace in Liberia became a hostage to fortune because of Taylor's failure to restructure the armed forces. In Sri Lanka, one of the thorniest issues is the question of security-sector reform and whether the LTTE retains an autonomous military structure. Similarly in Afghanistan, a precondition for peace is the concentration of the means of violence through building up the Afghan National Army and disarming warlord militias.

The case studies also highlight the importance of coercive approaches being incorporated into a wider framework of peacebuilding. Most peace operations involve balancing coercive inducements with positive inducements, a combination of various sticks and carrots (military, political and economic) involving a wide range of actors who constitute peacebuilding capability in war zones (Miall, Ramsbotham and Woodhouse, 1999). The viability of negotiated solutions for civil wars rests on the assumption that the conflict parties share a common values framework within which differences can be negotiated. In the case of Sri Lanka this may hold true, since both parties have political goals regarding the nature of the Sri Lankan state. However, in armed conflicts involving competing warlords, in which there is in effect no state left to fight over, the pursuit of mediated settlements becomes more problematic.[10] Non-state military actors may have a limited interest in the international legitimacy or the incentives that diplomats can offer. Knowing when not to act appears to be an important lesson from the case studies. In Liberia it has been argued that the international response precipitated the humanitarian crisis because it stalemated a situation that otherwise would have been decided through a military takeover (Outram, 1999).

The case studies also show how, in the context of a peace process, the state finds it difficult to engage with the non-state and vice versa. As Kissinger (1969: 214) noted, in civil wars the guerrilla group wins if it does not lose. But this dynamic changes when the non-state actor goes to the negotiation table. A balance of military forces does not translate into political symmetry at the negotiation table, since states are better able to engage in the international diplomatic arena. In Sri Lanka, the breakthrough which led to peace talks was Wickramasinghe's willingness to accede political symmetry to the LTTE. Also significant was the willingness of international actors including the Norwegians to recognize the LTTE as equal partners in the peace process. Arguably the downside of such an approach is that it rewards violence; other groups such as the Muslims who did not take up the gun were at least initially left out of the peace talks.

Whether international intervention can open up peacebuilding space is determined largely by the types of (dis)incentives that are deployed to deal with spoilers. The options include coercion, benign neglect, criminalization and co-option (Stedman, 1997). Coercion, as already mentioned, has been employed half-heartedly and inconsistently. Possibly a neutral peacekeeping force on the ground in 1991–92 in Kabul could have averted the power vacuum that followed, but there was never any international interest in putting troops into Afghanistan. Benign neglect tended to be the default setting of international actors, but this allowed the combat and shadow economies to thrive. Neglect involved simply avoiding the question of how to take the violence out of the economy and concentrate the means of coercion. Criminalization was attempted through sanctions in Afghanistan and Liberia and proscription of the LTTE in Sri Lanka. In Afghanistan, one-sided sanctions appeared to have limited effect on the military capacities of the warring factions but probably increased the vulnerability of the general population.[11] An arms embargo proved impossible to enforce. Although the question of international recognition was one of the few bargaining chips that the international community had in relation to the Taliban, this was never used in a coherent way in relation to other sticks and carrots. In Liberia, more targeted sanctions on individual warlords did appear to have an impact. New sanctions were applied to Liberia on 7 May 2001. This included a ban on the export of diamonds from Liberia and travel sanctions on senior government officials and spouses. It also involved a tightening of the existing arms embargo by prohibiting the sale or supply of arms and related material and banning the provision of military training to the government. Finally the co-option strategy has been tried to an extent in Liberia and more recently in

Afghanistan and Sri Lanka.[12] Though this may buy short-term peace, it may not work in the long run. The nature of the end game and how war is curtailed have an important impact on the kind of peace that emerges. In Afghanistan an administration built purely around the factions who supported the GWOT may have shaky foundations. How the new dispensation is legitimized is crucial.

Coherence

Just as consent-based approaches tend to assume that warring groups have common values, the idea of policy coherence is based upon an assumption of common interests and values among the interveners. This, as the research highlights, is rarely the case. First, the case studies show a lack of coherence over time: as Western governments or the international political climate change, so do policies towards a country. US policy towards Afghanistan or the Indian approach to peacemaking in Sri Lanka are illustrative of this temporal inconsistency.

Second, there was a lack of coherence between different countries. As might be expected in Afghanistan, Iran and Pakistan pursued mutually incompatible approaches. But even between Western governments there were marked differences.[13] The overall picture is characterized by complex multilateral responses in which authority and accountability are diffused and there is often confusion over mission, mandates, capacities and credibility. In the absence of consensus on fundamental objectives, success in peacemaking is unlikely. For example, the conflicting objectives of Russia and the US in the Minsk group have hindered conflict resolution in the Nagorno-Karabakh conflict.

Third, there was a lack of vertical coherence, in the sense of coordination between different conflict resolution tracks. Negotiations tended to be elite-driven and there were limited efforts to include a wider cross-section of society in peace processes. A critical question is how one strikes the right balance between a narrow focus on key political actors and potential spoilers, and a more inclusive approach that builds wider ownership around the peace process. Peace processes may marginalize civil society groups which might otherwise have played an active role in building a sustainable peace. Peacemakers were perhaps constrained by sovereignty issues (as in the case of Sri Lanka), or focused more on buying off the warlords in the interests of short-term peace but at the expense of justice and long-term human security (as in the case of Liberia). The Armenia-Azerbaijan peace negotiations have involved an extremely small group of actors, primarily the high-level leadership, with talks being conducted in extreme secrecy. As one US diplomat stated: 'If you're dealing with fundamental issues of compromise it may not be possible to flesh them out in public.' However, the narrow base of the peace talks has been criticized, first because it failed to address the spoilers, including extremist political parties on both sides who have opposed compromise, and second, because it did not build links with Track Two and Three processes (Vaux and Goodhand, 2002). As the same US diplomat argued, 'Finding a solution at the negotiating table is not the hardest task... the more difficult task is for the presidents to take it to their people and persuade them that it's in their interests' (cited in Vaux and Goodhand, 2002: 28). There is a tension between the normative and pragmatic positions on this issue. How far is public participation in a peace process viewed as inherently desirable as a right and how pragmatically desirable is it in terms of effects?[14]

Finally, there was a lack of horizontal coherence, as the military, diplomatic and development establishments followed divergent and sometimes contradictory policies.[15] The sticks and carrots that might affect the calculations of conflict stakeholders have often not been applied in an intelligent and coordinated manner. For instance, while international actors have provided support for the Moldovan peace process, there have been no attempts to regulate the activities of Western companies in Transdniestria who contribute to the negative stalemate that has developed around the conflict. The case studies demonstrate there may not always be a smooth convergence between the values and objectives of foreign policy, trade and international aid.

Timing and Time Frames

It is evident from the case studies that the time frames employed by external actors tend to be far too short in relation to the processes they are seeking to address. Interveners were often unaware of the long-term histories of the countries they were dealing with and did not look far enough into the future when developing strategies. Also opportunities were missed because interveners had not geared up sufficiently to a particular phase of the conflict. For example, with hindsight, Afghanistan in 1991–92[16] was one such turning point, where more robust and timely intervention might have tipped the balance towards peace.

There is an important nexus between the mediation and implementation phases. The post-conflict moment represents either an opportunity for change or a return to normalcy. International interventions and particularly their sequencing may create the incentives for progressive change or a return to the status quo ante. Perverse sequencing may create the wrong incentives. For instance, the admission of Armenia and Azerbaijan to the Council of Europe arguably created a disincentive for change. It removed an important source of leverage in relation to the conflict and to domestic willingness to reform. Furthermore, elections may also create the wrong incentives in a highly politicized and conflictual environment. They raise the stakes and increase the probabilities of violence, which is why many argued for the postponing of parliamentary elections in Afghanistan. Elections may also be part of the international community's exit strategy. Conflict entrepreneurs realize this and simply wait out the peace agreement.

Peace Versus Justice

Although this is a vast topic, which is beyond the scope of this study, it is important to stress the constant tension in peace processes between stabilizing the situation and creating the mechanisms for reconciliation and justice. The absence of justice may be the primary reason for the absence of peace (Nathan, 2004: 3). The challenge of finding a common language of peace which involves truth-telling and establishing forms of transitional justice comes across in all case studies. At the time of the research, in Sri Lanka populations in the south tended to talk about peace, whereas communities in the north talked about justice. Resolving the Armenia-Azerbaijan conflict may require a history commission, in which both sides come to terms with the injustices of the past and find a common language of peace (Vaux and Goodhand, 2002: 29). In the post-conflict moment, what may be regarded as best practice internationally can become obstacles to viable political solutions (Ottaway, 2002: 1021). For instance, attempting to bring warlords to account for war crimes in Afghanistan may have the effect of destabilizing an already fragile peace process. However, the best short-term solutions are not something that should necessarily be institutionalized. Balancing the short term with the long term and what is desirable with what is possible is something that clearly has to be done on a case-by-case basis, based upon a careful analysis of the context. Since 9/11 the balance appears to have shifted decidedly in favour of hard security issues, to the detriment of questions of justice. A powerful illustration of this is the US arming and financing of commanders in Afghanistan in order to hunt down Al Qaeda and neo-Taliban operatives.

Aid, Conflict and Peacebuilding

An Overview of the Cases

Although the significance of international aid varied from case to case, it was an important facet of the response to conflict. In this section the supply-side characteristics of aid are explored. This involves a comparative analysis of aid regimes and donor policies. The political and operational space for NGO peacebuilding is shaped, to a large degree, by the architecture of aid and donor policies. Supply-side factors appear to have been more influential than demand factors. Aid flows respond to political variables and strategic considerations. Therefore, just as conflict was examined through a political economy lens, the same analytical lens can be applied to the transnational sector, which can best be understood as a political arena and as an aid market characterized by organizational insecurity, competitive pressures and fiscal uncertainty (Cooley and Ron, 2002).

The Evolution of Aid Regimes

Although an international political economy perspective helps explain the commonalities between aid regimes from country to country, aid regimes are also shaped by the particular political economies of individual contexts. Different conflicts create different types of aid markets. Duffield's (2001) argument that emerging political complexes are analogous to organisms which grow, adapt and transform themselves can be extended to aid regimes. They tend to reflect and mirror the idiosyncrasies of the particular conflicts they seek to address.[17] For instance, patterns of aid delivery mirror the patterns of security and insecurity in a country. Similarly the architecture of aid often replicates the organizational characteristics of warfare: in contexts where conflict is networked and decentralized the architecture of aid is likely to combine similar features. Aid, like violence, may be mimetic. For example in Afghanistan during the cold war period, the aid regime reproduced the pattern of the conflict, with Soviet aid going to populations under its control in the cities and Western aid going to resistance-controlled areas in the countryside.

Aid regimes therefore evolve and change according to the influence of a range of international and domestic factors. In Sri Lanka, for example, the aid system took on a very different character after 1977 as a result of both domestic factors (the change to a liberalizing government) and international factors (the growing international consensus on structural adjustment and liberalization). But the application of the norms of liberal governance was in practice very different from the orthodoxy. Donor–government interactions involved a great deal of bargaining, watering down and adaptation of policy prescriptions. The Washington consensus was applied selectively, based on political and institutional interests (Herring, 2001). In Afghanistan three 'generations'[18] of international aid reflected shifting responses to changing ground realities and cycles of international engagement and neglect. Both countries, but Afghanistan in particular, experienced a freeze–thaw pattern of assistance driven less by an objective assessment of needs than narrow political interests, public opinion and media images. The inadequacy and unevenness of funding are striking across the cases. Donors discriminate among crisis countries and their engagement with any one country fluctuates with little reference to objective needs.

Apart from the transition countries, the key features of the aid regimes were well established by the end of the Cold War period. To a great extent the structures and institutions in place at the beginning of the millennium were a product of an earlier era, and arguably institutional reform had not kept pace with changing global and national contexts. This parallels the failure of peacemaking strategies to adapt to changing realities, as mentioned in the previous section.

Aid, the State and Conflict

The conflict analysis in Chapters 2 and 3 placed the state in the foreground. Effective states are responsive to a broad range of interests, and are able to contain and manage grievance and prevent latent conflict from becoming violent

(Goodhand, 2003: 641). Therefore, the institutions of the state largely determine the net capacities for change in the peacebuilding triangle. The aid regimes in each country were found to have an important and sometimes critical influence on the capacities and legitimacy of the state.

Aid regimes and the institutions of aid-giving and -receiving are an extension of North–South relations in international politics. Aid donors do not just provide guidance, they assert interests and in doing so they challenge (and compromise) state sovereignty. The idea of unfettered state sovereignty was never a reality for states like Afghanistan, Kyrgyzstan or Moldova that were located on the margins of empires and the state system. But a historical reading of aid policies across the cases shows an extremely mixed record in terms of their impacts on sovereignty, governance and conflict. Aid policies may have impeded, rather than promoted, the emergence of effective, legitimate states. What was pursued in the name of economic development, good governance and conflict prevention may have had the opposite effect.

Cold War aid policies were found to be a significant factor in the origins of conflict. They had the effect of bolstering unaccountable elites, distorting state–society relations and undermining social contracts. The default setting is for aid to flow to those who wield power (Boyce, 2002b: 240). In Afghanistan, aid flowed to an urban elite, contributing to the bifurcation of the Afghan economy and society. In Sri Lanka, the adverse effects of donor policies were less about the sticks associated with structural adjustment than the carrots of development funding. Aid flows reinforced horizontal inequalities, leading to ethnic scapegoating which exploded into violent conflict in 1983. Soviet development policies created eggshell states that were dependent on Moscow and in which there were important disjunctures between social and political boundaries, between nation and state.

Apart from aid policies contributing to the causes of conflict, there was some evidence of aid playing a role in sustaining violent conflict. In Afghanistan, aid donors were in fact the conscious agents of state collapse. During the course of the conflict the donor community built up a humanitarian shadow state or parallel universe (Donini, 2003a), which sidestepped the remnants of the Afghan state. This caretaker government, as some agencies described themselves, was externally-driven and expatriate-dominated. Few Afghans had positions of seniority (Atmar and Goodhand, 2002). In post-Taliban Afghanistan roughly three-quarters of government expenditure is paid for and is directly executed by donors. This does little to build the legitimacy of the government or solidify the peace process. In Sri Lanka, the division of the country into zones of relief and development accentuated the political and economic disparities between north and south. In Nepal, where aid has financed more than 50 per cent of the country's development budget (Bray et al., 2003: 128), the default position of donors once conflict had broken out was to provide humanitarian aid and adopt an indefinite wait-and-see approach.

The Radicalization of Aid and Peace Conditionalities

Though the politicization of aid was as much a feature of the Cold War as the post–Cold War environment, the focus on peacebuilding—or aid securitization as Duffield calls it—was new. This manifested itself in a number of ways, including the mandate expansion of the World Bank in Sri Lanka and the Strategic Framework process in Afghanistan. Both development and humanitarian aid, it was assumed, could be redesigned or withheld, in order to support peacebuilding or discipline recalcitrant regimes and actors.

Humanitarian minimalists objected vigorously to the intrusion of politics and the pollution of humanitarian principles.[19] However, the case studies question such a fundamentalist position. It rests upon an ideal-type notion of humanitarianism, which conceives it as entirely separate from and involving different guiding principles from development assistance. According to Macrae (2001), development aid is political, as it involves dealing with a recognized, legitimate government—in other words, one with juridical and empirical sovereignty. Humanitarian aid is targeted at the individual and is politically unconditional. The distinction between development and relief is therefore seen as political not technical.

However, this neat distinction rarely appeared to exist (or in fact to be desirable) in any of the cases. First, these categories meant little to those living in contexts of chronic political instability. Second, as the case studies demonstrate it is not always easy to make a clear-cut distinction between a legitimate stable state and an illegitimate failed state.[20] Third, in practice the division between relief and development was blurred because aid agencies tended to work with a mixture of humanitarian and development funding. Even in Afghanistan where the lion's share of funding over two decades had been short-term humanitarian assistance, NGOs used rolling funds to implement programmes which were neither conventional development nor conventional relief. They subverted donor categories by using various forms of assistance more creatively, just as communities did with different types of agency projects. The closer one got to the field, the more meaningless the binary distinction between political development and apolitical relief became.

The problem for the most part was not that donors began to take an interest in peacebuilding, but first, that they did not pursue it in a way that was serious enough or smart enough. And second, that aid became a substitute for, rather than complementary to, political engagement in the peace process. In Afghanistan during the 1990s humanitarian conditionality had limited leverage, and the links between outside influence, internal compliance and results on the ground were weak. As one donor in Afghanistan noted in 1998, a simplistic and confrontational response had limited impact: 'You can't socially engineer a country by shouting out principles.' In Sri Lanka, though many of the smaller bilateral donors refocused their policies on peacebuilding, the Japanese and the ADB, the two largest donors, continued to work around conflict (Goodhand, 2001a).

The Afghan case study in particular highlights the lack of correlation between donors' ambitions and the resources they brought to the table. There were
insufficient resources to meet humanitarian needs (consolidated appeals were
consistently underfunded), never mind to build peace. The lack of a realistic
fiscal policy to pay for peace reflected the political disengagement of Western
governments.

Donors, NGOs and the Aid Marketplace

Donors' decisions are not simply determined by external political pressures.
Aid agencies themselves also exercise a degree of independence, with their
internal incentive systems and institutional agendas generating a momentum of
their own (Boyce, 2002a). Political will is important, but so too is institutional
performance.[21]

In many respects the case studies confirm global trends outlined in Chapter
4. To a considerable degree the aid regime, and in particular donors' role in it,
actively discourages good NGO practice and consequently limits the space for
peacebuilding. The aid sector in the 1990s became increasingly marketized,
which in turn had a powerful homogenizing effect on NGOs, something that
Smillie (1999) refers to as the 'crisis of conformity.' In this aid market, material constraints rather than normative aspirations may better explain aid agency
behaviour.[22] Securing new funding becomes an ever-expanding part of the
NGOs' function, pushing other concerns—such as ethics, project efficacy or
self-criticism—to the margins. In each of the case studies, NGO rent-seeking
behaviour was common, with organizations undermining competitors, conceal-
ing information and acting unilaterally. Interorganization discord is a predictable
result of existing material incentives (Cooley and Ron, 2002). What may appear
to be dysfunctional behaviour in relation to aid objectives may be an entirely
rational response to systematic and predictable institutional pressures (ibid.: 37).
These competitive pressures are likely to be more intense in armed conflict, as
NGOs rely more heavily on official funding for their relief work than they do
in development settings. The more unfettered the market, the more prevalent
the rent-seeking behaviour, characterized, for example, by Afghanistan in the
mid-1980s, with high levels of funding, many competing players, few barriers
to entry and low accountability standards. In Sri Lanka during the 1990s, on the
other hand, the aid market was more regulated—the existence of a state meant
there were barriers to entry such as registration and legal criteria—and there
were more controls on rent-seeking, the funding sources were more diverse, thus
decreasing interagency competition, and there was greater NGO self-regulation
because of an effective NGO coordination body.

Donor policies limited the space for NGO peacebuilding in a number of
other ways. First, though coordination mechanisms were in place,[23] they rarely
led to joined-up policy and practice on the ground.[24] Coordination arrange-

ments were resisted by donors for various reasons: they limited donors' room for manoeuvre in terms of pursuing commercial and political interests through aid programmes; they were costly in terms of administrative time and expense; and there were genuine disagreements over policies and priorities. For instance, the approach of the Norwegians and Canadians in Sri Lanka was fundamentally different from that of the Japanese. These frictions could not be addressed simply through calls for better coordination.

Second, donor involvement with civil society was often hamfisted and naïve. In Afghanistan the UN encouraged the proliferation of Afghan NGOs, but then failed to provide sustained support. Elsewhere, particularly in the transition countries, a weak analysis of civil society led to a policy of picking winners and equating civil society strengthening with support for Westernized NGOs based in capital cities. Donor agencies tended to focus on the short term and the easily measurable, concentrating on the physical infrastructure of civil society—the 'forms rather than the norms' (Edwards, 1999).

Third, short time frames and a project-based approach discouraged more innovative and high-risk activities. Donor time frames were particularly short in Liberia and Afghanistan, where 6–12 months' funding was the norm: 'As donors we always want the quickest return and the biggest bang for our buck' (multilateral donor, Peshawar, August 1998). This had a range of negative knock-on effects, including: the bypassing of local NGOs (as transaction costs were often greater); discouraging NGOs from thinking long-term about their role in areas such as local institutional development and strengthening civil society; fostering shallow careers that were patched together and involved either moving from one agency to another or from one conflict to another; encouraging aid project monocultures.

Fourth, the introduction of Western managerialism and the consequent demands for log frames and the use of rational planning techniques undermined the traditional NGO comparative advantages of flexibility, responsiveness and innovation. Donors encouraged NGOs to avoid risk (rather than assess risk and decide whether the opportunities merited taking a risk) and to minimize overhead costs, so that establishing capacities in strategic analysis and research on the causes of conflict are treated as unnecessary luxuries. The donor obsession with impacts and a culture of concrete results also encourages NGOs to talk up their results and leads to an understating of the less tangible but possibly more significant impacts of NGO activities on social relations, norms and leadership that was noted earlier.

Therefore, the case studies reveal a serious problem with bad donorship. In general donors did not come close to meeting the standards that they routinely demand of NGOs. And NGOs, because of their dependence on official funding, were reluctant to or unable to lobby for changes in donor policies and practices. Overall, it was found that NGOs were less constrained by donor policies where there were pockets of high-quality funding, that is, flexible, long-term, with low conditionalities, from a number of the smaller, conflict-sensitive bilaterals, as was the case in Sri Lanka. There were few unambiguously positive examples of good donorship. Notable exceptions were in Afghanistan in the funding relationships between NORAD/Norwegian Church Aid and a number of Afghan NGOs, including ADA; in Sri Lanka Norway's support for the National Peace Council; and in Kyrgyzstan the SDC's relationship with the Foundation for Tolerance International. In each case the core ingredients were the fairly obvious ones (though quite uncommon) of a long-term relationship, core funding, flexible arrangements and trust that had developed over time. To a certain extent they depended upon personal relationships and individuals who managed to make things work in spite of, rather than because of, the system. It was probably also significant that the Norwegian and Swiss governments did not have a strong political axe to grind in the respective country, thus giving the donor agency the space to pursue policies guided by development and humanitarian criteria, rather than political interests.

NGOs and the International Response to Armed Conflict

Although civil wars are often treated as internal disorders, the case studies highlight the culpability of international actors in failing to avert or actively promoting state crisis. The case studies demonstrate that contemporary conflicts are as much about failures in global governance as crises in domestic authority. Can NGOs themselves play a role in constructing, constituting or expanding the peacebuilding space within which they operate? What are their effects, if any, on global governance? Can NGOs play a role in humanitarianizing politics? Or is humanitarianism simply the continuation of politics by other means? This study has largely focused on the question of how NGOs affect the dynamics of conflict and peace in countries affected by armed conflict. The question of whether and to what extent NGOs can influence the response of Western governments and intergovernmental organizations to armed conflict is a critical one, but largely beyond the scope of this study. A more optimistic, perhaps Kantian perspective, is that they have socialized state elites towards humanitarian and peacebuilding norms, reflected in a greater willingness to intervene on humanitarian grounds and an expanded role for civil society in multidimensional peace operations. NGOs have perhaps benefited from and helped bring about the growing mobility between high politics and low politics referred to earlier.

An alternative reading of current trends is that because INGOs are rooted in Western societies and receive funding from Western governments, they are ultimately the agents of Western security concerns. Increasingly, it is argued that NGOs are becoming supply-side extensions of government systems (Fowler, 2005: 5). The very notion that they are nongovernmental can be called into question. LNGOs operate within the same logic of this system and they are viewed by many as simply an extension of the North–South relationship in international politics. As Wickramasinghe (2001: 170) argues in the case of Sri Lanka, NGOs serve to create new circles of power in Sri Lankan society: 'the timid and sometimes servile civil society of Sri Lanka is being used by transnational forces as a way of transforming more efficiently domestic politics and society'. NGOs therefore operate in the Westphalian system and consequently reproduce the flaws of that system.

These two positions are not mutually exclusive and the case studies provide evidence for both. But the balance of evidence suggests that multi-mandate humanitarian NGOs involved in relief and development work have very limited autonomy because of their position in the aid market. Consequently they have tended to replicate, rather than challenge, the flaws in the international response. In Afghanistan they inadvertently legitimated first a policy of one-sided intervention and second a policy of containment and arm's-length engagement. In Sri Lanka, NGOs provided donors with an alternative means of keeping engaged while avoiding the crucial question of state reform. NGOs were themselves the willing or unwilling accomplices in this process. Similarly in transition environments NGOs followed the money, but were more reticent about challenging a transition model that arguably undermined human security.[25] Their dependence on official funding, combined with the lack of a significant constituency in either their home countries or areas in which they operated, meant they had limited influence over the calculations and behaviour of international actors. This influence may be further eroded as Western governments increasingly deploy military and private-sector organizations to engage in humanitarian and reconstruction work.

NGOs' limited, or sometimes inadvertent, effects at a macro level, can be set against their concrete benefits at the community level. Perhaps they should be held accountable for their impact on the latter, rather than on the wider processes over which they have limited influence. But neither should their political effects, particularly their legitimating role, on the international response to conflict be ignored, as this has an influence on the peacebuildng space, and ultimately the type of peace that emerges.

Conclusion

This chapter has examined the external dimensions of peacemaking and peacebuilding in the case study countries. It has been argued that the international political and policy environment has had a major influence, both positive and negative, on peacebuilding processes. To understand what is going on in these different cases, one's starting point should be to assume that international actors do not necessarily have an interest in expanding the space for peacebuilding. The hard national interests of dominant powers usually trump proclaimed concerns with human security, and the assertion of these interests may reduce the space for peacebuilding.

However, the case studies also suggest that it is too simplistic to view peacebuilding as simply the foisting of an apparatus of international hegemony on powerless, marginal states. Interventions in the various cases involved multiple actors and a complex mixture of competing priorities and interests, which in turn interacts (and clashes) with the goals and projects of various domestic actors. In fact the case studies suggest that the importers of peacebuilding have a great deal more agency than is frequently attributed to them. An analysis of the alliances formed between exporters and importers in specific cases appears to be key to understanding how and why certain interventions increase or decrease the peacebuilding space.

Based on an analysis of contextual factors, one can begin to identify defining features of environments that are more or less conducive for NGO peacebuilding. A specific mix of structural, dynamic and contingent factors create different types of peacebuilding ecologies. Key factors identified were: first, the nature of the conflict—the roots of hostility and capacities for change, with a particular focus on the state and state–society relations; second, the international response to conflict—the strategies, capacities and agendas of the peacemakers, the robustness and coherence of the response; and third, the nature of the aid regime—the architecture of aid and its relationship to the recipient state, the type of funding available, the policies and practices of donors and the position of NGOs in the aid regime. In addition there may be more idiosyncratic and contingent factors such as a drought or a change of government. Applying the above criteria to a comparative analysis of the cases, one can identify more or less challenging environments for NGOs in peacebuilding terms. Broadly the level of difficulty ranges from extreme (Afghanistan, Liberia, Nepal), to moderate (Sri Lanka, Moldova, Armenia-Azerbaijan), to low (Kyrgyzstan). However, at the subnational level the picture is more complex, since one can identify peacebuilding niches even when the wider context is unpromising.

To conclude, it has been argued in this and the last chapter that wider contextual factors have a critical influence on the extent to which NGOs have higher- or lower-level impacts on peacebuilding processes. But the analysis, so far, has not focused on the agency of NGOs themselves and their ability to create space or room for manoeuvre. Those who view NGOs as simply the agents of the liberal peace underestimate the reflexivity and autonomy of the NGOs themselves. The case studies also show that organizational performance is an important factor in its own right, and this question is turned to in the next chapter.

7

NGO Programming and Capacities for Peacebuilding

This chapter details the ways in which NGOs have responded to the challenges of working in or on conflict. It examines the programming, organizational and relationship-building capacities required by NGOs working in unstable environments. The chapter explores whether there are generic capacities that all NGOs working in areas of conflict should develop, or whether there are distinctive capacities or 'peaceabilities' that are unique to NGOs aiming to build peace.

Introduction

Violent conflict is less about breakdown than about reordering and transformation. This observation might be applied not only to the societies and polities in which wars take place, but also to the international organizations that respond to them. Wars have exposed profound weaknesses in the way international agencies conceptualize and respond to them, which in turn has led to a process of reordering within the international response system. For NGOs, armed conflicts have also been a crucible for organizational change.

The previous chapter explored the contextual factors largely beyond the control of NGOs that determine the space for peacebuilding. In this chapter the analytical focus moves inside NGOs. Research and debates on conflict, peace and humanitarianism commonly lack an organizational perspective.[1] However, the case studies show first that organizations are important and play a role in shaping peacebuilding outcomes. Second, they highlight the complexity and differentiation both between and within NGOs. NGOs differ in terms of mandates, identities, performance and so on. They also can be many things at the same time. Organizations are socially constructed (and reconstructed) in everyday actions and in order to understand them one must observe the 'everyday politics of NGOing' (Hilhorst, 2003). This chapter examines and compares everyday NGOing in the case study countries, in order to gain an understanding of the internal factors that influence NGOs' capacities to work in and on conflict. It examines in turn the programming, organizational and relationship-building dimensions of NGOs.

NGO Programming for Peacebuilding

Programming Mix

The scale, focus and mix of NGO programmes varied between contexts, depending on the type and intensity of the conflict, the needs of the population, the funding environment and the agency mandate. In all countries, mandates tended to expand during the course of the conflict. NGOs that had started out in relief increasingly broadened their focus to include development, rights and peace objectives. Although some niche agencies maintained a clear focus on relief/protection (ICRC, MSF), rights and advocacy (Amnesty International, Sri Lanka) or conflict resolution (NPC, Sri Lanka; MICOM, Moldova; FTI, Kyrgyzstan), most were generalists who provided a range of services. For example, CARE, Afghanistan's programme, spanned relief and protection in Kabul, livelihood support in the east, refugee women's education in Pakistan and advocacy on Afghan rights and gender issues in the US. Whether external assistance comes from a relief, development or conflict resolution budget line is less important than whether and how it strengthens an individual's or group's portfolio of entitlements, enabling them to better manage interlocking risks. Therefore, a hybrid approach evolved, based on the mainly intuitive understanding of NGO staff, that different types of interventions are required in different types of settings to build different forms of human security. As Box 7.1 shows, NGOs contributed to peacebuilding indirectly or directly through a range of different programming approaches.

In theory multi-mandate organizations have the potential to exploit synergies between overlapping relief, development, rights and peacebuilding opportunities and between their service delivery, capacity-building and advocacy roles. In practice, simultaneously pursuing multiple objectives often led to tensions and trade-offs. First, mandate expansion tended to happen in an ad hoc and reactive way. Consequently insufficient thought was given as to how one strengthened the synergies while minimizing the tensions and costs associated with a hybrid strategy. Second, NGOs' transient relationships with communities and their shallow understanding of local coping strategies meant they were often poor at matching responses to the requirements of individual contexts. Third, NGOs often lacked the necessary range of technical skills or the organizational structures to support such a rich programming menu. Oxfam's institutionalization of the relief-development divide at the country and head-office level is one example. Another was NGOs' weakness, across the board, in listening and participatory approaches.[2]

Box 7.1   Indirect and Direct Approaches to Peacebuilding

Indirect approaches
• Conflict-sensitive relief, e.g. Oxfam resettlement projects, eastern Sri Lanka.
• Supporting local leadership, e.g. CCA/Christian Aid, eastern Sri Lanka; NCA, Afghanistan.
• Human rights monitoring/protection, e.g. ICRC, CCA, Afghanistan.
• Governance, e.g. constitutional reform and ICES in Sri Lanka; judicial reform, Liberian NGOs; election monitoring, CPA, Sri Lanka.
• Local capacity-building/civil society strengthening, e.g. Christian Aid, eastern Sri Lanka.
• Socio-economic development/alternative livelihoods, e.g. EHED community development programmes, eastern Sri Lanka; Afghanaid, northeast Afghanistan; Mercy Corps International, micro credit, Ferghana Valley.

Direct approaches
• Conflict prevention, e.g. conflict-monitoring, Tolerance International, Kyrgyzstan.
• Mediation/conflict resolution, e.g. between warring parties, ICRC in northern Sri Lanka; between and within communities, ADA in Uruzgen, Afghanistan; EHED in eastern Sri Lanka; MICOM, Moldova; human rights NGOs, Nepal.
• Building peace constituencies, e.g. NPC in southern Sri Lanka; CPAU, Afghanistan.
• Reconciliation, e.g. ADA community development and reconciliation in Afghanistan; Lutheran World Service trauma counselling, Liberia; QPS, community mediation programme, eastern Sri Lanka.
• Security sector, e.g. SCF (UK) programme with child soldiers, Liberia; de-mining NGOs, Afghanistan.
• Advocacy/education, e.g. ICRC, IHL dissemination; Oxfam, cut conflict campaign; Listening to the Returned/Displaced, Oxfam, SCF, Sri Lanka; children zones of peace, SCF, Sri Lanka; BBC 'New Home, New Life', Afghanistan.

Therefore the overall picture is one of multi-mandate NGOs struggling to find an optimum balance and programming mix in complex, constantly changing environments. Three key sets of tensions can be identified as agencies moved from relief into new programming areas.[3] First, there was the tension between relief and development. In Sri Lanka, for example, depending upon whether it was in cleared or uncleared areas, the LTTE or the SLAF objected to development programmes. The very haziness of rehabilitation allows an avoidance of long-term commitment and enables donors and NGOs to hedge their bets.[4]

Second, there was the tension between relief and rights. In Sri Lanka, for instance, SCF(UK)'s shift in focus from relief to child rights entailed a significant reduction in operations, which undermined its credibility with local partners. More common was the reverse problem of NGOs prioritizing operationality over bearing witness or advocating on rights violations. A silent witness could thus become a complicit witness, particularly when it failed to pass on information about abuses to actors who could potentially expose or address them.

Third, there was the tension between relief and peace. The reasons for getting involved in peacebuilding were complex and mixed, involving a range of external (donor pressures, funding opportunities, community demand, media profile) and internal (field-based learning, product champions, religious mission, country desk support) factors. The case studies revealed a considerable level of ambivalence within and among NGOs about whether and how to incorporate peacebuilding approaches. Within the same organization there were often very different understandings of, and approaches to, peacebuilding. Most NGOs running field operations saw peacebuilding as a potential by-product of their work, but few actively scanned the environment for peacebuilding opportunities, or incorporated peacebuilding as an explicit objective in their programmes.

Purists argue that the tensions and trade-offs between relief and development, or peace and rights, cannot be fudged, they are fundamentally incompatible with one another, amounting to different positions about the ends and means of humanitarian action. However, the research findings support neither a minimalist nor a maximalist approach to programming. In certain contexts a minimal relief response was the most appropriate and the only possible response, for example, eastern Sri Lanka in the early 1990s or Liberia during the height of the conflict. In practice, aid workers in multi-mandate agencies tended not to see rigid boundaries between rights-based, developmental or humanitarian approaches. Programming decisions and day-to-day project work were delimited by a combination of factors including organizational mission and risk threshold, the conflict context and individual staff members' own values. Good practice involved a contingent approach that was grounded in situational analysis. Activities were adjusted to take account of the contingencies posed by different types of conflict and diversity among aid recipients. NGO fieldworkers on the whole make judgements about what is desirable and what is possible based upon an analysis of the local context at a specific time. In Afghanistan, Nepal and Liberia the political space was perceived to be more limited, while in Sri Lanka and Kyrgyzstan the opportunities to work on conflict appeared to be greater. Peacebuilding may be the outcome of a variety of programming approaches and skilful practitioners make conscious choices about the blend and mix of activities, according to the constraints and opportunities of the operating environment.

No choice is cost-free. A maximalist approach may lead to serious organizational pressures. Apart from the additional time and resources required—ADA in Afghanistan, for example, made a significant investment in staff training, adjusting implementation schedules and educating its donors—an explicit focus on peace risked endangering access to conflict-affected communities.[5]

But there are likely to be costs attached to a minimalist approach in terms of missed peacebuilding opportunities. An ability to exploit windows of opportunity[6] by responding to high-risk but high-opportunity moments in a conflict is a central challenge for NGOs. There may be an analogy here with desert ecology. During the drought years, plants remain dormant. There is only a brief window of opportunity when the rains come, and during this time there is a period of intense activity. Similarly, NGOs in terms of peacebuilding may have to undergo long periods of drought, but if they can identify when the 'rain' is coming and respond quickly and appropriately when it does, they may have a disproportionate impact. In Sri Lanka off-site NGOs which focused on human rights and political lobbying were better placed to respond quickly, because they were unencumbered by projects. Such organizations often had a comparative advantage in high-risk, high-opportunity situations. The same applied to specialist mediation or peace-focused NGOs whose credibility and effectiveness depended less on implementing projects than the quality of their analysis, their personal relationships and their mediation skills.

The evidence from Sri Lanka indicates that multi-mandate NGOs by virtue of their presence in the northeast played an indirect 'climate-setting' role. It was essentially a holding operation, which involved conflict-proofing communities, keeping civic spaces open and nurturing local leadership. But niche NGOs could at certain times in the conflict open up spaces for peacebuilding. In this sense the two types of NGOs had different but complementary roles, though a lack of strategic relationships between the two meant this was rarely exploited.

Ways of Working

The case studies exposed the severe limitations of a project-based approach to humanitarian action in general and to peacebuilding in particular. The reification and resilience of the project-based approach and its continuity over time and from area to area were striking. In Afghanistan the diversity of the environment could be contrasted with the monochrome nature of the programming. The same key elements of an agriculture project, for instance, would be replicated by NGOs from one district to another with virtually no adaptation. The tunnel vision of the project system prevented the emergence of more innovative programming.[7]

International NGOs were found to be surprisingly weak in the area of local capacity-building and advocacy. Reflective and participatory approaches were often overtaken in emergencies and the imperatives for speed tended to marginalize local actors. INGOs, in spite of their claims to be capacity-builders and lobbyists, still tended to go operational in emergencies and focus on service delivery. This appears to be a deeply ingrained reflex of INGOs, who cited concerns about neutrality, politicization and corruption, and created an unhelpful duality between pure humanitarian aid and impure southern development. By putting the humanitarian dilemma entirely in the hands of expatriates, such an approach disempowered local humanitarians and their institutions (Christoplos,

1998). The LNGO success stories indicate the shortcomings of such a view. NGOs like ADA in Afghanistan, NPC in Sri Lanka and FTI in Kyrgyzstan were the result of long-term partnerships with international organizations that had a commitment to and an understanding of capacity-building.[8] It is hard to avoid the conclusion that INGOs' foot-dragging on capacity-building is at least partly coloured by hard organizational interests. In the final analysis, LNGOs are viewed as much as competitors for funding as potential partners. Although in many respects it is too early to tell, the tensions between international and domestic civil society actors are likely to be heightened by the GWOT. Domestic political elites play the terrorism card to undermine the position and legitimacy of supposed dissidents, making it more difficult for international actors to engage with progressive elements in civil society.

Donors and NGOs who simplistically equated civil society with NGOs avoided the state and ignored 'uncivil' elements in civil society. Though Bastian (1999) argues for a more political and more sceptical approach to civil society, this was lacking among most of the multi-mandate NGOs. The more successful peacebuilding interventions involved a capacity-expanding element and tended to focus on the interface between state and society, as for example with NPC in Sri Lanka.

To an extent, the coherence agenda championed by donors represents an advocacy opportunity for NGOs to hold donors to their own rhetoric. But in practice NGOs were reticent about holding donors and states to account. This varies between agencies: Oxfam, for example, has a long tradition of maintaining a critical distance from government policies and pressures. Wilsonian NGOs, on the other hand, tend to align themselves more closely behind government policies. However, this varies from context to context: CARE, who many view as a classic Wilsonian NGO, has been one of the most vocal advocates for a more coherent and thoughtful international engagement in post-Taliban Afghanistan.

Therefore, it is in the areas of capacity-building and advocacy that the disjuncture between discourse and practice was greatest. The reasons for this are varied but include short-term time frames and funding, a lack of strategic analysis, the inherent difficulties of capacity-building as a project and institutional interests. Although it may not be the determining factor, it did appear that NGOs with a larger proportion of independent funding were more willing to challenge donors, advocate on sensitive issues and experiment with innovative approaches.

NGO Capacities for Peacebuilding: Hearts and Minds

Research on peacebuilding has tended to focus on what organizations actually do. Much less has been written about the internal workings of NGOs engaged in peacebuilding. To an extent the organization is treated as a 'black box' and ethnographic studies of development agencies remain relatively few in number (Lewis et al., 2003: 543). This is a serious omission, as peacebuilding approaches raise important questions about agency mandates and capacities. The case studies highlight the importance of NGOs developing the right combination of heart and mind. The former is taken to mean having a clear normative and ethical position and being able to communicate it consistently. The latter is taken to mean having the organizational intelligence to analyse and learn from situations, to know one's own capacity and use that capacity to good effect. These two 'peaceabilities' are examined in greater detail below. This is followed by an analysis of leadership, staff and organizational structures and management, in other words the head and body of the organization. The section finishes with the crucial question of accountability.

Mandates, Values and Culture: The Organizational Heart

The case studies revealed great variability among agencies in how espoused values and principles were understood and put into practice, particularly between the field and head office. In Oxfam, for example, while field staff in Sri Lanka were advocates of community peacebuilding, UK-based staff from the Emergencies Department were critical of such an approach:

> the rationale for humanitarian intervention is strictly limited and should remain so… particularly with regards to impartiality… we distribute according to need and if we don't the whole thing becomes hi-jacked… having criteria overlaid is very dangerous… the Geneva Conventions are not concerned with peace. (Emergencies Department staff member, Oxfam, HQ)

These types of tensions, which were essentially about clashing world views, have probably grown in recent years, reflecting the expanding mandates of humanitarian organizations. At one level, these debates were about ethical concerns and whether certain core values should be elevated above others. Humanitarianism, rights and peace are often treated by aid workers as separate theologies practised in different churches (Smillie, 2003: 187). This partly accounts for the depth of feeling such debates generated: ego and power drives are often strongest when cloaked by moral rectitude (Edwards, 1999; Harrell-Bond, 1986).[9] On another level the debates are also tied up with hard institutional and personal interests. They can be interpreted as a form of jockeying between individuals and departments in order to prove their worth within the organization and consequently to attract funding, power and/or status.[10] Humanitarianism is bound up with a strong culture of self-justification. Because of NGOs' dependence on official funding, there are strong institutional incentives to portray humanitarianism as indispensable (Terry, 2002: 228; de Waal, 1997).

The shared, consensual language employed by NGOs tends to paper over the fragmentary tendencies in the cultures and practices of agencies. NGOs are characterized by ambiguity, competing subcultures, processes of ideological negotiation and ongoing conflict. Although the activist culture of relief workers versus the process-oriented culture of development workers may be something of a caricature, it is still one that many practitioners recognize and relate to. Organizational culture, defined as the system of knowledge, technologies, practices and power relationships (Lewis et al., 2003) in an agency, is an important factor shaping NGOs' capacity to work effectively in or on conflict. Oxfam and SCF in Sri Lanka both experienced a major disjuncture between the rapid introduction of organizational changes and the much slower pace of cultural change.[11] NGOs such as ADA and FTI with a relatively successful track record in peacebuilding managed to develop a level of coherence at all levels of the organization around values, mission and purpose. This was perhaps easier in a relatively small, one-country NGO that had exceptional leadership and strong donor backing, compared for instance with a more complex, multicountry NGO. Faith-based NGOs may also find it easier to build and sustain coherence around mission and values. The peacebuilding and reconciliation activities of EHED, a Catholic church NGO in Sri Lanka, and Lutheran World Service in Liberia were guided by a strong sense of religious mission. On the other hand, such a powerful organizational culture may act as a block to change. As one interviewee in EHED argued, the conservative and largely welfarist approach of the religious hierarchy tended to prevent a more radical approach to peacebuilding from emerging: 'We have to go beyond the praying level—we need to link justice to peace and bring out the injustice of the current situation. We have to build on the concept of a right to peace, like the right to life.'

Therefore the internal dynamics and the unseen conflicts or 'infra-politics' (Scott, 1997) in an organization had a critical impact on their external activities. In addition to organizational culture, the wider societal and political culture must be considered. NGOs are part of broader societal structures and sets of meanings. Although local NGOs are often assumed to be more embedded and therefore prone to battlefield bias, this was not necessarily found to be the case. For example, CARE Afghanistan was colonized in the 1980s by the Hezb-i-Islami, a radical Islamic political party. This inevitably had an influence on how different groups in Afghan society and other NGOs related to the organization. In contrast, EHED, though socially embedded, was generally perceived to be politically neutral. The Catholic church's crosscutting ties meant that it had a unique position in Sri Lankan society, enabling it to play an intermediary role spanning the ethnic divide. Organizational and individual identities were important determinants of legitimacy, access and, to an extent, leverage. What intervening agencies brought to the bargaining table was in some cases less important than who they happened to be and who they happened to know.

The history or genealogy of an NGO plays an important role in determining its position in society, its perceived legitimacy and consequently its potential role as a builder of peace. In contexts where there is no history of NGO activity, but donor funding has rapidly spawned an embryonic NGO sector, as occurred in Afghanistan and Kyrgyzstan, their legitimacy and scope to act as political or social changes agents may be circumscribed. In Sri Lanka, with its long tradition of civil society activism, NGOs were seen by some segments of society, at least, to be credible and legitimate political actors.

Analysis and Learning: Developing the Mind

NGOs acquired data and information through a number of different methods, ranging from the informal and ad hoc (chats with colleagues and beneficiaries in the field, or on the cocktail-party circuit in Kathmandu or Islamabad) to the formal and technical (food security/early warning, livelihood analysis, child rights monitoring, PRA assessments, etc.). Although the case studies reveal a trend towards greater technical proficiency in data collection, programming performance was still held back by poor empirical analysis and theoretical modelling. First, in war zones hard data are difficult to come by and unlikely to be value-free. Second, analysis and knowledge tended to be extremely fragmented. Needs assessments were usually limited to short-term objectives and there were unlikely to be standardized and aggregated data at the national level.[12] Third, aid actors may also have an interest in massaging the figures. As Terry (2002) notes, there is a culture in relief organizations that trains the eyes on the positive and blinds them to the negative. Agency survival may depend upon a narrative that their activities make a difference between life and death (ibid.). Fourth, in emergencies analysis is likely to be undervalued. Relief agencies tended to place a greater premium on doing than on understanding. This was reflected in the limited investment over the years in building up the aid community's knowledge bank of a particular country.[13] A limited emphasis on listening skills meant that programmes sometimes bypassed rather than built upon community coping strategies and initiatives. The example of LTD/R in Sri Lanka shows that more participatory approaches were possible even in fluid, conflictual environments. Fifth, analysis tended to be mandate-driven, with a focus on immediate organizational and project concerns at the expense of the wider context. Many NGOs did not extend their analytical gaze sufficiently beyond projects; by both looking upwards, that is, thinking more strategically about their interventions in the wider context, and looking downwards, that is, with greater disaggregation of communities, groups and individual households. Nor were feedback loops sufficiently developed between field realities, practice and policy. This particularly applied in Afghanistan in the 1980s and 1990s, as country offices based in Pakistan were several steps removed from field realities. Evaluations tended to focus on the details of project implementation, their role being more one of system maintenance than critical questioning.

NGO practices changed over time and some forms of analysis were valued more than others at different stages of conflict and with different generations of aid. For example, in Afghanistan first-generation NGOs delivering crossborder

Table 7.1 NGOs' Working Assumptions in Afghanistan

Some aid agency assumptions, working hypotheses	Research findings	Programming implications
Conflict has led to state collapse and the breakdown of societal institutions.	Conflict has led to new forms of governance at national and local levels.	Develop a more nuanced understanding of emerging forms of governance; support forms of governance that help sustain lives and livelihoods.
Aid may have a significant impact on the incentive systems and decision-making structures of warring groups.	Aid in relation to other resource flows is relatively insignificant and its impact on decision-making is likely to be negligible.	Stop conditionalities on aid; be aware of the potential negative impacts. Strengthen advocacy for political and diplomatic initiatives.
Social relations/social capital have been depleted/eroded; there has been a breakdown of trust.	Social capital has been central to people's survival; redistributive networks continue to function.	Better understanding of social networks. Greater focus on the software aspects of programming.
Coping strategies have been destroyed by conflict.	Coping strategies have been differently affected but in general have been robust.	Better understanding of coping strategies—more focused support to prevent groups from moving from coping into survival. Support risk-spreading activities.
Vulnerability is due to poverty.	Vulnerability is due to powerlessness and the denial of rights.	Better understanding of the politics of vulnerability. Stronger focus on rights and protection.
Support for subsistence agriculture is central to livelihood support; Afghanistan is a nation of peasant farmers.	Livelihoods have become more diversified as a result of the war. Market entitlements have been central to coping and survival (and profiting).	In addition to supporting productive activities, think more about protecting market entitlements—terms of trade, access to markets, engaging with the private sector, etc.
Aid has been central to people's survival.	Aid has been important for certain groups at certain times but in general has not been central.	Improved early warning systems and targeting of humanitarian aid.

Source: Bhatia and Goodhand (2003).

relief assistance were very poor at project-related analysis. A solidarity position eroded the humanitarian principles of impartiality and neutrality and affected the ability of NGOs to make critical judgements. On the other hand, aid agencies needed to be politically astute, since security depended on a network of contacts. Some, such as the Swedish Committee for Afghanistan, kept extensive dossiers of field commanders about their political, tribal and religious affilia-tions, resources and support base. By the early 1990s a second-generation aid strategy placed greater emphasis on professionalization, project management and aid effectiveness. The typical staff profile of aid agencies changed and technical experts and aid managers came in to replace the 'Afghan experts' and political fixers.

As mentioned in Chapter 5, underlying assumptions about processes of political and social change were rarely made explicit or questioned. Table 7.1 highlights some of the working assumptions commonly held by NGOs in Afghanistan, which are contrasted with the research findings. These findings have practical implications for how aid agencies could reorientate their policies and programmes.

The research supports the findings of other studies that NGO understanding of the political economy of war was relatively weak and not sufficiently factored into strategic planning (Le Billon, 2000; White and Cliffe, 2000; Collinson, 2003). There was also limited systematic analysis of the interactions between aid interventions and the dynamics of peace and conflict. One of the major blocks to learning was the short-term contracts of NGO staff (particularly expatriate staff). Consequently, careers in humanitarian aid tend to be broad but shallow, which militates against the long-term, locally grounded approaches required for peacebuilding. Other blocks to learning included the perverse incentive systems operating in NGOs. These included the pressures to disburse money and the tendency to play to internal audiences rather than listening to external stakeholders.

Leadership

Allen's (1992) account of post-conflict reconciliation and healing processes in Uganda argued that the charisma of the healers as well as the therapies them-selves are enormously important. A similar argument can be made in relation to peacebuilding: the charisma of the product champion may be at least as important as the product itself. The importance of personal relationships and individual intuition should not be underestimated (Uphoff, 1992; Leonard, 1991).[14] In some cases, particularly in young organizations, it was individual leadership rather than the institution that made the difference. In organizations like ADA and FTI, for example, the challenge was one of how to routinize charisma (Garcia, cited in Sorbe, Macrae and Wohigemuth, 1997: 65). Innova-tors and individuals who take risks and have the authority to effect change may influence the formal and informal rules in organizations and by so doing change incentive structures. For example, two dynamic and committed Afghan leaders who worked for Norwegian Church Aid played an important role in diffusing ideas about peacebuilding and conflict resolution to its partners and the wider aid community.[15] Such actors are interface experts because they master languages and cultures prevailing in different social domains (Hilhorst, 2003: 219). In this case, the Afghans were able to mobilize support and talk the language of both the foreign aid community and key elements of Afghan society.[16] Conversely, a conservative, risk-averse leadership may constitute a block to change, by resisting experimentation and innovation. Given the importance of leadership, the more or less constant rotation of senior NGO staff, particularly within INGOs, was a serious constraint.

Staff

As the business literature stresses, the focus of any successful enterprise is the relationship between customers and frontline personnel (Hock, 1995). NGO strategies, policies and projects are ultimately mediated through and operationalized by field staff. As has been noted elsewhere, the key determinant of good or bad practice was often the quality of frontline staff: 'Successes were often the product of serendipities and circumstances, of creative individuals making the best of difficult circumstances, often without institutional support and stretching their mandates to the limit' (Minear, 2002: 185). A nuanced understanding of the practitioner's world view is required, which examines their processes of 'sensemaking' (Weick, 1995). The problem is often one of confusion rather than ignorance (Christoplos, 1998). For instance, EHED and SCF staff felt strong external (and moral) pressures to provide relief (deontological ethic), while there were countervailing organizational pressures to be more developmental (teleological ethic). Head office people occasionally dismissed the welfarist attitudes of frontline staff, but deontological ethics were an understandable response in the circumstances, and furthermore, often helped build trust with communities. The 'let them eat empowerment' (ibid.) approach (or 'let them eat child rights' in the case of SCF) tended to come from NGO staff who were several steps removed from the field. The tensions between head office and the field was often less about skills and knowledge than about values, priorities and clarity about preferences.

Walkup (1997) identifies various psychological coping mechanisms that are employed by field staff to cope with high levels of uncertainty and stress. One is to become defensive. Another is to externalize by transferring guilt towards other factors, like politics or donors. Reality distortion and the creation of false illusions is another. Elements of all three could be detected in the case studies. Minimalists tended to most commonly employ the first two strategies ('doing good shouldn't be criticized', 'everything is beyond our control'), while maximalists were more likely to employ the last one, born out of a desire to do more in the face of widespread suffering ('we have to go beyond "just" providing palliatives'). Staff burnout was found to be a significant factor limiting NGO performance. This was not only about the stresses of negotiating with the Maoists, the Taliban or community organizations. The constant pressure to service the organization was also a major source of stress. The research revealed a significant mismatch between the expectations and demands of head office and the time and capacities of field staff to meet these demands. Though multi-mandates increasingly deployed technical specialists for particular tasks, frontline staff, who were often relatively young and inexperienced, were expected to be proficient in an impossibly wide range of skills and methodologies, from gender analysis, to livelihoods assessment, to do no harm analysis. The overall picture was of a growing dissonance between an increasingly rich and sophisticated programming menu and the overstretched capacity of frontline staff to translate this into something that was programmable. The growing emphasis on technical skills and servicing the organization meant that contextual knowledge was increasingly undervalued: 'Today's international relief professional is like the multinational executive who feels able to operate in any part of the world because she knows the way the firm works. However, she very seldom knows the way the country works' (Slim, 1995: 121–2). The 'contextual innocence' (Minear, 2002) of frontline workers on occasion limited NGOs' abilities to exploit peacebuilding opportunities. This factor more than any other differentiated Oxfam's intervention in Mullipottanai from ADA's in Khas Urugzen, as outlined in Chapter 5.

The successful cases of conflict-sensitive relief and development programming indicate that generic skills in conflict analysis and peacebuilding can usefully be absorbed and used by frontline staff. However, this did not apply to the more specialist conflict resolution and mediation skills of staff working for the niche peacebuilding/mediation NGOs like NPC, FTI and MICOM. These skills could only be developed through a dedicated focus and long-term experience. Finally, it is perhaps insufficiently recognized that NGOs' support for training and internal capacity development represents a massive investment in human capital often in an environment where opportunities for training and education are extremely circumscribed. Although NGOs frequently bemoaned the fact that staff often moved on after receiving this training, in the wider scheme of things this was less important than their role in helping stimulate and nurture social energy.

Losing Control? Managerialism and Peacebuilding

Earlier chapters described the trend towards NGOs' growing dependence on official funding. The bilateralization of funding has been associated with a deepening of donor involvement in the design and management of programmes. Growing external control brings the risk of conditionality and politicization. Big NGOs that primarily depend on official funding run the risk of becoming executing authorities for government policy. Top-down accountability pressures have been the primary driving force behind the trend towards professionalization in the NGO sector, one of its primary features being a concern for results-based management. Most NGOs studied have adopted rational planning tools such as strategic planning and log frames. Although there may be benefits attached to such changes, it is important to recognize the costs. First, they tend to consume staff time that might otherwise be spent monitoring projects and talking to beneficiaries. In some cases, a period of organizational introspection led to a weakening of long-term, field-based relationships, which in turn undermined the quality and reliability of an agency's analysis. Paradoxically, donors encouraged NGOs to engage with peacebuilding while employing modalities that undermined their capacities to do so effectively. Good practice often emerged in spite of the frameworks adopted by NGOs. Creative practitioners learned to adapt or subvert rational planning methods.[17] They may play the donor game by filling out the requisite log frame, but when it comes to actual implementation they experiment and adapt according to the individual context. What is happening can be illustrated diagrammatically—see Figure 7.1.

NGO efforts to improve practice have focused on the central circle, that is, increasing the area of what can be controlled. This was done through scaling up activities, particularly expanding the size and range of service delivery programmes, while improving reporting, monitoring and evaluation procedures, organizational restructuring and professionalization. Energies were directed inwards at servicing the organization, often at the expense of external relationships and consequent efforts to understand the wider context.

However, organizations operating in today's armed conflicts may need to adopt more appropriate organizational forms. As Duffield (2001) argues, the natural sciences have moved beyond the Newtonian view of the cosmos—that of a vast and perfect clockwork machine governed by exact mathematical laws—towards post-Newtonian ideas of complex systems that are analogous to organisms. This also throws light on how institutions and organizations function in war zones.[18] Insurgency groups, for example, may be more of a virtual than a formal organization, involving loose networks that lack a clear hierarchy and centre, and have the ability to mutate and adapt to constantly changing conditions; they may be composed of small teams of individuals, who are highly motivated and have a clear sense of mission but maintain considerable room for manoeuvre in the field; value is placed upon developing local knowledge or intelligence, with an emphasis on being close to the people and on influencing others by winning hearts and minds.

Some of these characteristics might equally be applied to businesses operating in a turbulent and fast-changing private-sector environment. The business literature categorizes them as 'adhocracies' or chaordic organizations, that is, having systems that are complex, adaptive and self-organizing (Mintzberg, 1994; Hock, 1995). This is not to argue that NGOs should model themselves on guerrilla organizations or internet companies. But the research highlights the need to achieve a better fit between organizational structures, systems and processes, and the demands of the operating environment. Evidently, what is required to deliver a large-scale relief programme is different from that needed to support

Figure 7.1   Getting the Right Balance for Peacebuilding

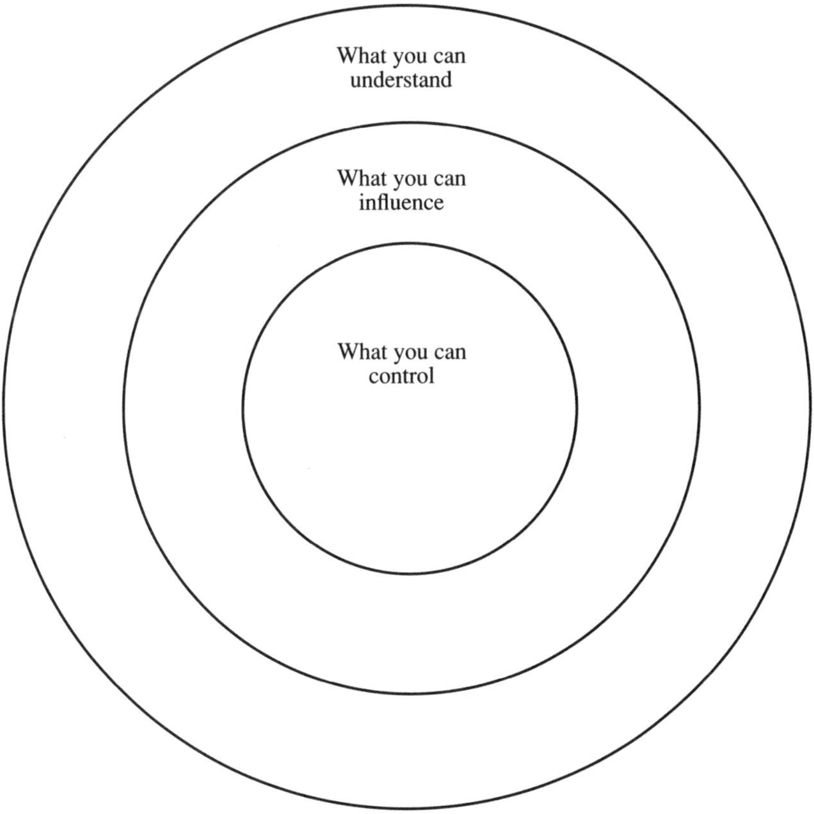

a conflict mediation process. Moreover, much depends on the maturity, size and complexity of the organization. However, the case studies suggest the relative focus and organizational energies devoted to controlling, influencing and understanding should be reconsidered. This means getting rid of the illusion, which log frames tend to induce,[19] that everything can be controlled. External control cannot create certainty of outcomes. Chaordic organizations are not chaotic messes; they combine order with disorder in the sense of having clear values, strategies and principles, combined with freeflowing and decentralized structures and decision-making processes. This creates greater space for individual creativity to react to circumstances. Linked to a more realistic appraisal of what can and cannot be controlled is an appreciation of how one can ally with other actors to effect desired changes (see below). Finally, the case studies show a mismatch between the complexity and dynamism of the operating environment and the planning methods employed by NGOs. Humanitarians tend to distrust strategic planning (Kent, 2004). As Kent argues, speculation and reflection are devalued as an academic luxury, a diversion from the proper focus on finding immediate and practical solutions to problems. NGOs, like most other organizations, tend to seek the least dissonance and the least disruption (ibid.: 7), and consequently there is a tendency to fall back on preprogrammed responses and standard operating procedures.

Accountability: The Heart of the Matter?

For many years the standards of accountability[20] applied to aid agencies in war zones were much more lax than for those working in development settings. Generally accepted principles of good practice for development practitioners, such as participation, gender equity, monitoring and evaluation, were suspended for relief workers. They were seen as either naïve or expensive luxuries in emergencies. Relief workers were also to an extent insulated by a duty-based ethic, whereas development workers were increasingly encouraged to be accountable for the consequences of their actions; in emergencies doing good was seen to be enough. As outlined in Chapter 4, this has changed over the last decade and relief agencies have been forced to take seriously the accountability revolution.[21]

The research indicates that this has not been an easy transition. The thorny questions of who are you accountable to and what are you accountable for remain difficult ones for NGOs to answer. While these questions are problematic in development settings, conflict tends to bring them out in sharper relief. First, as NGOs increasingly work in intensified political engagements, the problem of managing multiple relationships (see below) and consequently multiple accountabilities becomes more acute. Second, the question of what NGOs should be accountable for has become more complex and contentious as the objectives of humanitarian assistance become increasingly unclear.

The shift towards results-based management and a contracting culture has led to an emphasis on functional accountability (short-term, such as accounting for resource use and immediate outcomes) rather than strategic accountability (accounting for impacts that NGO action has more widely and on other organizations) (Lewis, 2001: 144). For example, audit reports on humanitarian assistance have been largely confined to issues of financial probity and the conduct of specific operations, and have thus largely avoided questions of strategic accountability (Macrae et al., 2002: 7). Few have questioned the accountability of the donors themselves (ibid.).

The research found, unsurprisingly, that how NGOs manage their bundle of accountabilities has a major impact upon their legitimacy and consequently their performance. Whether the focus is on relief delivery, human rights monitoring, conflict resolution or a combination of all three, the ability to balance multiple accountabilities is crucial. By allowing one line of accountability to dominate, other accountabilities are eroded. The research highlights the distorting effects of too little or too much upwards accountability. Afghan solidarity NGOs are illustrative of the danger that when accountability falls below a certain level, ineffective or illegitimate actions are likely to increase. In this case the lack of NGO accountability was seen by bilateral donors as a comparative advantage, since they acted as convenient middlemen, obscuring the original source of funding (Atmar and Goodhand, 2002: 23). Conversely, too great a focus on upward accountability, which in most cases meant functional accountability, drains organizational energies and erodes downwards accountability towards primary stakeholders. The research reinforces concerns that NGOs are becoming too close to the powerful and more distant from the powerless (Hulme and Edwards, 1997). This problem is perhaps accentuated in conflict, since life and death may literally depend on close links to power-holders. The accountability problems are also far more complex since agencies, as well as being held accountable to the relevant laws of a country, may also be held to account by the alternative rules and regulations of competing centres of power—whether it is the LTTE, the Taliban or local commanders.

Therefore, dependence on donors for funding and on state and non-state actors for access may create perverse accountability pressures which distance NGOs from their clients. Evidently upwards accountability is important and NGOs must be able to account for their use of resources and demonstrate effects and effectiveness. Resistance to this by NGOs damages their credibility and legitimacy, and the inability of some conflict resolution NGOs to systematically demonstrate impacts undermined both their credibility with donors and their actual practice, as assumptions were rarely questioned and practice became increasingly habitual. However, the Achilles heel of most NGOs in this study is primarily that of downward accountability. This is particularly the case where NGOs are dependent on official funding and it is magnified further when funding quality is low. This was the case in Afghanistan and the transition countries, where the existence of donor-funding created local NGO sectors overnight, and there was little time or incentive for such organizations to build up a natural constituency.

Partly in response to these problems, there has been a proliferation of codes and principles in recent years, including the Red Cross Code of Conduct, the SPHERE programme, the Humanitarian Accountability Project, the Local Capacities for Peace Project (LCPP) and the International Alert code of best practice. Only the final two of these explicitly address peacebuilding and the others are primarily concerned with humanitarian relief practice. It was beyond the scope of this study to examine these initiatives in detail but a number of short observations can be made based on the field research. First, there is a risk of them becoming exclusive and turning into vehicles to defend the interests of well-resourced and established humanitarian organizations (Hilhorst, 2003: 210). LNGOs have been minority voices in such exercises, and although attempts have been made to bring them on board later, this sometimes smacks of tokenism.[22]

Second, there are concerns that such initiatives are part of the inexorable shift towards the marketizing of the humanitarian community. Their harsher critics argue that essentially it is about PR and the need for NGOs to repackage themselves as a result of public scrutiny and criticism in the 1990s. Third, as already mentioned, the codes have largely been promoted by humanitarian minimalists and the overall thrust is to go back to basics, focusing on technical standards for relief delivery. Much less has been done in the area of peacebuilding, although this is an area that many of the large multi-mandate NGOs are now involved with. Fourth, NGOs have embraced the codes very lightly. The Code of Conduct, for example, has not really filtered down to the field level and many NGO fieldworkers were unaware of its existence.

There is clearly no such thing as a perfectly accountable NGO, but the case studies reveal that accountability to 'the person in need' (Vaux, 2001) was often notional at best. The examples of good practice all evolved out of a process of consultation, listening and participation. But these by themselves are not a panacea. Whose voices are heard involves making political choices. For example, the Feminist Majority, a US-based lobbying group, chose to listen to the voices of a vocal urban minority of Afghan women. Downward accountability has to be balanced with other lines of accountability and mediated through the NGO's mandate and the values of its staff. However, ultimately in order to have a sustained impact on peacebuilding processes, NGOs must be able to demonstrate their legitimacy through responsive accountability.

NGO Relationships for Peacebuilding

The strength of NGOs supposedly lies in their ability to act as bridges, facilitators, brokers and translators (Edwards and Fowler, 2002: 9). They are viewed as a crucial part of the 'connective tissue' of a vigorous civil society (ibid.). As mentioned in the section on accountability, NGOs have to deal with competing loyalties and interests, involving donors, beneficiaries and the organization itself. These interests conflict with each other at least as often as they overlap. The combined and interrelated trends of the shift to contracting, the scaling up of service delivery and the introduction of managerialism all affected the quality and diversity of NGOs' external relationships. This does not mean that NGOs retreated into their humanitarian shells, disavowing all contacts with the outside world. On the contrary, organizational survival dictates a strong focus on external relations. But the weighting and prioritization of external relationships changed. Public name recognition and donor contacts were the key to gaining profile and market share. Clearly this cannot be de-linked from community-level relationships altogether, but as Hillhorst notes, 'There is no necessary correspondence between an NGO's worth, the way it manages its image and the way it is perceived by the outside world' (Hillhorst, 2003: 8). Richards in his book *Fighting for the Rainforest* (1996) on the war in Sierra Leone interprets the violence and atrocities of the RUF as a form of ritualized theatre, which is acted out strategically for internal and external audiences. NGO programmes have something of this theatre-like quality about them (though clearly with very different objectives and methods from the RUF):

> In practice the professionals' work is more than a translation: it is a production, large parts of which must be achieved without the subjects of development. They must construct an entire theatrical scenario for the project, including the dramatic conceit, the sequences of plot, the set and props, and the casts of stars, and of thousands. (Craig and Porter, 1997: 233)

The link between NGO productions and real life may sometimes be a tenuous one: 'the point is that representations are not just a neater and simpler version of reality, but may be completely unrelated to reality' (Hillhorst, 2003: 215). As Lewis et al. (2003: 546) note, there is frequently a slippage between development text and effect. Narratives are created not only for external audiences. They may also be an essential part of the process of practitioners' sensemaking. In several instances, programmes appeared to continue exactly as before, only a new narrative had been created around them:[23] last year it was a resettlement programme, but this year it is a peacebuilding programme.

Some of the perverse incentives created by the pressures of contract fever were mentioned in the last chapter, including undermining competitors, hoarding information and acting unilaterally. External relationships were distorted by the rush for contracts, and none more so than the relationship with communities. It was noticeable that in Afghanistan and Nepal, having a monopoly of presence and a long-term engagement in a particular locale, led to stronger agency-community relationships. The ability to build long-term, high-quality linkages with a variety of stakeholders was found to be critical for NGOs working in or on conflict. NGOs that were more locally grounded, like ADA, NPC and FTI, were better able to adapt to the changing conflict environment and exploit opportunities when they appeared. These NGOs developed and actively maintained a dense network of relationships from the micro to the macro level. This gave them a cutting edge in terms of their ability to conduct social analysis,[24] to withstand external shocks[25] and security risks, and to exert leverage.[26] This was also combined with an ability to manage the conflicting demands of multiple stakeholders. In highly politicized, conflictual environments, these demands and pressures tend to be accentuated, often endangering the integrity and independence of the organization. Pressures came from a variety of sources, including warring groups (e.g. LTTE, Maoist and Taliban restrictions on NGOs), donors (e.g. conditionalities in Afghanistan), or civil society groups (e.g. pro-war civil society organizations in Sri Lanka). NGOs like ADA and NPC were better able to withstand such pressures because of a strong network of counterbalancing relationships, a nuanced political analysis, good negotiating skills,[27] and a clear sense of their own values and identity. Having access to funding that was either from diverse sources (like ADA), independent or 'free' money (like EHED), or high-quality (NPC and FTI) were key factors. Moreover, NGOs could to some degree create room for manoeuvre in relation to donors: 'Despite the fundamental inequality between funding agencies and NGOs the latter can sometimes if not turn the tables at least develop a substantial countervailing power, allowing them to secure stable funding and to negotiate the terms of accountability' (Hillhorst, 2003: 219). Seemingly contractual relationships were entangled with a range of other factors including moral obligations, personal friendships and ideological positions. For example, Norwegian support for NPC was related to the government's political position, the norms and values of individuals on the ground and personal friendships.

The overall probabilities of peacebuilding outcomes will likely be maximized through a combination of more flexible, context-sensitive responses from multi-mandates and a more optimal division of labour between specialist agencies and multi-mandates (White and Cliffe, 2000). In the case studies, however, the division of responsibilities was rarely optimal. There were various attempts at interagency strategic coordination in all countries, the Strategic Framework in Afghanistan in the late 1990s being one of the most high-profile. Unfortunately, the Strategic Framework process was perceived by NGOs as a UN-led initiative and increasingly tied to donor countries' political agendas. As a result there was limited NGO buy-in. The learning from this and other examples of strategic coordination[28] is that institutional arrangements need to be light but robust, and strategic collaboration on specific issues, rather than comprehensive coordination, is more likely to succeed. A significant impediment to a more optimal division of labour was the 'humanitarian laager' mentality of a number of the specialist relief agencies. The refusal of some NGOs operating in northeast Sri Lanka to talk to human rights agencies was one extreme example of this. The humanitarian minimalist position of insulating oneself entirely from the politics of the conflict and the international response, though increasingly rare, still hindered the evolution of more collaborative and complementary relationships.

Finally, the research indicates that the overriding NGO focus on service delivery was at the expense of developing more strategic relationships for coalition-building, strategic lobbying and policy analysis. Although NGOs are serious players in the humanitarian marketplace and the wider international system, they are still reluctant to use their collective weight to leverage change. Events in Afghanistan before and after the fall of the Taliban demonstrated NGOs' high level of dependence on official aid sources, which limited their room for manoeuvre in terms of challenging donors' policies towards the country. INGOs working in Afghanistan played a limited role in their home countries to counteract the negative media portrayal of the country, which in turn influenced donors' policies towards the country. In contrast, SCF in Sri Lanka arguably focused too much on their national policy-influencing role at the expense of their field-level relationships.

Events in post-Taliban Afghanistan highlight the need for NGOs to place a stronger focus on coalition-building. If they do not, they are likely to become increasingly marginal actors, as the military and the private sector become more involved in humanitarian and reconstruction activities.

Conclusion

Context clearly plays a key role in determining peacebuilding outcomes, but so too does organizational performance. The choices made by NGOs regarding their programming, organizational capacities and relationships increased or decreased their room for manoeuvre in terms of peacebuilding. It is not possible to read off from the case studies generic 'peaceabilities' which are required by NGOs to work in or on conflict. But one can identify a number of factors that enhanced NGOs' abilities to support peacebuilding processes.

First, the empirical evidence does not support either a minimalist or maximalist approach. The findings are more nuanced and contingent than this. Good practice involved contextualized programming, which meant a flexible blend and mix of activities according to particular peacebuilding ecologies. Multi-mandates had the potential to build upon synergies between different activities and approaches, although in practice there were often tensions and trade-offs involved in attempting to do so. In general multi-mandates played more of a 'climate-setting' role than an explicit peacebuilding role. Their programmes helped maintain civic space and stimulate social energy. On the other hand, niche organizations, which were able to function better in high-risk, high-opportunity settings, were better able to directly support peacebuilding processes.

Second, organizational capacities had a significant influence on NGO programming. Being able to develop the right combination of heart and mind was found to be critical. Building a level of consensus around mandates, values and ethical deliberation was the sine qua non for any form of intervention in conflict. Contextual analysis was another, and in many cases NGO action had got ahead of understanding. A range of factors were important in developing a mindfulness of conflict and peace dynamics, including: political sensitivity to equity and proportion in project benefits; flexibility in project design and implementation; monitoring and evaluation which included some form of peace and conflict impact assessment (PCIA); a clear ethical framework; strong linkages with society; and an ongoing field presence.[29] A clear lesson from Afghanistan in the 1980s and the late 1990s was that agencies with weak or distorted accountability and an inability to demonstrate impact or effectiveness in a reasonably rigorous manner were more vulnerable to co-option into the agendas of others. Many of these cardinal rules of good development practice have yet to be adequately learned by NGOs operating in areas of armed conflict. Although increased access to donor funds permitted an increase in the size and numbers of NGOs in many contexts, the downside to this included a growing emphasis on contracting, short time frames, a project approach to peacebuilding, risk avoidance and the stifling of creativity, innovation and flexibility. NGOs that managed to diversify their funding or had access to untied money were able to insulate themselves from such pressures and were more likely to pursue long-term and innovative approaches.

Third, NGOs with a diverse and dense network of relationships, which were able to manage their bundle of competing accountabilities, were better able to work in or on conflict. The case studies suggest that NGOs are less embedded in the communities in which they work than they frequently claim to be, and this was an obstacle to more grounded and contextualized programming.

8

Politics, Policy and Practice

This final chapter briefly revisits the main findings and explores how NGOs' performance might be improved. It focuses on three key areas, the interrelated challenges of understanding, funding and action. In other words, how can analysis, donor support and NGO activities be improved, in order to achieve better humanitarian and peacebuilding outcomes? It is beyond the scope of this study to address operational issues in significant detail, but some of the key challenges are identified, along with how they may be tackled in order to move towards improved practice.

Introduction

The first section of the chapter summarizes the research findings and examines their implications for emerging theory, donor policy and NGO practice. As stated in the introduction, the intention was never to stand back and maintain a safe academic distance from the object of analysis. The goal was always to engage with actually existing practice, not only to provide a commentary on what was happening in the field, but also to identify how improvements can be made. A political economy framework was adopted, in order to analyse armed conflict, NGO behaviour and their impacts on peacebuilding. This led to the conclusion that the most important challenges facing NGOs are primarily political rather than technical. It is less about finetuning projects than making choices about where and how NGOs should position themselves in relation to the political economy of war and the response system in which they are firmly embedded.

These choices might usefully be framed using Hirschman's (1970) three positions of loyalty, exit and voice, in order to explore the questions of policy reform and improved practice. In the context of this study the loyalty position can be interpreted as keeping quiet and leaving things as they are. Exit is taken to mean the classical Dunantist position of separating oneself out from the conflict and the response in order to maintain the distinctiveness and independence of humanitarian action. Voice is interpreted as engagement with the conflict context and response system in order to enlarge the peacebuilding space. Given

171

the critical nature of the research findings, it is clear that the first position is neither credible nor tenable. Few practitioners, policy-makers or academics would subscribe to keeping things as they are, even though there are strong covert institutional pressures to do precisely that. The second and third positions provide different but possibly more promising avenues for exploration. The finding that NGOs' role is limited by actors and institutions further up the political chain may be interpreted to support the exit position; if NGOs are part of a dysfunctional system that reinforces hegemonic interests, then aligning themselves too closely to this system may be counter-productive. Arguably, they should seek to insulate themselves as much as possible and attempt to maintain their humanitarian space. On the other hand, the finding that NGO performance does make a positive difference and translates into tangible peacebuilding impacts—even though these are limited by both the structures of aid and the structures of conflict—may support a voice position. Political engagement, combined with a pluralist approach involving incremental changes in practice, may create room for manoeuvre and ultimately perhaps wider systemic change. Both perspectives, therefore, have some merit and validity in the context of this research and both are explored in the final section.

Summary of Findings

NGO Impacts

Assessing the impacts of NGOs' activities involved making judgements about the extent to which interventions strengthened or undermined human security in locally defined terms. This was easier when NGO interventions were targeted at the micro level and the impact chain was consequently shorter. But for interventions involving long impact chains—for example the activities of policy lobbying groups in Colombo or human rights activists in Kathmandu—the task of tracing the cause–effect linkages was far more difficult. It is not possible to identify predictable linear patterns of cause–effect relationships. Just as similar background conditions can lead to armed conflict in one context and not in another, the same types of NGO interventions may have very different effects in one setting from another. This highlights the importance of the contingent and the idiosyncratic. However, it is possible to make conditional generalizations and discuss plausible scenarios.

NGOs' interactions with conflict and peace. All NGO interventions have an impact of one kind or another. Whether an intervention has explicit peace-building objectives or not, it influences the conflict context. For the purpose of this study, three types of impacts were posited: first, the impacts of conflict on NGOs; second, the impacts of NGOs on conflict; and third, the impacts of NGOs on peacebuilding. In practice, the interactions are more complex, multidirectional and mixed than this model suggests, but it represented a starting point for exploring the connection between NGOs and conflict and peace.

First, the research revealed how conflict has a range of direct and indirect effects on NGO programmes. Overall, it was found that compared with governmental and intergovernmental organizations, NGOs had a higher tolerance of risk, were more flexible and were better able to conflict-proof themselves and their activities, particularly in borderlands where sovereignty is contested, as shown by crossborder operations in Afghanistan in the 1980s and NGO activities in northeast Sri Lanka or the midwest of Nepal.

Second, a range of conflict-fuelling effects were identified. The idea of doing no harm was found to be misleading, since in practice all interventions have some kind of negative effects. However, overall, it was found that the extent to which NGO programmes do harm has been exaggerated. Far more significant than humanitarian aid was the role of development assistance in contributing to the origins of conflict. And in terms of sustaining conflict, other resources such as arms, drugs or remittances were more central to the combat and shadow economies.

Third, a range of positive political, economic and social effects on peacebuilding processes were highlighted. Multi-mandate NGOs with an operational presence could play an important stabilizing role, protecting local leadership, stimulating social energy and stemming human capital flight. This represented a holding operation. It involved building community resilience, which enabled households and individuals to better manage interlocking risks, and in this sense countered the dynamics of bottom-up violence. In more conducive environments, off-site, dedicated peacebuilding NGOs were able to leverage impacts at a macro level.

The research findings provide a corrective to the often overblown assessments of NGOs' potential to either fuel violence or build peace. Findings from extreme cases or outliers have been generalized in the literature to build up a new orthodoxy of aid-driven resource wars. This is partly due to the geographical bias of the aid and civil wars literature towards Africa, where some of the most egregious examples of aid fuelling conflict can be found. The flip side of this new orthodoxy is a belief in the transforming potential of aid, the idea that assistance can somehow be the 'Archimedean lever for the perpetual peace' (Rieff, 2002: 333). The case studies show that NGO assistance is rarely central to people's coping and survival in crises, even though it is axiomatic among aid agencies that it is central. As de Waal (1997: 1) notes, 'humanitarianism is generally a footnote to the story of how people survive in famine'. Moreover, humanitarianism is not purely a Western enterprise. The role of community networks, diasporas, Islamic and other faith-based relief agencies and the national and local governments were in most cases of greater importance than the more visible but more transient interventions of international relief agencies. NGOs are therefore rarely either the main coping mechanism or a significant change agent in contexts of chronic political instability.

Elevating the importance of NGOs serves a coalition of interests. Competition for funding and profile between NGOs leads to exaggerated claims; donors, like NGOs, need success stories to improve their standing and generate further funding; Western political leaders can buttress their legitimacy at home while avoiding pressure to account for final policy outcomes. This dynamic of scriptwriting for success operates at all levels of the aid chain and it is not unique to humanitarianism and peacebuilding. As Scott (1990: 2, cited in Mosse, 2004: 663) notes in relation to development projects: 'The public transcripts of development are sustained by the powerful and the subordinate, both of whose interests lead them to conspire to misrepresent'. Humanitarian intervention is important as an idea as well as a practice. It is a mobilizing metaphor, which brings together a multitude of contradictory interests that are translated into a single politically acceptable model.

The Space and Scope for NGO Peacebuilding

It has been argued throughout this book that NGOs do have agency or context freedom, but this is constrained and shaped by a range of structural factors at the global, national and subnational levels. To paraphrase Marx, they can make history, though not in contexts of their own choosing. At the global level, although inter- and intra-state armed conflicts have declined in the last decade, NGOs continue to operate in some of the most chronically insecure borderland regions of the world. They are doing this at a time when there has been an unprecedented level of international activism in response to global disorder. The regulative rules of the post-colonial sovereignty game, which involve the classical principles of non-intervention and reciprocity, no longer work in an unequal state system, in which it is necessary to compensate for weaknesses in substantial statehood (Sorensen, 2000: 11). A hybrid system has emerged. On the one hand, there is evidence of a transition from government to security governance, denoting a shift towards a fragmented mode of policy-making which includes state and non-state actors. On the other hand, as Hirst persuasively argues, states remain the key locus that ties together the various levels of governance:

> States because they are territorial and if they are legitimate, are able to speak authoritatively for their populations and to make international commitments that are binding and that will be enforced... The forces that are supposed to be supplanting the state in a globalizing world—multinational companies, NGOs, virtual communities—can do neither of these things, precisely because they are neither territorial nor inclusive. (Hirst, 2005: 43)

Global governance and the UN have not escaped state power and neither have NGOs, which are still firmly national rather than cosmopolitan: they continue to base themselves, pay taxes and recruit their staff in home countries.

Transnational governance and specifically the humanitarian complex needs state power; like TNCs they depend upon the security and stability provided by non-market public power. Also, unlike private companies, NGOs depend upon states for a growing part of their funding, to the extent that in some cases the nongovernmental label is questionable. As Hirst (2005: 46) argues, states do not necessarily lose power by sharing power. They may share power with other agencies and institutions in order to stabilize their external environments.

Viewed from this perspective, NGOs may be less autonomous than they think and are more likely to act as a product of power than a check on power. Events following 9/11 perhaps confirm this view, in that the reassertion of state power has led to growing pressures on NGOs. These pressures vary from place to place and between different categories of NGOs. The space and choices for large multi-mandate NGOs operating in Iraq are obviously far more limited than for, say, a niche NGO like MSF operating in Sri Lanka. In the 1990s NGOs were part of a global response system, which despite its failings, did play a role in contributing to declining levels of armed conflict (HSC, 2005). The GWOT risks undercutting the gains made during this period and NGOs are finding themselves part of a global order that produces disorder while claiming to deal with it.

At the country level, the research has highlighted that there are more and less difficult environments for peacebuilding. Difficulty is defined in terms of peacebuilding space, which is a product of the interactions between three key factors: the roots of hostility; the local capacities for change; and the international response. The first two factors are endogenous and relate to the conflict context, and the third, an exogenous variable, relates to various forms of international intervention[1] (Tracks One, Two and Three). Afghanistan in the 1990s, for example, combined in extreme form all the characteristics of a difficult case: the roots of hostility were deep (widespread death and destruction; multiple, hostile factions; longstanding political and economic grievances; regional interests), the local capacities for dealing with conflict were limited (state collapse, ethnicized social relations, weak governance structures) and the international response was half-hearted and had perverse impacts (limited support for UN mediation, one-sided sanctions; politicized aid; arm's-length engagement).

While ultimately every context is unique, with its own configuration of power, structures, actors and beliefs or grievances, the case studies highlight the failure of international actors to engage sufficiently with the complexity and the politics of armed conflicts—they are treated primarily as emergencies. In most cases there was a failure to match responses to the demands of particular contexts, because of the intrusion of interests other than the human security of affected populations. NGOs are unlikely to have a significant impact on peacebuilding processes when: first, the basic preconditions for building peace are not there (including deep-rooted hostilities and limited local capacities for change); second, they are part of a dysfunctional international response; and third, they are dependent on official aid donors and part of a competitive aid market which discourages experimentation and risk-taking.

To some degree these rather dismal conclusions support the liberal peace thesis, which argues that NGOs have simply become the agents of Northern security policy (Duffield, 2001). However, the case studies also show a more varied picture and greater room for manoeuvre than this framework implies. Structures do not shape outcomes in a deterministic way and processes of change are complex, contingent and unpredictable. Even with optimal structural conditions, peacebuilding is not just about getting the outside politics right. Peacebuilding outcomes can never be engineered by outsiders alone, and individuals and agencies can, for better or for worse, create room for manoeuvre and influence the probabilities of peace or war. Much depends upon the specifics of the aid market in each country. An unfettered market, characterized by Afghanistan in the 1980s and Kyrgyzstan in the 1990s, encouraged rent-seeking behaviour. The more regulated market of Sri Lanka in the 1990s, with more diverse sources of funding, some of it high-quality, gave greater space for NGO experimentation and risk-taking.

At the subnational level the picture is even more varied. The policy discourse in its attempt to provide a single, coherent and overarching framework hides the diversity of the operating environments and NGO practices. Moreover, although humanitarian minimalists argue that the pursuit of peace should be left to politicians and diplomats, this is to misunderstand actually existing conflict and contemporary practice. Top-down, elite-led peace processes failed to bring peace in the case study countries. A focus on the high politics of the state, without complementary measures to address the deep politics of society, achieved limited success. NGOs potentially have a comparative advantage in this area, though they did not always meet its demands. The question is not whether NGOs should play a role in peacebuilding—since they are already doing this—but how they can do it better.

NGO Performance

Although the case studies reveal the diversity of NGOs, it is possible to identify some common patterns in terms of their performance. These are summarized in the next section, with a particular focus on the kinds of activities and organizational capacities that are more or less likely to support peacebuilding processes.

Programming. First, there is no such thing as a model for best practice. The research points to the specificity of history and context. Good practice in one context or situation may be bad practice in another. For multi-mandate NGOs the challenge was less about doing different things than doing things differently, in other words, mainstreaming conflict sensitivity into all programming activities rather than initiating bolt-on peace projects. Second, the case studies exposed the limitations of a project-based approach, particularly in relation to longer-term interventions with development or peacebuilding aims. Examples of good practice could be found where NGOs conceptualized what they were doing less in terms of implementing projects than supporting strategies, individuals and processes.

Third, the research supports neither a minimalist nor a maximalist position, as applying either approach dogmatically means ignoring the operating environment. Practitioners, for the most part, did not see rigid boundaries between relief, development, rights and peacebuilding. Good practice involved developing the optimal mix of activities, which were delimited by a range of factors including mandate, risks threshold, the conflict context, and individual preferences and values. Fourth, multi-mandate NGOs were less able to pursue high-risk, high-opportunity strategies than niche NGOs because of their operational presence. In the main, multi-mandates were part of a holding operation, although niche NGOs were often better equipped to respond to high-risk, high-opportunity situations. Fifth, the spaces for peacebuilding were constantly opening and closing and good practice involved reading individual peacebuilding ecologies and responding to opportunities when they appeared. Sixth, positive examples of peacebuilding in most cases had a capacity-building or multiplier effect built into them. The operational reflex of INGOs and the expatriate-dominated view of humanitarianism were found to be serious constraints.

Organization. Debates about relief, development and peacebuilding frequently lack an organizational perspective. Maximalists in particular appear to assume that NGOs can be all-knowing and all-seeing, and have unlimited management capacities and skills. The case studies show that NGOs frequently lacked the organizational capacities to deliver relief effectively, never mind build peace. Going beyond relief has important organizational implications. If the requisite capacities are not developed, there are likely to be severe internal tensions.

Overall, NGOs were found to have 'personal energy but contextual innocence' (Minear, 2002: 187). A range of factors impeded analysis and learning, including: a cultural bias towards action rather than reflection; a focus on immediate project concerns rather than the wider environment; a lack of emphasis on listening and participation; and the rapid turnover of staff, particularly those in decision-making positions. One of the main factors distinguishing NGOs that worked on conflict from those working in conflict was the sophistication of the former's conflict analysis. To work on conflict requires staff with specific expertise in this area.

The adoption of Western management techniques, which donors have encouraged, undermined NGOs' comparative advantages of flexibility and responsiveness. Growing organizational introspection has been at the cost of external relationships, contextual analysis and flexible programming. These tendencies are accentuated by an overreliance on official funding, leading to too great a focus on upward accountability. None of these findings is particularly new and they have been described and analysed elsewhere (Edwards and Hulme, 1995; Smillie, 1995; Lewis, 2001). But they are perhaps more pressing in relation to conflict, first: because NGOs rely to a greater extent on official funding for their relief work; and because they have less independent money when operating in conflict-affected areas, the scope for innovation and risk-taking is more limited. Second, it is precisely in areas of conflict where greater flexibility and innovation are needed, and the limitations of managerialism are most evident.

Finally, the case studies show that the capacity of NGOs to support peace-building processes depends to a great extent on the quality of leadership and frontline staff. Often good practice was the result of creative practitioners stretching organizational mandates and subverting the rules to get things done or respond to opportunities.

Relationships. A clear lesson from the case studies is that if NGOs are to increase the space for peacebuilding, they must collaborate more strategically with one another. But the rush for contracts impedes the development of strategic link-ages. It also means that NGOs are less close to the ground than is commonly assumed. A shift towards developmental and peacebuilding approaches required NGOs to be more embedded in the societies in which they intervene. ADA, EHED and FTI in Afghanistan, Sri Lanka and Kyrgyzstan respectively were closer to achieving this than the INGOs studied. Relations with communities were frequently transient and shallow. Concerns about neutrality and keeping a distance from the fray impeded the development of more grounded community-based relations. The post-9/11 environment has further exposed these tensions, particularly in frontline states like Afghanistan. The GWOT has created even stronger pressures for INGOs to become embedded in the international response system, rather than in the societies they are assisting.

Implications for Theory, Policy and Practice

This final section highlights some of the main implications of the research findings for theory, policy and practice. As discussed in earlier chapters, con-temporary wars have induced a crisis of theory as well as a crisis of policy and practice. They have prompted academics, practitioners and policy-makers to revise the way they think about and respond to armed conflict. Some involve deep superstructural changes to the response system and others are concerned with improving policy and practice within the current international architecture.

Implications for Conflict and Peacebuilding Research

The research indicates that the gap between academic theory and NGO practice is still a wide one. As Mack (2002) notes, policy is often determined by organi-zational mandates, past practice and politics, with little reference to the findings and prescriptions of academic researchers. There are also significant points of contention and gaps in the research literature on conflict and peace. Where there is a degree of consensus, the findings are often poorly communicated to the policy and practitioner communities. The results are 'lost in translation' and rarely lead to substantive changes in policy or practice.

To address the research gaps, more empirically based research in areas affected by conflict is required. Armed conflicts usually become research-free zones; when the fighting starts, serious research stops. But this study and others (Richards, 1996; Ellis, 1999; Collinson, 2003; Barakat et al., 2002) demonstrate that this does not necessarily have to be the case. Research can be conducted in live war zones and produce valid results. This study has involved three levels of analysis:

- macro level, i.e. the broader contextual factors that set the parameters for humanitarian action, including the nature of armed conflicts and the wider international response to them;
- community level, i.e. localized responses and forms of adaptation to armed conflict, community coping and survival strategies, etc;
- agency level, i.e. the internal characteristics and nature of humanitarian agencies and the humanitarian system they are embedded in.

These categories broadly correspond with Macrae's (1999b) tripartite division of humanitarian research challenges into those involving studying up, studying down and studying sideways. A number of tentative theoretical and empirical implications can be drawn from these three levels of research.

Macro level (studying up). The research focus of those studying contemporary wars has tended to be on internal problems and external solutions (Lund, 2001). This study suggests that there should be a rebalancing of the analytical centre of gravity, which would involve a greater focus on external causes (global governance, international development policies, transnational networks) and internally generated solutions (domestic governance, rebuilding social contracts, transforming war economies).

The old war–new war dichotomy is a singularly unhelpful way of conceptualizing civil wars today. The Sri Lankan, Afghan and Liberian cases, like many other conflicts, are hybrid wars involving strong continuities with the Cold War period as well as new elements linked to globalization and the reordering after the Cold War. Terms like 'complex political emergencies' or 'post-modern conflicts' have become a kind of shorthand for a category of 'bad new wars' (Kalyvas, 2000). There are perhaps two key theoretical implications here: first, the need for a more historically informed analysis; second, the need for a more disaggregated examination of civil wars. Multicountry, econometric studies have perhaps encouraged the belief that one can simply read off risk factors to predict the onset of conflicts. However, the case studies indicate that a more nuanced analysis is required. Although quantitative analyses have value and have helped advance understanding in important ways, they certainly do not have unique explanatory powers and they need to be complemented by the thick descriptions and analyses generated by case study research.

There is broad agreement that greater analytical sophistication can be achieved by integrating political, economic and social perspectives, along with an appreciation of dynamics, actors and contingent factors. However, there is still no convincing explanation of why difficult pre-existing conditions lead to conflict in some places and not in others. The same applies to why similar types of peacebuilding interventions work in one context, but not in another. Findings from the case studies suggest two promising lines of enquiry. First, process-based approaches drawing on complexity theory could potentially advance the understanding of mobilization dynamics, the role of leadership and 'boundary activation' (Tilly, 2003). Second, the understanding of armed conflicts could be enhanced by studying the interconnections between peace, war and other forms of violence. The rather embryonic idea of ecologies of violence (Sambanis, 2003) is based on the assumption that civil wars share common determinants with other forms of violence. Similarly, there may be distinct, but interlinked ecologies of peace, both in the middle of war and in the transitions from war to peace. Research attention has tended to focus more on the peace–war, rather than the war–peace, side of the bell-curve. Declining levels of intra-state conflicts have been attributed to the growth of international activism and the spread of democracy in the 1990s (HSC, 2005; Gurr, Marshall and Khosla, 2001). But there is limited solid research to explain whether, and if so, why, this may be the case. We know more about the underlying causes of war than we do about the causes of peace. Therefore more research is required on the political economy of peace as well as the political economy of war. Key issues include why people choose not to fight; the incentive systems and mobilization dynamics related to peacebuilding; the role of peace entrepreneurs; and transitions from war economies to peace economies.

Research has increasingly focused on the links between state crisis and civil wars (Cliffe and Luckham, 1999, 2000; Milliken and Krause, 2002). This study has also focused on the role of the state and state–society relations, because this seems to be at the heart of the question of why people turn from politics to violence. A state-centred (rather than state-centric) approach provides a lens for studying greed and grievance dynamics, questions related to re-territorialization, or changing state boundaries, and overlapping sovereignties, the role of non-state military actors, civil and 'uncivil' societies, and the role of borderlands. All were highlighted in the case studies and all require further study.

The case studies show that external intervention is less about humanitarian concerns than asserting liberal or national interests. Clearly, one should abandon naïve ideas about benign and neutral third-party interventions. Intervention in the modern era is less about Kantian principles than those of Clausewitz. However, bemoaning lack of political will, which is a way of apportioning blame, does not advance our understanding. Analysis of international responses, like analysis of civil wars, needs to be disaggregated. This would involve more research into the complex and changing institutional dynamics of international organizations and actors and how responses are influenced as much by the response system as the conflict itself.

Community level (studying down). An unambiguous message coming out of the research is that place matters, and researchers as well as humanitarian practitioners need to take context more seriously.[2] Studying up needs to be complemented by studying down. Inferences from the elite level about the mass level are problematic (Kalyvas, 2000: 9). History is written by the court scribes of the state or the discontented intellectuals (Moore, 1966), and it is the job of the peasant to stay out of the archives (Scott, 2000: 6). An analytical focus on the subaltern level involves reading history 'against the grain' (ibid.). Contemporary wars are about localization as much as globalization, and this suggests a need to engage more seriously with what is happening locally. Notions of peace and security were bound up with local definitions of these terms. An analysis of ecologies of violence and ecologies of peace needs to be rooted in an understanding of people in relation to place.

This research has drawn upon the concept of human security to go beyond realist notions of peace and security. Though it is recognized that human security, like civil society has become a point of convergence for very different ideological strands, it is nevertheless useful for thinking about how communities survive and cope in civil wars. It helps focus attention on how households mitigate and manage interlocking risks in contexts of chronic political instability. This takes us beyond the more common needs-based analysis associated with humanitarian interventions. It also focuses attention on political risks and vulnerability. A more politically informed analysis highlights forms of resistance, leadership and social energy. These are areas that have been under-researched.

Agency level (studying sideways). Studying upwards and downwards helps place NGOs and their activities in context, providing a less NGO-centric view of the world. NGOs must be understood against the backdrop of wider historical and structural changes: 'International NGOs are the result of accumulation processes in developed capitalist countries and accompanying societal changes... They began to expand into developing countries under particular historical circumstances. They become allies of certain social and political forces' (Bastian, 1999: 48). Studying up and down provides a more distant (and more critical) vantage point for assessing the role of NGOs, which challenges some of the central tenets of NGO lore.

However, studying sideways is also necessary to generate insights into how the humanitarian regime works in practice. Structuralist critiques do not take us very far in this respect, as they tend to downplay the agency of individual actors and organizations. Duffield's (2001) groundbreaking work on the strategic complexes of the liberal peace has perhaps gone furthest in mapping out the complicated mutating institutional arrangements that constitute the international response to conflict. However, there has been limited work at the country level that examines how the aid regime or complex functions and interacts with conflict dynamics over time.

Implications for Donor Policy

> ... many countries are happy to sign up to conflict prevention and peacebuilding in theory, but deeply reluctant to engage in practice. This is because conflict is by its nature risky and development departments tend to be risk averse. But it is clear that the risks of non engagement outweigh the risks of action. (Short, 1999: 7)

The research shows that the first-order questions are less about the choices and policies of aid agencies, than the interests of core powers and the structures of global governance. It has been argued that there are strong continuities between the Cold War, post-Cold war and post 9/11 environments, not least in terms of the abiding and central role of territorial states within the international system. A multilateralist consensus of sorts did emerge in the 1990s on the limits of military force in international affairs and an expanded concept of collective security (Tschirgi, 2003: 11). However, there was never a coherent doctrine or set of institutional arrangements for peacebuilding (Tschirgi, 2004). In practice, its implementation was uneven, reflecting to a large extent the interests of dominant powers. 9/11 exposed the fragility and the limitations of such a multilateral consensus when hard security interests were threatened. Many of the gains of the 1990s on human rights, poverty eradication, good governance and the rule of law are being undermined as a result of the hardening of the security agenda.

However, as this and other studies show, traditional security approaches are an inadequate response to the diffuse and multifaceted threats faced by populations in the developing and developed world today. Militarized peacebuilding runs the risk of creating the disorder it claims to address. The Human Security Report that was published for the first time in 2005 represents an important and timely reminder of the need to view human security and peacebuilding as a global public good and a collective responsibility.

Donors, like NGOs, are enmeshed in a wider international response system and to an extent the scope for improved policy and practice is shaped by factors higher up the political chain. At the heart of the issue is the strategic calculation of hegemonic states. Are their interests best served by unilaterally pursuing short-term strategic goals, or do they gain in the long term by promoting human security through multilateral institutions, and in so doing help stabilize their external environments? To prioritize peacebuilding as understood in this study would mean significant changes in a number of interrelated areas, including the following.

• Developing a response system with a strong multilateral core and expanding democratic practices within the sphere of global governance. This would include substantive reforms of the UN.[3] It would also mean investing in and building the capacities of regional organizations.

• Changes in the spending priorities (and budgets) of Western governments. For instance, one only has to compare the $10 billion that is spent per year on humanitarian and post-conflict peacebuilding with the $749 billion on global military expenditures (Smillie and Minear, 2004: 24) to get a sense of where priorities currently lie. As already argued, 'bargain basement' peacebuilding simply does not work (Ottaway, 2002).

• A stronger focus on conflict prevention by means of tackling structural violence and the proximate causes of conflict, rather than simply responding to the outbreaks of armed conflict and humanitarian emergencies when they occur, which, as argued earlier, are themselves manifestations of deeper structural crises. This would also involve Western governments recognizing their own role in the creation of structural violence at a global level and taking steps to address this.

• A commitment to stronger domestic ownership of peacebuilding processes. The externally driven and liberal 'state-lite' approach to peacebuilding has been part of the problem. There is a need to abandon the illusion that external actors have the sole capacity and legitimacy to resolve intra-state crises and rebuild societies anew. As this research has shown, institutions are the key to managing, resolving and recovering from armed conflict, and none is more important than the institutions of the state. This suggests a need for approaches that prioritize the state, rather than privileging other actors from the private sector or civil society.

These are just some of the factors which could positively affect the political framework of aid-giving. As mentioned earlier, aid actors now find themselves in the paradoxical situation of having more funding and a closer relationship with high politics than ever before, yet feeling a deep sense of unease with this situation. This is due to the perception that the goals of development and humanitarian actors have become increasingly subordinate to the national security interests of powerful states. The research findings suggest that development and humanitarian funding can make a significant contribution to peacebuilding, but not when it is hitched so closely to other political objectives. There needs to be much greater clarity about what exactly development and humanitarian actors can and should be expected to do, and what their relationship to other policy objectives should be. It may be more useful to think in terms of strategic complementarity rather than coherence. In other words, to what extent can development and humanitarian interventions retain their distinctive qualities and goals, but also contribute to broader peacebuilding objectives?

Having argued that donors are constrained by the wider political and economic landscape, their policies can be a significant factor in determining peacebuilding space. The research provides plenty of evidence of bad donorship which has an impact on the overall effectiveness of the aid system as well as NGOs' performance. Improvements in the international response to war depends in no small part on changes in donor policies and practices.

First, the need to reform humanitarian financing is particularly urgent. The case studies highlight the ad hoc and voluntaristic nature of humanitarian financing. Essentially it is a 'casino economy' (Smillie and Minear, 2004), which encourages unruly competition and the duplication of resources. Funding needs to be adequate, flexible and predictable (ibid.), and the creation of a global humanitarian fund in which donor countries make statutory contributions makes a lot of sense.

Second, if donors are to work more seriously on conflict, this means addressing the question of sovereignty in a more coherent and honest way, as opposed to the current tendency to talk about policies but not polities, while promoting approaches which undermine the sovereignty and capacity of the state. Countries affected by conflict need special provisions. These may include measures that aim to reduce the effects of economic globalization, provide distributive justice, and reduce economic uncertainty and state weakness. There may also be a need for a greater focus on protection and social safety nets. Without the fiscal policies to pay for peace, a rhetorical commitment to peacebuilding achieves little. 'Peacebuilding-lite' has involved ambitious targets of political and social engineering, but with limited financial or political resources to back it up. There is a major mismatch between the objectives, the means and the final results.

Third, developing a greater sensitivity to context and to conflict dynamics would form a strong basis for improved donor practice. This means developing the requisite skills, capacities and systems to become more adept at conflict analysis. The case studies show a significant disjuncture between local and international discourses in relation to conflict, partly because of the types of contacts and networks that donors utilize, which tend to be very capital-city focused and aid-centric. Incentive systems are not structured so as to reward a greater focus on listening and analysis. Staff received insufficient training and skills in the area of conflict analysis,[4] though some donors, including DFID and the World Bank, have begun to invest more seriously in this area.[5] Greater contextualization should lead to responses that are more firmly anchored in the societies concerned.

Fourth, donors must be prepared to meet the standards that they demand of those they fund. The aid system is shot through with a lack of accountability.

The case studies highlight the inconsistency of donor behaviour, the absence of meaningful coordination and the lack of coherent policies over time. 'Aid is directed according to narrow political interests, public opinion and media images' (Munslow and Brown, 1999: 215). Some of the major donors are characterized by a combination of ambition and impatience. There are no ethical frameworks or benchmarks for donors to make them behave more consistently across cases. There is a need for serious engagement with the question of donor accountability and what good donorship[6] might look like. The types of initiatives that have been introduced to improve NGOs' performance and accountability could be considered and adapted in relation to donors.

Fifth, donors need to pay more than lip service to notions of ownership and trust. There will always be a tension here that is not necessarily resolvable. This particularly applies to peacebuilding, as it so clearly touches upon the question of sovereignty. Debates on peace conditionalities, for instance, often centre on 'ways donors can more effectively impose their will, if necessary by ganging up against governments who do not behave the way donors think they should' (Uvin, 1999: 21). Yet in Sri Lanka, arguably, donors were too respectful of sovereignty and worked blithely around the conflict. The tension centres on having clear principles (and conditions) related to peacebuilding, while recognizing that without a degree of trust and local ownership, nothing is likely to change. However it is difficult to encourage trust and cooperation in a system which encourages the opposite incentives, 'with built-in asymmetries between "donors" and "recipients", layer upon layer of conditions and constraints, bucketfuls of outside interference, and continuous changes of dogma and fashion' (Edwards, 1999: 10). Although there is no magic bullet, addressing some of the perverse incentives in the aid system and developing clearer conditions—what Edwards calls 'light but robust'—may be a way forward.

The remaining implications are concerned specifically with how donors relate to NGOs. It should be noted that there was great variability between cases and donors. But in spite of the uneven nature of donor policies and practices, a number of common weaknesses can be identified and tentative solutions put forward.

First, the contracting culture and accountability revolution introduced by donors has had adverse impacts upon NGO practice. These include growing competition between NGOs, a culture of conformity, a tendency to hide failure and therefore not learn from practice, and a stifling of innovation and risk-taking. Donors need to rethink the validity of attempts to control from afar. The examples of good practice show the importance of building trust over time, supporting organizations and individuals (and not just projects), and encouraging risk-taking and creativity.

Second, the compartmentalization of relief and development funding constrained NGO programming in protracted crises. Most of the conflicts in this study were neither classical relief nor development contexts. The lack of funding for activities in this indeterminate grey zone limited the opportunities for NGOs to engage in peacebuilding. This division is based more on bureaucratic convenience than an analysis of the context and the coping strategies of those living in areas of chronic instability. 'The organization of bilateral and multilateral agencies into divisions in which there is little overlap between relief and development has created dysfunctional fiefdoms in which rules, compartmentalisation and independence have become more important than the job to be done' (Smillie, 2001: 186).

Third, donors need to rethink how they conceptualize and engage with civil society. In general donors were found to have a shallow understanding of the processes they were trying to influence. As Jenkins (2001) notes, donors suffer from a historical amnesia when it comes to civil society. In spite of the evidence from the case studies of its contested and decidedly 'uncivil' nature, donors view civil society as 'a sort of political ombudsman, reflecting the values of impartiality, fair play, and commitment to public welfare.' (ibid.: 268). The result is a rather naïve and skewed engagement with civil society. In the main this has consisted of support for NGO service delivery rather than civil society strengthening. Spending imperatives create perverse incentives to cherrypick those organizations based on capital cities, which literally and metaphorically talk the same language.

Three alternative ways of working emerge from this analysis. First, donors could reconceptualize their support of civil society in terms of peacebuilding portfolios. They could work towards a better spread of high-risk and low-risk activities, based upon a fine-grained analysis of the context. Their civil society programme might be conceived as an investment risk portfolio, in which they endeavour to achieve the right balance between risk and assurance. The key point is that risk assessment is different from risk avoidance. Donors' aversion to risk has led to missed peacebuilding opportunities: 1991–92 in Afghanistan and 1994–95 in Sri Lanka are two cases in point. Moreover, risk-taking is not about getting others to take risks for you. It must involve donors putting their own resources and credibility on the line, by providing long-term support for key organizations and individuals. Second, the research points to the importance of individual peace entrepreneurs, and donors could explore creative ways of providing support to individuals (as well as organizations) who may play a role in generating social energy and opening up spaces for peacebuilding. Finally, the research suggests the critical importance of timing. Donors' bureaucratic procedures mean that it is difficult to access funding quickly, often for small, low-profile activities which may be of a high-risk and high-opportunity nature. Setting up country-level peace trust funds could be one way of addressing this problem. Such trust funds would constitute a source of money that could easily be accessed by peace entrepreneurs or peace-related organizations when opportunities arise.

Implications for NGO Practice

The research shows the need for humility on the part of those who intervene and those who study conflict and peacebuilding: 'understanding the limitations on coercion and kindness alike may be the beginning of wisdom in the post Cold War era' (Minear, 2002: 187). Attempts to improve practice always run up against the question of political feasibility. However, continuing with business as usual (the loyalty position) is not a viable option. Contemporary conflicts have exposed severe limitations in the policy and practice of aid-giving. This final section identifies some of the key implications of the research for NGO practitioners and policy-makers and funders, and tentatively outlines ways in which things might be done differently. It does not get down to the level of individual NGOs or individual projects. The focus is on NGOs as a collectivity, and how they can improve their bargaining position and room for manoeuvre. This will hopefully contribute to better humanitarian and peacebuilding outcomes in war zones.

NGOs and the politics connection. As argued in Chapter 4, there has been a convergence between relief, development and peacebuilding in recent years. Because the scope of humanitarianism has broadened, aid agencies have had to renegotiate their relationship with political, military and diplomatic actors. This has been a fraught process, boiling down to the question of how humanitarian NGOs should engage with the international and domestic political realms. What should be the nature of the connection between NGOs and politics?

These options can be explored drawing upon Hirschman's (1970) ideas of exit and voice that were introduced earlier. First, exit is taken to mean the conscious choice of NGOs not to engage with the political realm. This represents the classical Dunantist response; it is about suspending moral judgement in order to create a narrow incontestable humanitarian space. Minear (2002) argues that humanitarian action can contribute significantly to peace and security, but that it cannot do this by harnessing itself too tightly to an often flawed political process. Therefore, he argues, humanitarianism should insulate itself from politics. But voice is about engaging with, and seeking to influence, the wider political context in which humanitarianism takes place. As Hirschman (1970: 16) notes, 'voice is political action par excellence'. Voice and exit, used in this sense, are not all-or-nothing or mutually exclusive. An NGO may combine the two, in different combinations in different contexts. This can be explored further in the matrix (Figure 8.1) below.

Box 1 represents the classical Dunantist position, based on the hardwon wisdom of ICRC. Box 3 is a more recent variant of humanitarianism, which retains a strong focus on impartiality, but combines this with speaking out and engagement in the political sphere, sometimes referred to as disobedient humanitarianism. NGOs like MSF are able to play this role partly because they keep their government funding below certain limits[7] in order to maintain their independence; this is a form of exit deployed as an option in order for the organization to retain its own voice. Boxes 2 and 4 involve responses that are far removed from traditional notions of humanitarianism. The principal actors are large multi-mandate NGOs, though Box 4 is also occupied by niche lobbying organizations for whom voice is their raison d'etre. The Wilsonian NGOs, occupying Box 2, experienced rapid growth in the 1990s, largely as a result of increased official funding for disasters. Their pragmatic focus on the technical and the operational and their reliance on government funding has meant a limited capacity or willingness to exercise voice. The scope for independent action for Wilsonian state humanitarian NGOs has probably decreased even further since 9/11 (Stoddard, 2003). Box 4 represents the most difficult position for multi-mandate NGOs to occupy, because it involves combining operationality (in non-traditional areas) with a commitment to political engagement.

Responses in Boxes 1 and 2 are clearly important, particularly in the acute phases of an emergency. Without these more instrumental approaches fewer people would receive assistance or protection, and for such NGOs, voice may be an expensive luxury. There is therefore a need to think carefully about the costs of voice—how it may affect questions of access, positioning and funding. But exit in the form of minimalism may buy limited humanitarian space in some of today's conflicts, where all NGOs may be seen to be associated with a Western liberal (or imperial) cause. Minimalism, for instance, did not protect ICRC in Iraq, leading some to question whether copyright humanitarianism is possible

Figure 8.1 Exit and Voice: Options for NGOs

		EXIT	
		YES	NO
	NO	*Box 1 Dunantist* Narrow humanitarian focus; strict neutrality and impartiality; narrow humanitarian focus.	*Box 2 Wilsonian* Broad multi-mandate focus; focus on service delivery; following the line of government funders, e.g. US/Wilsonian NGOs.
VOICE	YES	*Box 3 Political humanitarian* Narrow focus; minimizing or refusing official funding; exit emergency if humanitarian space no longer exists, e.g. MSF, Rwanda Humanitarian advocacy.	*Box 4 Political maximalism* Broad multi-mandate focus or niche advocacy and peacebuilding NGOs; political advocacy/dissent, e.g. European NGOs, Oxfam, Amnesty.

in such hyperpoliticized emergencies. Exit in such cases may mean literally leaving the scene, as for instance MSF did in Afghanistan in 2004.

However, minimalists use the word 'politicization' in a pejorative way, though the evidence from the case studies suggests that there can be good and bad politicization. Donor practice in Afghanistan in the 1980s was evidence of the latter, while the support of conflict-sensitive bilateral donors like the Norwegians in Sri Lanka and the Swiss in Central Asia was evidence of the former. The minimalist position on the politics connection may also be contradictory and sometimes even disingenuous. Its advocates tend to view themselves as being above or superior to politics, and yet see no problem in overriding sovereignty by pressing governments on relief provision, or even running surrogate states, as in the case of Afghanistan. It is not always clear whose interests are served, besides those of the humanitarian agencies themselves, by having assistance activities hived off and unpolluted by politics. Though some view the period of political disengagement from Afghanistan as a humanitarian golden age because of the lack of political intrusion, for most Afghans this was a dark age when the country descended into a regionalized civil war and Western attention turned away.

Some of the more radical critics of NGOs would argue that it is not possible to exercise political voice through transnational organizations. The growth of the latter in their view signals an exit from politics. As Hirst (2005: 14) notes, most modern forms of transterritorial power are inherently non-inclusive and they violate basic expectations of self-governance, as they are inaccessible to collective action. Chandler (2004) further argues that the growth of transnational activism signifies the attenuation of political community rather than its expansion, since it is only in the domestic political sphere where political leaders can be held to account. Accountability of international bodies through national publics is at best indirect and weak. Internationalizing responsibility effectively leads to no accountability:

> ... in the not so recent past it was religious leaders and moral authority figures who 'intervened' in other people's struggles in the hope of bringing a peaceful resolution by bearing witness to the suffering and attempting to help. Today the collapse of a broader political or moral framework has led to individuals claiming their own moral right of intervention without any legitimacy derived from a collective authority. (Chandler, 2004: 338)

For Chandler, voice would involve foreign activists rechannelling their political energies into their own societies rather than other people's. The evidence from the case studies supports Chandler to the extent that there is a need for a more honest engagement by NGOs with the politics connection. This would mean NGOs being clearer about the kind of politics that they stand for, and being more conscious about the political choices that they make. But the case studies also suggest that there are many other legitimate ways to exercise voice, and for NGOs this can mean simultaneously engaging with political processes at home, in the international sphere and with partners and constituencies in the countries where they work.

It is doubtful whether avoiding political processes rather than engaging with them best serves the primary stakeholders of humanitarian action: 'The humanitarian imperative cannot be pursued effectively by seeking to maintain artificial barriers between the humanitarian and the political. Instead aid agencies should consciously engage in political processes in order to realise their objectives' (Weiss and MacFarlane, cited in Minear, 2002: 77). Arguably by engaging with politics in a smarter and more robust way, NGOs can play a role in humanitarianizing politics. To an extent this appeared to be happening during the 1990s with humanitarian concerns increasingly forcing their way up the political chain. The environment is perhaps less conducive now, but the need to be politically engaged has probably increased, as O'Brien (2004: 39) argues: 'The "with us or against us" political culture in today's foreign policy… makes politics a singularly unattractive field with which to engage. But engage we must, for politics is too important to be left to politicians.'

One might also argue that humanitarianism is too important to be left to humanitarians. Humanitarian problems can rarely be addressed only with humanitarian solutions. NGOs therefore need to think carefully about how they can mobilize political actors to accept their humanitarian responsibilities. For NGOs to engage more explicitly in the political sphere involves making difficult choices; it is important to recognize the constraints on such choices and the trade-offs they typically entail.

First, it makes little sense for all NGOs to gravitate towards either Boxes 1 or 4. Actually existing humanitarianism is polyarchical, and this diversity constitutes one of its strengths. Though there are strong political and economic pressures on NGOs to conform to standardized approaches and models, these should be resisted. A variable humanitarianism (Slim, 2004) is best equipped to deal with the diverse needs and challenges of today's world.

Second, if NGOs are to exercise voice in a more robust way, this means being more honest about declared and hard interests. For example, the logic of institutional self-preservation means that NGOs almost never reject funding opportunities. If they made a more realistic assessment of their potential impact—rarely do they make the difference between life and death—and their own political and normative positions, then they might be more willing to say no and retain a degree of control over their work.

Third, if voice is to involve more than the courtly politics of influencing friends in high places, NGOs need to focus on constituency-building, so that they are more grounded, both in their own societies and the societies in which they operate.

Fourth, as Hirschman (1970) notes, the power of voice is greatest in markets where there are few buyers, or where a few buyers account for an important proportion of the sales. In the aid market there are many NGO buyers, and as a result power remains largely in the hands of the donors. But, around six or seven major NGOs account for up to 55 per cent of humanitarian funding. This could potentially put them in a strong bargaining position if they were prepared to exercise their voice in a more coordinated way. As it is, voice is often experienced by donors as a form of low grumbling which, in effect, amounts to little more than blowing off steam. Clearly negotiations and bargaining do not take place among equals, but arguably NGOs have greater leverage now than at any other time, since the international response system is so dependent on them and humanitarian issues are so high on the political agenda. Having spent the previous 10 years complaining about the lack of political engagement, it makes little sense, now that political actors are involved, for NGOs to retreat back into their humanitarian shells.

NGOs and the conflict connection. As previously noted, there is no such thing as a non-impact, and whether intentionally or not, NGOs affect the dynamics of conflict and peace. Few NGOs would now confine themselves to a duty-based ethic and the idea that humanitarianism should limit itself to the act of giving. Most would accept a measure of the responsibilities associated with a consequentialist ethic. The implications of such a teleological ethic is that practitioners have to think more seriously about context and be conscious of the effects of their actions.

The dogmatic either-or nature of the minimalist-maximalist debate is unhelpful and does not reflect actually existing practice. Borrowing Uphoff's (1992) phrase, there is a need for more 'both-and' ways of thinking. Communities living in chronic emergencies are likely to need both food aid and development assistance at the same time. As Christoplos (1998: 16) argues, NGOs should keep 'developmental goals firmly within a framework of humanitarian values, while providing space for finding a locally sensible mix of both'. But maximalists, like the liberals who prescribe democracy and an open market for war-torn societies, tend to believe that all good things come together. Neither recognize sufficiently the tensions involved in pursuing multiple goals and the danger that one may undercut the other. Humanitarian practice may sometimes involve making least-worst choices that are unavoidably of an 'either-or' nature. No form of intervention is cost-free in terms of risks for the organization or for those receiving assistance. The key is to be self-conscious, to deliberate and to make informed decisions about how to manage them.

A shift towards more expansive approaches should not simply involve relabelling activities while continuing with business as usual. INGOs in emergencies often pay lip service to the idea of civil society capacity-building while continuing with service delivery. Similarly, though NGOs may be unwilling to frame their task more comprehensively, they sometimes cloak their relief and development programmes in the broader jargon of peacebuilding. Though minimalists frequently point to the costs of a more expansive approach, they are less willing to acknowledge the opportunity costs of not engaging with peacebuilding.

Finally, it is clear from the research that if NGOs are serious about conflict, then they need to think beyond projects and explore ways of providing ongoing support for individuals, strategies and processes. A stronger focus on capacity-building and advocacy would be part of this. NGOs need to simultaneously become more localized, that is, develop closer and more longstanding relationships with local institutions and actors, and more globalized, that is, develop analyses, strategies and relationships which enable them to lever changes at a macro level. This does not mean that all NGOs should aim to become maximalists. The Sri Lanka case indicates, for example, that a better division of labour between multi-mandate and niche NGOs could have led to more sustained peacebuilding outcomes.

Improving contextualization. The research shows that NGOs cannot be effective in the area of peacebuilding unless they have a substantial knowledge base about a conflict and its political and socio-economic context. Some argue that humanitarian NGOs can never develop a sufficient level of analytical sophistication to have a credible role in peacebuilding (Schloms, 2003). The research findings show this not to be the case: NGOs like ADA and EHED did have the contextual understanding to perform such a role, though many other NGOs did not.

A more systematic approach to analysing conflict and peace interactions through conflict assessment methodologies is increasingly employed by NGOs. But the key is not to try to measure and prove impacts but to improve analysis and learning processes. Stronger political analysis is essential so that NGOs can better situate their relief work in a larger political context. Cliffe and Luckham (2000: 292) describe a more politically informed approach as a kind of 'humanitarian Machiavellianism', involving a more accurate and honest appraisal by aid agencies of uncomfortable political realities.

NGOs operate in situations where knowledge is always incomplete and many of the conditions with a bearing on decisions are unknown at the time the decision is made. In diverse, unpredictable environments, practitioners must learn to cope with uncertainty and employ 'quick and not-too-dirty' methods to achieve 'optimal ignorance' (Chambers, 1984). The gap between action and understanding could be narrowed by some relatively simple mechanisms, such as listening to key stakeholders, planning expatriate staff employment so that dramatic losses in institutional memory are minimized, and mounting annual scenario-building workshops for groups of NGOs. Speculation and reflection are undervalued and agencies are reluctant to stray too far from the ways that they traditionally interpret the world around them (Kent, 2004).

Managing and organizing for peace: pluralism and adaptability. Those who seek to promote peace in war zones are not engaged in simple problem-solving exercises (identifying the cause of the problem and selecting the best solution available), but are intervening in a mess that usually defies the reductionist logic of linear cause-and-effect chains. The technocratic belief that problems can be thought through is inappropriate for interventions in which knowledge is limited and uncertainty high (Hulme, 1995: 226).

Two practical implications can be indicated. First, NGO practitioners should adopt a pluralist approach. In diverse and rapidly changing environments a pro-forma approach may provide the practitioner with a sense of security, but not much else. A pluralist approach is about keeping options open and widening, not narrowing choices, which is precisely how poor people cope and survive in complex and turbulent environments. As Porter, Allen and Thompson (1991) argue, the greater the level of uncertainty the greater the desirability of having as many options available as possible. They advocate a 'methodological anar-chism' which should lead to 'less external control, less pretence that control creates certainty of outcomes and more space for individual creativity to react to circumstances' (ibid.: 203). Evidently a pluralist approach may encourage an unjustifiably voluntaristic view of what is possible. Pluralism lacks a hard political edge and needs to be complemented by an appreciation of how wider political structures limit individual room for manoeuvre. More thought could be given about how to politicize and add nuance to the pluralist discourse (Christoplos, 1998).

Second, NGOs need to think seriously about how to organize and manage for complexity. Though NGOs recognize complexity, they do not take its implica-tions on board sufficiently in terms of policies and organization. In fact, the more complex the environment and task, the greater the tendency to compartmentalize and departmentalize (Kent, 2004). The ability to adapt to fast-changing contexts is one of the ultimate measures of an organization. As well as fitting responses to contexts, there is a need to think more carefully about which organizational forms are appropriate for which tasks in which particular contexts.

Conclusion

This study offers a corrective to overblown accounts of NGOs' damaging or positive effects in situations of chronic political instability. They are a small part of the story of violent conflict or peace. An exaggerated view of their role serves many interests, including those of politicians, donors and NGOs themselves. It has been argued that there is a need for a sense of proportionality and humility on the part of outsiders aiming to build peace. But an awareness of one's limi-tations should not blind practitioners and policy-makers to the peacebuilding opportunities that arise in contexts affected by armed violence. The research shows that individuals and organizations can and do create peacebuilding spaces, leading to positive outcomes. The precondition for improved policy and practice must be a more honest and serious engagement with the complexity and the politics of such contexts.

Acronyms

AAD	Afghanaid
ADA	Afghan Development Association
ADB	Asian Development Bank
ANGO	Afghan nongovernmental organization
AREU	Afghan Research and Evaluation Unit
BBC	British Broadcasting Corporation
CAA	Christian Aid Abroad
CAFOD	Catholic Agency for Overseas Development
CAP	Consolidated Appeal
CARE	Co-operation for American Relief Everywhere
CBO	community based organization
CCA	Cooperation Centre for Afghanistan
CHA	Consortium of Humanitarian Agencies
CHAD	Conflict and Humanitarian Affairs Department of DFID
CIA	Central Intelligence Agency
CPA	Centre for Policy Alternatives
CPAU	Co-operation for Peace and Unity Network
CPE	complex political emergency
CSO	civil society organization
DDR	Disarmament, Demobilization, Reintegration
DFID	Department for International Development
DRC	Democratic Republic of Congo
EC	European Commission
ECOMOG	Economic Community of West African States Monitoring Group
ECOWAS	Economic Community of West African States
EHED	Eastern Human Economic Development Centre
EU	European Union
FDI	foreign direct investment
FTI	Foundation for Tolerance International
GDP	gross domestic product
GWOT	Global War on Terror

HSR	Human Security Report
ICES	International Centre for Ethnic Studies
ICISS	International Commission on Intervention and State Sovereignty
ICRC	International Committee of the Red Cross
IDPM	Institute for Development Policy and Management
IFI	international financial institution
IHL	international humanitarian law
IIGA	Interim Islamic Government of Afghanistan
INGO	international nongovernmental organization
INTRAC	International NGO Training and Research Centre
IPKF	Indian Peacekeeping Force
IR	international relations
IRDP	Integrated Rural Development Programme
ISAF	International Security Assistance Force
ISI	Inter-services Intelligence Agency (Pakistan)
JCDC	Joint Committee for Democratization and Conciliation
JPO	Joint Policy of Operations
JVP	Janatha Vimukht Peramuna (People's Liberation Front)
KPF	Kalmunai Peace Foundation
LCPP	Local Capacities for Peace project
LFA	log frame analysis
LNGO	local nongovernmental organization
LTD/R	Listening to the displaced/returned
LTTE	Liberation Tigers of Tamil Eelam
MICOM	Moldova Initiatives Committee of Management
MSF	Médecins Sans Frontières
NCA	Norwegian Church Aid
NGO	nongovernmental organization
NPC	National Peace Council
ODA	Official Development Assistance
ODI	Overseas Development Institute
OSCE	Organization for Security and Cooperation in Europe
PPHO	Principles and Protocols of Humanitarian Operations
PRA	participatory rural appraisal
PRT	Provincial Reconstruction Team
QPS	Quaker Peace and Service
RNA	Royal Nepalese Army
SCA	Swedish Committee for Afghanistan
SCF	Save The Children, UK
SEDEC	Social Economic and Development Centre
SF	Strategic Framework
SRSG	Special Representative to the Secretary General
TACIS	Technical Assistance for Commonwealth of Independent States

TNC	transnational corporation
TRO	Tamil Rehabilitation Organization
UF	The United National Islamic Front for the Salvation of Afghanistan
UN	United Nations
UNDP	United Nations Development Programme
UN DPKO	United Nations Department for Peacekeeping Operations
UNGA	United Nations General Assembly
UNHCR	United Nations High Commission for Refugees
UNICEF	United Nations Children's Fund
UNMIL	United Nations Mission in Liberia
UNOCHA	United Nations Office for the Coordination of Humanitarian Assistance to Afghanistan
UNOPS	United Nations Office for Programme Support
UNSC	United Nations Security Council
UNSG	United Nations Secretary-General
US	United States
USAID	United States Agency for International Development
WFP	World Food Programme

Notes

Chapter 1

1. The major legal points of reference are the Fourth Geneva Convention Relative to the Protection of Civilian Persons in Times of War of 12 August 1949; the Additional Protocol I of 1977 Relating to the Protection of Victims of International Armed Conflicts (Articles 51–3); and Additional Protocol II Relating to the Protection of Victims of Non-International Armed Conflicts.

2. See for instance MacFarlane's analysis of humanitarian aid during the First World War, the Spanish Civil War, Vietnam and Biafra (MacFarlane, 2000).

3. The global funding for humanitarian assistance increased by more than a factor of five during the 1990s, to $4.365 billion in 1999 (Minear, 2002: 3).

4. The main exceptions to this are studies by Anderson (1999), MacFarlane (2000) and Collinson (2003).

5. Globally the nongovernmental sector commands one-third of multilateral aid flows.

6. Although some argue that NGOs have made less progress in the area of account-ability than was hoped for in the early 1990s (Edwards and Hulme, 1995).

7. The following section draws upon Goodhand, J. (2006) 'Preparing to intervene' in Yanacopulos, H. and Hanlon, J. (eds) *Civil War, Civil Peace,* Open University, James Currey, Oxford, UK, pp. 259–79.

8. IDPM/INTRAC, 'NGOs and peacebuilding in complex political emergencies', funded by ESCOR/DFID, 1997–2000, and INTRAC 'Conflict assessment project', 2000–01, funded by CHAD/DFID.

9. Historically, the separation of inter-state conflicts from other conflicts has been well established in international law. Inter-state conflicts were traditionally handled by international institutions such as the UN, the International Court of Justice and regional organizations. Internal wars were left to the domain of the states themselves. This is a basic tenet of the UN Charter and was seen as an untouchable principle during the Cold War (Wallensteen, 2002: 71).

10. But this definition excludes the Rwandan genocide—as it refers only to battle-related deaths—and armed conflicts between non-state warring parties.

11. These include: 'post-modern conflicts'; 'complex political emergencies' and 'emerging political complexes' (Duffield, 2001); and 'situations of chronic political instability' (Collinson, 2003).

12. For example, the Soviet-backed Najibullah regime in Afghanistan promoted a policy of national reconciliation in the early 1990s, arguably as a strategy of regime maintenance rather than as genuine peacebuilding.

13. This definition can be criticized because of its focus on the internal dimensions

199

of conflict and peacebuilding. Given the focus of this study on the country level, this definition is appropriate, but it is recognized that the international and regional aspects of peacebuilding are also crucial and have to a large extent been insufficiently recognized by international actors.

14. There is an extensive literature on multi-track diplomacy with different ways of categorizing and analysing the various tracks (Ramsbotham and Woodhouse, 1996; Miall, Ramsbotham and Woodhouse, 1999; Stedman, Rothchild and Cousens, 2002).

15. This kind of distinction has in my view been one of the weaknesses of 'peace-building approaches from below'. Even if NGOs' intervention focuses primarily on the community level they must be aware of and attempt to make linkages to Track One peacemaking and the politics of the state.

16. It is a term that lacks a sharp policy edge and it is perhaps often used because it allows analysts to avoid pointing the finger at which specific entities are responsible (Weiss, 2001: 424).

17. In this book the definition of Salamon and Anheier (1999) will be adopted, which outlines five essential characteristics: formal, private, non-profit-distributing, self-governing and voluntary. Although NGOs are a category firmly established in the language and accreditation procedures of the UN, the term does not do justice to the diversity and range of organizations that fall under this label. In this study the focus is on 'third-party' organizations (as opposed to membership organizations such as churches and trade unions), both international and national NGOs.

18. According to Gurr, Marshall and Khosla (2001), who grade conflicts in terms of intensity from 1 to 10, with 10 representing 'total destruction', our case study countries were graded as follows: Azerbaijan, suspended, 3; Moldova, suspended, 4; Afghanistan, ongoing (high), 7; Nepal, ongoing (low), 1; Sri Lanka, ongoing (high), 5; Liberia, sporadic, 4. Kyrgyzstan was not included.

Chapter 2

1. Some of the main ones include: the Uppsala Conflict Data Project published by the Stockholm International Peace Research Institute; the Causes of War Project at the University of Hamburg; the Correlates of War Project, University of Michigan; the PIOOM in Leiden, the Netherlands, which includes human rights violations; the Minorities at Risk Project, University of Maryland, which focuses on the subset of conflicts which involve ethnic minorities. The *Human Security Report,* published for the first time in 2005, draws upon these and a number of other sources of data.

2. See also Bates (2001) and Olson (2000). Olson views 'stationary bandits' as the forerunners of modern states. They emerged as the most powerful actor in a territory previously occupied by 'roving bandits'. By controlling territory and concentrating the means of coercion, incentives gradually emerge to provide protection and public goods as well as extracting resources from the population.

3. The late state-builders' task of forging a nation has also been hampered by the arbitrary nature of the boundaries drawn up by the colonial powers.

4. As Michael Mann (1999: 45) argues in the conclusion to his article 'The Dark Side of Democracy', the tendency of Western countries to make 'pious denunciations of the machinations of evil leaders' in the South unaccompanied by constructive or comprehensive actions, smacks of hypocrisy, 'since we ourselves live in ethnically cleansed states'.

5. A point made by Clapham (2002). See also Uvin (1998).

6. For instance, Gurr, Marshall and Khosla (2001) attribute the declining levels of conflict in the second half of the 1990s to a wave of democratization globally.

7. This, however, is frequently contested. For instance, as Mann (1999) argues, modern liberal democracy did not emerge out of social harmony. It was built upon extraordinarily high levels of violence: the 20th century's death toll through genocide was over 60 million, which was used, according to Mann, as a deliberate instrument of modern state policy.

8. Gurr (2000) usefully distinguishes between established and new democracies.

9. For an excellent critique of the new wars thesis, see Kalyvas (2000).

10. According to Sambanis (2003), living in 'bad neighourhoods', i.e. neighbour-hoods with undemocratic countries and countries experiencing ethnic wars of their own, increases a country's risk of having a civil war threefold.

11. Entitlements are defined by Sen (1981) as a 'set of commodity bundles that a person can command in a society using the totality of rights and opportunities that he or she faces.

12. This extension of the entitlement framework leads to five main categories of entitlements: direct, market, civic, public and extra-legal.

13. Uvin (1998), writing about Rwanda, traces the roots of the genocide back to failed development policies and a legacy of discrimination.

14. As Sambanis (2003) notes, government repression increases opposition and if repression is incomplete it can lead to violence. Violence, therefore, is the result of either lack of accommodation or incomplete repression.

15. As Sambanis (2003: 12) notes, 'Everyone is a potential rebel if the net (expected) economic benefits of rebellion are greater than the net benefits of the status quo'.

16. See Ballentine and Sherman (2003) for a more balanced treatment of the 'greed and grievance' debate. Based on case study research, they conclude that 'very few contemporary conflicts can be adequately captured as pure instances of "resource wars" or conflicts caused by "loot-seeking", on the part of either insurgents or state actors. Economic incentives and opportunities have not been the only or even the primary cause of these armed conflicts; rather to varying degrees, they interacted with socioeconomic and political grievances, interethnic disputes, and security dilemmas in triggering the outbreak of warfare' (p. 260).

17. Richards' (1996) and Ellis's (1999) finely drawn analyses of conflict and social transformation in Sierra Leone and Liberia respectively point to the importance of his-torical and sociological detail when thinking about contemporary conflict.

18. As Duffield (2004) notes, deciding between them (good or bad) and checking the latter in favour of the former are a matter for practical ethics and politics.

19. See, for instance, Coletta and Cullen (2000) for an examination of the links between violent conflict and the transformation of social capital, based upon case study research in Cambodia. Rwanda, Guatemala and Somalia. See also Goodhand, Hulme and Lewer (2000) for an analysis of the political economy of conflict and social capital in Sri Lanka.

20. See Harris (2002) for a powerful critique of how development agencies have used (and abused) the notion of social capital, and also Fine (2002) for an even more critical perspective on social capital and the World Bank.

21. In Afghanistan Schetter (2001) notes that 'a German treatment of the subject concludes that there are about 50 [ethnic groups], while a Russian study claims 200'.

22. Ignatieff captures this idea nicely in his phrase 'the deadly dynamic of nar-cissism of minor difference' (1998: 71). To illustrate how relative deprivation works, though Catholics had higher living standards in Northern Ireland than the Republic of Ireland, it was their deprivation relative to Protestants in the north that generated griev-

ance (Woodwell, 2002).

23. Similarly Horowitz (1985) argues that conflict potential is maximized when ethnicity overlaps with class.

24. Women's roles become particularly prominent in wars about national identities, as 'women in most societies take the major responsibility for passing on cultural identities to children and play active roles in supporting exclusive and aggressive ideologies about nationalism' (Pankhurst, 2003: 158).

25. This is evidently changing, with a number of women standing in the parliamentary elections in 2005 and winning seats.

26. Though, as Pankhurst (2003) notes, there has been a contradictory tendency to reify women as peacemakers while excluding them from peace settlements.

27. In Somalia, for instance, there has been a globalization of economic relations with the emergence of the transshipment and remittance economy, while there has been a localization of politics, with new forms of governance emerging at the local level (Bradbury, 2003).

Chapter 3

1. Since the royal coup in February 2005 international support has been less forthcoming and there has been a freeze on military assistance. However, the US still has a strong predisposition to make a connection between the Maoists and global terrorism.

2. Whether this has in turn created conducive conditions for the sustainable resolution of the conflict is of course another question. At the time of writing the ceasefire has become increasingly fragile and few of the preconditions for a political settlement are in place.

3. India, for instance, has an important impact on conflict and peacemaking in Sri Lanka and Nepal. Similarly Moldova comes under the Russian and Ukrainian spheres of influence.

4. The Taliban, in contrast, managed to concentrate the means of violence (with external support) and consequently had empirical sovereignty. But it was never recognized and therefore lacked juridical sovereignty.

5. The military in Afghanistan has historically become the focus for a number of contests of authority between the state and the tribes (Cramer and Goodhand, 2002: 898).

6. The role of the police force came out strongly in the case studies, in terms of citizens' perceptions of their day-to-day (in)security. People's attitude towards the police was a good litmus test of their faith in the state. In Kyrgyzstan, for example, there was very limited trust in the police. As one informant noted, getting a position in the police force is like getting a 'hunting licence', such is the level of corruption.

7. As James Scott (2000) notes, marginal areas such as mountains, deserts, marshes and forests are inhabited by those who have resisted the state's attempts to concentrate and fix populations in space.

8. Similarly in Liberia, even during the height of the conflict, in most areas people experienced long periods of relative calm and normality, interrupted by battles or skirmishing (Utas, 2005: 139).

9. Similarly in Nepal, human rights legislation has not been implemented because of weak monitoring mechanisms and a lack of political will to enforce them.

10. Milliken and Krause (2002: 765) usefully distinguish between state failure and state collapse. As they note, 'state maintenance (in whatever weakened or decayed capacity) is still the norm, and state collapse the exception'.

11. It has been argued that Kyrgyzstan's entry into the WTO has had a destabilizing

effect both politically and economically.

12. A disturbing example of the latter is the young children acting as porters crossing the border at Torkham between Pakistan and Afghanistan carrying a range of commodities from scrap metal to drugs.

13. As the Moldovan Human Development Report, 2000, concluded: 'the losses to the national economy of Moldova due to illegal activities in the Transdniestria region are comparable with the entire volume of financial asssistance obtained by the Moldovan state from international financial institutions' (UNDP, 2000: 26).

14. See World Bank (2003). In this influential report drafted by Paul Collier and colleagues entitled 'Breaking the Conflict Trap. Civil War and Development Policy' it is argued that such are the terrible costs of civil war it represents 'development in reverse'.

15. The Sheriff company in Transdniestria is a beneficiary of the shadow economy and a good example of the nexus between security, political and economic interests. Created by a former policeman from Bendery, the company controls a chain of supermarkets and fuel stations and has major investments in the telecommunications and construction sectors. It has good connections with President Igor Smirnov and has been declared tax-exempt. Sheriff has poured its 'dirty' money back into the community by building a football stadium and a cathedral (Kemp, 2005: 3).

16. Luckily this approach was not pursued and the IMF innovatively worked with the informal money exchange system when introducing a new currency into Afghanistan.

17. The Tamils are a minority in relation to the Sinhalese, but the Sinhalese also feel that they are a minority in relation to the much larger Tamil population in south India.

18. Nordstrom (2000) makes this point in relation to the shadow economy in Mozambique.

19. The LTTE, however, has not been entirely successful in eradicating internal divisions, and the emergence of the breakaway Karuna faction in 2003 exposed long-standing tensions between eastern and northern Tamils.

20. For example the government of Sri Lanka's arming of Tamil militant groups and Afghan warlords using ethnic divisions to mobilize support.

21. See, for instance, Stedman (2001, 2002). He defines spoilers as 'leaders or factions who use violence to undermine peace implementation' (Stedman, 2002: 9).

22. For instance, Pakistan always had concerns that a stable Afghanistan would be pro-Indian.

23. Although the combat and shadow economy evolved in Sri Lanka, and probably became increasingly significant, greed never displaced grievance as the primary motivation for the conflict. The two primary actors were oriented towards changing or (retaining) the laws and administrative procedures of society (Keen, 2000: 23). In Afghanistan, on the other hand, economic incentives clearly became a central factor in the continuation of the war. Warlords had few interests in putting the state back together. The shadow economy increasingly undermined the economies and political stability of neighbouring countries, further complicating conflict resolution strategies.

24. Paul Collier and colleagues (World Bank, 2003) use the term conflict 'proneness'.

Chapter 4

1. Although figures are notoriously difficult to gauge with any accuracy, the number of development NGOs registered in OECD countries is believed to have increased from 1,600 in 1980 to nearly 3,000 by 1993. The expenditure of these organizations has grown in the same period from $2.8 billion to $5.7 billion (Hulme and Edwards, 1997). There

are thought to be nearly 29,000 international NGOs alone (Lewis, 2002: 372).

2. The concept of the liberal peace derives from a long tradition of Western liberal theory and practice (Tschirgi, 2004; Paris, 2004; Richmond, 2005).

3. According to Woodhouse (1994), conflict resolution and third-party peace-making are grounded in two broad ideological traditions: first, Gandhian ideas of non-violent action, and second, pacifist teachings of religious groups such as the Quakers.

4. NGOs involved in conflict resolution have been subdivided by Voutira and Brown (1995) into three types of organizations with differing approaches: 'Model A NGOs', specialist organizations with a 'pure' focus on conflict resolution, training, preventative diplomacy, etc., e.g. Saferworld, International Alert; 'Model T NGOs', multi-mandate organizations which include conflict-related work within their overall focus on development or relief activities, e.g. Save the Children, Catholic Relief Services; 'Model B NGOs', focus on peace, rights and justice, with an emphasis on independence from governments, e.g. Balkan Peace Team, Christian Council of Sweden.

5. NGOs' supporters, for example, argue they have played a role in socializing state elites and improving norm recognition and institution-building in the area of human rights. They have helped modify the behaviour of actors in international politics towards a more pacific and democratic ethos, creating opportunities for dialogue, consultation and monitoring. For example, NGOs were influential in securing the international ban on landmines (Simmons, 1998).

6. Richmond (2001) categorizes this as a 'third generation' hybrid approach, involving a combination of traditional diplomatic and military instruments with softer non-traditional conflict resolution approaches.

7. This extremely benign view of civil society has been criticized. Voutira and Brown (1995: 29) argue that a weak understanding of civil society and its relationship with the state is one of the chief failings of conflict resolution NGOs: 'The future of conflict resolution activities and mediation practices largely depends on our ability to acquire a more coherent understanding of the relationships between state and civil society.'

8. The UN Security Council has authorized nearly 40 peacekeeping or peace enforcement operations over the last decade. UN peacekeeping, for instance, peaked in 1993 at 78,000 troops. But if NATO and UN missions are included, by 2001 the number of soldiers in international peace operations had soared to 108,000 (ICISS, 2001: 71).

9. In 2002 UN peacekeeping cost about $3.6 billion. The approved peacekeeping budget for 2004–5 was $3.8 billion).

10. For a sceptical treatment of *The Responsibility to Protect* see Chandler (2004), who argues that essentially it gives moral authority to new, more direct forms of Western regulation. Similarly Bellamy (2002: 33) describes humanitarian intervention as a 'Trojan horse used by the powerful to legitimize their interference in the affairs of the weak'.

11. Opposition to international activism in Darfur may be a sign of this.

12. For instance, Western disengagement from Afghanistan at the end of the Cold War had a range of regional and international blow back effects, including regional instability, terrorism and the narcotics trade.

13. Partly in response to a critical evaluation in 1997 (Sorbe, Macrae and Wohige-muth, 1997), International Alert developed a code of conduct which aimed to guide it in making ethical and principled decisions about how and where the organization would work. This is symptomatic of a wider trend towards professionalization in the conflict resolution sector.

14. For useful background on the roots, roles and impacts of development NGOs see: Korten (1987); Salmon and Anheier (1999); West (2001); Edwards and Hulme (1996); Hulme and Edwards (1997); Van Roy (1999).

15. The Millennium Development Goals set in September 2000 by aid donors were

arguably the product of this new found space for development actors.

16. For instance, multi- and bilateral aid agencies pledged more than $100 billion in so-called post-conflict assistance to some three dozen war torn countries in the past decade (Boyce, 2002b: 8).

17. For example, in Bosnia donors have attempted to link aid to protection of human rights, cooperation with the international war crimes tribunal and the right of people displaced by ethnic cleansing to return to their homes.

18. In relation to NGOs in Croatia it has been noted: 'Any application for funding, any explanation of the nature of democratization; any plans for future development; all seem obliged to include [civil society] as a central concept. Yet it is almost always undertheorised, insufficiently concretized in terms of specific practices, and rarely subject to critical scrutiny' (Stubbs, 1995: 6).

19. It has been argued that one of the reasons for the decline in development aid in the 1990s was that with the end of the Cold War the West no longer had a political incentive to compete with the East on development assistance (Cosgrave, 2003).

20. One indicator of the growing prioritization of conflict by the UN system is the growth in the number of Special Representatives of the Secretary-General (SRSGs). At the beginning of the 1990s there were only a handful, but by the end of the decade there were more than 30 (Jones, 2003: 217).

21. Which has subsequently been renamed the Conflict Prevention and Reconstruction Unit.

22. For instance the UK government established in 2001 the Global Conflict Prevention Pool and the Africa Conflict Prevention Pool in order to combine the knowledge and resources of the Ministry of Defence (MOD), DFID and the Foreign and Commonwealth Office (FCO). The objective of these new arrangements is to deliver 'a more strategic and cost-effective approach to conflict reduction' (DFID/MOD/FCO, 2003: 3). There is a perception that DFID is losing influence in relation to MOD and the FCO as a result of these new institutional arrangements.

23. NGOs may be complicit in humanitarianizing emergencies, which is something that has a long history: 'Interpreted largely through the eyes of relief agencies, Biafra became a humanitarian problem, excusing the UN and virtually every western government from direct involvement' (Smillie, 1995: 106).

24. In the First World War, for example, when Entente powers feared that some assistance provided by the Belgian Relief Commission to civilian victims in Belgium and German-occupied France would be diverted to the German military. British approval was conditional on 'stopping the leaks' (MacFarlane, 2001: 1).

25. Gresham's Law is the rule whereby, with no regulation, debased coinage drives pure coinage out of circulation (de Waal, 1997).

26. Copyright humanitarianism is understood to mean the classical Dunantist notion of humanitarian action.

27. As detailed in Table 1.1, in the 1990s we saw a steady move rightwards to include development, human rights, and conflict resolution and peacebuilding.

28. These represent the tools through which agencies negotiate a framework of respect or humanitarian space for the delivery of aid. The Geneva conventions and protocols draw a clear division between politics and the purposes and conduct of war, on the one hand, and assistance to victims, on the other.

29. This draws upon Bebbington (2004: 344), who makes similar comments in relation to academic debates on social capital.

30. There is, however, no clear line between humanitarian and non-humanitarian aid. Commodity-based definitions are problematic, but so too are definitions by agency mandates or the effects of aid. The last is theoretically the best but practically the most

difficult, since methodologies for assessing the impacts of aid on peace and conflict are underdeveloped.

31. Mosse (2004) is referring here to the discourses around development policies and projects, but his analytical framework provides a useful way of looking at the discourse and practice of peacebuilding.

Chapter 5

1. An alternative definition is Chris Roche's (1998): 'lasting or significant changes in people's lives'. This recognizes that humanitarian interventions may not have lasting or sustainable impact but they may be significant because they save lives or protect basic rights.

2. As Uphoff (1992: 399) notes, 'Phenomena and relationships range along a continuum from near certainty to near impossibility, with few normal distributions because there are many more possibilities than probabilities. The tension between probabilities and possibilities is ever present in the social universe since... the desirable possibilities are more numerous than are present probabilities.' This especially applies to development and peacebuilding where the most probable outcomes are seldom the most desirable ones.

3. The most well-known being Operational Lifeline Sudan (see Duffield, 2001; Vaux, 2001).

4. In 1999, for instance, a workshop conducted by Oxfam (GB/I) in eastern Sri Lanka on community reconciliation was curtailed by LTTE military cadres who felt that 'now was not the time for reconciliation'. But NGOs like Quaker Peace and Services and the Kalmanai Peace Foundation were able to continue community-based peacebuilding throughout this period in the same area, because they kept a low profile and were locally embedded.

5. The fact that NGO leaders in Sri Lanka working on political and peace-related issues are having an impact on the processes they seek to influence is shown by the threats they regularly receive from other political actors. For instance in May 2005 a number of the more prominent activists received death threats from an extreme nationalist group.

6. For instance Kyrgyz NGOs, particularly those working on the demand side of rights and democratization, were frequently threatened and intimidated by an increasingly authoritarian government before the Tulip revolution in 2005.

7. This tension between mandate-driven understandings of security and community-based notions of security comes out strongly in a report by Donini et al. (2005). This study compares the differing perceptions of security of communities, military actors in peace support operations and assistance agencies.

8. See Van Brabant (1998) for further discussion on security questions in relation to aid agencies.

9. In May 2004 five MSF staff members were killed in Afghanistan. Moreover, the development of 19 civil-military PRTs is cited by many humanitarians as evidence of this blurring of the lines.

10. For example, changing the policies and practices of Japan and the ADB in Sri Lanka would likely have a far greater effect on conflict and peacebuilding processes than micro-level changes to NGOs' programmes (Goodhand, 2001a).

11. One of the main exceptions to this is MacFarlane (2000, 2001) who examined in separate studies the links between aid and conflict, and aid and politics.

12. As an indication of the political and military role of the camps supported through aid flows, for refugees to receive aid they had to register with one of the seven Afghan political parties.

13. In Sri Lanka these tensions have been exposed by the post-tsunami response which has been dominated by large INGOs.

14. Apart from Afghanistan and Liberia where the state collapsed, in all other cases, though the state was a party to the conflict it continued to be an important source of entitlements, providing in most cases services that were far more central to people's survival than NGO aid programmes. In Sri Lanka in 1998, for instance, the annual costs of government dry rations to the northeast amounted to $60 million, around double the humanitarian assistance that year from foreign donors.

15. District leader.

16. NGOs are not solely to blame for these flawed transition processes and may in some respects have helped mitigate the conflict-fuelling effects of the transition through their welfare functions. But in the main they were prepared to accept donor funds without questioning the assumptions underlying the transition model.

17. For instance in the late 1990s in Afghanistan, aid resources had limited value to warring groups compared with the opium and smuggling economies, but because of the drought it was a significant part of the coping economy.

18. Another example of this is NGOs' involvement with Afghan carpet production, which runs the risk of deepening highly exploitative working practices for women and children. Direct entitlements may be temporarily strengthened, but at the costs of longer-term market entitlements.

19. With the possible exceptions of certain camp populations in Kabul, Azerbaijan and parts of northern Sri Lanka.

20. Another classic example of this is tube well programmes in southern Afghanistan which benefited the wealthy, particularly during the drought.

21. The post-tsunami response in Sri Lanka has also had conflict-fuelling distributional effects across a range of axes of tension: between the northeast and south, and coastal and inland areas; between the fishing and land owning castes; between the conflict-displaced and the tsunami-displaced.

22. A later evaluation of the water programme criticized Oxfam's decision to suspend it and estimated that it had put the lives of 1,800 people at risk as a result of drinking polluted water (Vaux, 2001: 127).

23. Another example of the conflict-dampening effect of NGOs in Sri Lanka has been in the area of election monitoring. There has been a noticeable drop in election violence since NGOs with international support became more involved in this area.

24. The Minister for Rural Development, Haneef Atmar, worked for several years with Norwegian Church Aid and was a committed advocate of community level peace-building. These perspectives have now been incorporated into government policy through programmes such as the National Solidarity Programme. Former NGO workers are also members of the Constitutional and Human Rights Commissions.

25. The Tamil Rehabilitation Organization (TRO), an international NGO which is essentially the humanitarian arm of the LTTE, could be seen in many respects as a Ministry of Welfare/Social Provision-in-waiting.

26. In Sri Lanka especially, there is a thriving subsector of NGOs whose focus is on promoting political change. For the leaders and members of such NGOs this does not represent an exit from politics so much as an alternative way of engaging with politics—and hopefully moving it in a progressive direction.

27. For instance, ICRC in Sri Lanka has on occasion helped mediate between the Sri Lankan government and the LTTE on questions of humanitarian access and provision.

28. Although many of these subsequently had to be closed because of a Taliban ban on NGO education programmes.

29. Kyrgyz NGOs, for example, have increasingly become part of the political landscape through their work with the independent media, advocacy on human rights and government legislation, election monitoring, etc. This growing politicization is

not without its dangers, however. As in a number of other nondemocratic contexts, government resistance to NGOs may be fed by the perception that they have become an institutional home for opposition individuals and parties or politicians-in-waiting (Fowler, 2005: 8).

30. If one accepts Hirshleifer's (1994) contention that the poor have a 'comparative advantage' in violence as they have less to lose, then socio-economic projects may play a role in decreasing the economic incentives to join militias.

31. There is a growing interest in diasporic finance, partly because of concerns about counter-terrorism, but also because of its potential contribution to development and poverty reduction. In spite of difficulties in specification and analysis, it is estimated that remittances are possibly four times larger than NGO transfers globally (Fowler, 2005: 18).

32. Nordstrom (2000) similarly draws upon research in Mozambique to highlight the ability of people and groups to create a counter-life world construct to challenge the politico-military one. Another example of this was a protest march organized by women in eastern Sri Lanka against the sale and consumption of alcohol. This was a challenge to their men folk (many of whom were heavy consumers of alcohol) and the LTTE (who derived substantial income from the market in illicit alcohol).

33. The Feminist Majority, a US-based Afghan women's solidarity organization, was one such example, though some question whether their confrontational approach ultimately helped the cause of Afghan women in response to Taliban repression.

34. Although strictly speaking this is not an NGO programme, NGOs were actively involved in an advisory and support role. Largely as a result of NGO and UN involvement, messages related to peacebuilding, health, drugs and mines awareness were incorporated into the soap opera. Star Radio in Liberia has also played a similar role in relation to issues such as peacebuilding and demobilization.

35. As Keen (1998: 320) notes, 'A major part of the problem is that aid organizations, in a sense, see their interest in promising a great deal, and then when they cannot deliver all that has been promised, disguising this fact.'

Chapter 6

1. During 2005 and 2006 the peacebuilding space closed significantly, due to a range of factors including: a change of government; the emergence of an LTTE breakaway faction; the failure to reach an agreement on a post-tsunami reconstruction mechanism; the assassination of the Sri Lankan foreign minister and the attempted assassination of the Commander of the Sri Lanka army by the LTTE; the election of a new president backed by Sinhaless nationalists; and escalating violence, particularly in the east. The potential for the resumption of full-scale war has increased significantly during this period.

2. Although with the benefit of hindsight one of the flaws of the negotiation strategy was the assumption that it was a bilateral conflict in which two parties could reach a deal and then deliver this to a clearly defined constituency. In reality there were multiple parties and many intra-group divisions. The peace process acted as a lightning rod for wider societal tensions and heightened the divisions between and within the various groups.

3. For example, in the US response to Afghanistan since 9/11 one can detect differing and sometimes contradictory approaches between the Pentagon, the Department of Defence and USAID.

4. See, for example, Stedman (2001), Wallensteen (2002), Stedman, Rothchild and Cousens (2002).

5. Third parties can create confidence between the conflicting parties and minimize the potential for cheating or free-riding: 'Third parties can thus ensure that the payoffs from cheating no longer exceed the payoffs from faithfully executing the settlement's terms. Once cheating becomes difficult and costly, promises to cooperate should gain credibility and cooperation should become more likely' (Walter, 1999: 46, cited in Hoddie and Hartzell, 2003: 315).

6. Norway also has the advantage of being seen by India to be a non-threatening actor.

7. Though the term itself is not a particularly useful one, as it tends to assume that political will is an immutable given. Rather than bemoaning its absence, it is more useful to analyse in particular cases the underlying reasons for political action or inaction.

8. For example on 27 October 1995 a donor conference on assistance to Liberia was held in New York. Only $145.7 million was pledged for Liberia's reconstruction, even as the international community pledged $6 billion for the reconstruction of Bosnia (Adebajo, 2002: 615).

9. See Bennet et al. (2003) 'Afghan elections: the great gamble', AREU Briefing Paper, November 2003.

10. Elbadarwi and Sambanis (2002) actually found that international interventions could have the effect of prolonging rather than resolving civil wars.

11. There were three UNSC resolutions between 1998 and 2000 which called on Afghanistan to surrender indicted terrorists and close terrorist camps, applied sanctions, including an arms embargo, and supported missile strikes.

12. In Afghanistan, for example, it has involved warlords taking key ministerial positions. In Sri Lanka part of the rationale for lifting the economic embargo to the northeast in 2002 was the belief that the economic attractions of the open economy would undermine the political project of the LTTE.

13. For example, there have historically been significant differences between the French and US positions, reflected in their support for different factions in the country.

14. There are also strong pragmatic reasons for being more inclusive. For example, the bilateral model of negotiations in Sri Lanka, which excluded key stakeholders such as the Muslims and nationalist groups in the south, has provoked a strong reaction from spoilers.

15. For example, in Sri Lanka the US simultaneously supported human rights organizations while arming and training the Sri Lankan armed forces, one of the main perpetrators of human rights abuses. In Afghanistan the diplomatic and assistance arms of the UN pursued different approaches toward the Taliban, based on fundamentally different analyses of the problem.

16. In 1991 with a US/Soviet rapprochement and changes in the Saudi Arabian and Pakistan positions in the aftermath of the Gulf War, the UN mission pushed for the establishment of a 'transitional mechanism'. The favourable regional alignments, the dynamics at the ending of the Cold War and the attention still focused on Afghanistan gave the 1991/2 initiative a concerted international tailwind. However, President Najibullah's announcement that he would leave office as soon as an interim government was formed served as a signal for other contenders to scramble for power. In retrospect stronger international support, including perhaps a neutral peacekeeping force in Kabul might have averted the power vacuum and infighting that followed.

17. According to Duffield, the 'strategic complexes of global governance' tend to imitate the nature of new wars themselves (Duffield, 2001: 45).

18. The idea of NGO generations was first developed by D. Korten (1987). Korten argued in this article that NGOs' strategies and approaches have evolved over time from a first-generation strategy of relief and welfare, to a second-generation strategy of

self-reliant local development, and finally to a third-generation strategy of sustainable systems development.

19. MSF, for instance, objected to the strategic framework process from the beginning as it felt humanitarian action should not be linked to other objectives, including peacebuilding.

20. The reflex action of humanitarians to work around the state appeared often to be based upon concerns for their own autonomy rather than the human security needs of the population.

21. Poor performance by international aid agencies during the 1990s has been widely commented upon: 'the frameworks to design, coordinate and deliver aid remain woefully under-institutionalized. Essentially the donor community improvises a new aid response for each country' (Forman and Patrick, 2000: 14).

22. The aid system is structurally integrated through resource transfers and NGOs are one of a number of organizations operating in this aid marketplace. It can be characterized as an oligopoly in which there are many sellers and few buyers (Bryans, Jones and Stein, 1999: 16), the buyers being national and multilateral aid organizations and the sellers the operational agencies, including the specialist UN agencies, NGOs and various other military and private-sector organizations.

23. In Afghanistan the principal coordination arrangements were through the Afghan Support Group (ASG) and the Strategic Framework process. In Sri Lanka the main international platform for donor coordination was the Development Forum, chaired by the World Bank, which was held every two years in Paris. At the country level UNDP took the lead coordination role.

24. This applied at both the national and local levels. For instance, after Jaffna was retaken by the SLAF there was a donor rush into the peninsula to support rehabilitation activities. This created huge transaction costs for the Government Agent and different line ministries, as donors set up their own pet projects, which often involved poaching the most able government staff.

25. There were some notable exceptions to this. For instance, SCF (UK) produced some excellent reports showing how transition policies have affected the lives of children in Central Asia.

Chapter 7

1. Marxists focus on structures and rational choice theorists on individuals. Neither pays much attention to organizations in general and NGOs in particular. The peacebuilding and humanitarian literatures tend to treat NGOs collectively as a homogenous group and individual NGOs as a single reality.

2. Though many agencies introduced PRA methodologies, in the field they tended to be used tokenistically and usually only at project outset.

3. In Table 1.1, the further rightwards agencies ventured along the horizontal axis the more politically sensitive it became and the more explicit the focus on peacebuilding.

4. As Christoplos (1998: 10) notes about rehabilitation, 'It is a marker for the fact that we don't know what we are trying to do other than keep people alive while increasingly looking for ways to increase local institutional capacity and avoid dependency.'

5. The LTTE, for example, would not tolerate NGOs working in the northeast explicitly focusing on peacebuilding.

6. The NPC, for example, was a response to the 1994 government-led peace process in Sri Lanka.

7. For instance, EHED's resettlement programme in Savukaddy, eastern Sri Lanka

missed the opportunity of linking the project benefits to a neighbouring Muslim community. Though the project was successful in achieving its stated objectives, a peacebuilding opportunity (a potential positive externality of the project) was missed.

8. Another success story is the Afghan de-mining programme, implemented purely by local NGOs and which from the beginning was based on a long-term commitment to building Afghan capabilities (Harpviken, 2002).

9. There are striking continuities between modern NGO workers and earlier missionaries in their deep-felt beliefs about what constitutes the good life. As Hopgood notes (2000: 21): 'Humanitarian activists remain as determined as earlier missionaries to effect widespread social change through transformation of personal identities.'

10. See Vaux (2001) for a fascinating account of the internal workings of Oxfam based upon 30 years experience of working within the organization.

11. As Edwards and Fowler (2002: 6) note, this is not uncommon: 'Changing or moving the boxes on the NGDO's organogram is a popular option for managers in this sector, as in others, but it is rarely effective without much deeper changes in culture and attitudes.'

12. This deficiency was exposed by the drought in Afghanistan, because of the lack of a nationwide model of food security assessment, surveillance and intervention.

13. It has been noted that some of the best anthropological work was done in the last century on the North-West Frontier (currently the Afghan–Pakistan frontier) by British colonial administrators. Incentives were paid for learning the language and developing an understanding of local politics, history, etc. The contrast with today's aid workers, on six-month to one-year contracts, is striking.

14. Leonard in his book on Kenyan bureaucracy analysed the biographies and strategies of 'positive deviants', people who used their environments productively rather than being trapped by them (Leonard, 1991: 11–12).

15. Both went on to hold senior positions in the Afghan Transitional Administration.

16. As Hilhorst (2003: 214) notes, how 'actors expand their room for manoeuvre depends on their effectiveness in enrolling others into their projects, which is called effective agency'.

17. One way of doing this is the time-honoured NGO tradition of 'rubber mathematics', which involves hiding administrative costs and inflating whatever cost the donor likes best. An NGO term for this is 'money morphing' (Smillie, 2001: 187). The overall impact of the accountability revolution has been to erode trust between NGOs and their donors and also, more worryingly, their beneficiaries.

18. For instance, the institutional arrangements that have developed around the opium economy in Afghanistan involve multiple networks which are dynamic, decentralized and constantly adapting to a range of external and internal factors, including weather conditions, demand, prices, changed political allegiances, and eradication and control regimes.

19. One NGO's log frames for conflict reduction, for instance, included objectives like reducing incidences of violence in a particular locale by 25 per cent. This is taking the compulsion to put a number on something to ridiculous levels. First, the unit of analysis was never specified, so it was not clear whether the figure applied to domestic violence, interhousehold disputes or armed violence. Second, it would have been impossible to measure. Third, even if it were possible to measure, it would have been impossible to attribute causality.

20. Accountability is defined here as 'the means by which individuals and organizations report to a recognised authority (or authorities) and are held responsible for their actions' (Edwards and Hulme, 1996).

21. This is not to suggest that NGOs working in development settings have put

their own house in order in relation to accountability. There have been a number of hard-hitting critiques of development NGOs which centre on the problem of accountability (see Wood, 1997).

22. Neither EHED nor ADA, for example, was involved in the SPHERE programme.

23. For example, NGO officers who had attended do-no-harm training might simply re-label existing activities as conflict reduction/peace building projects. One found it difficult to detect how do-no-harm analysis led to changes in actual practice.

24. NPC's high-quality social analysis was reflected in their research on the costs of conflict and on community perceptions of the peace process. This social analysis was built upon the foundation of a network of relationships extending from the village level into the macro policy arena.

25. ADA, for example, survived the forced closure of their education programme by the Taliban. Community support for this programme meant that over 45 per cent of the schools continued to function without external assistance. This indicates the importance of building long-term relationships that extend beyond the time frame of aid-financed projects.

26. NPC's strategy was partly to cultivate friends in high places. For example, they developed close contacts with parliamentarians and key embassy officials, which has enabled them to have an influence behind the scenes on peace issues.

27. ICRC's and CARE's slow and careful 'green tea' approach to negotiations with the Taliban made important gains relating to women's access to health facilities. Similarly, ICRC's quiet diplomacy between the LTTE and the government of Sri Lanka was successful in opening up a land route to the Wanni for humanitarian assistance. This might be contrasted with NGOs' failed negotiations with the Taliban over the relocation of NGO offices in Kabul in 1998. One person involved in the discussions commented that none of the NGO team had any previous training or experience in negotiation processes.

28. For example: the Consortium for Humanitarian Agencies in Sri Lanka; the EU-funded multi-agency rehabilitation programme for Afghan returnees in Eastern provinces; NGO attempts to develop common approaches to education provision in Afghanistan.

29. Van Brabant and Killock (1999: 38) highlight the effectiveness of organizations with a substantial field presence in Afghanistan, such as ICRC.

Chapter 8

1. It is recognized that the roots of armed conflict may be related as much to regional and international factors as to domestic issues.

2. This applies less to the work of researchers from disciplines like anthropology and history, than it does to many economists and to a certain extent political scientists and development studies researchers.

3. Many of these needed reforms are outlined in the Report of the Secretary-General's High Level Panel on Threats, Challenges and Change (UN, 2004). The establishment of a peacebuilding commission is one of the reforms that has gained high-level backing.

4. Certain types of analysis need to be strengthened. For example, analysis of poverty–conflict links are particularly weak and the same applies to the understanding of the political economy of non-state military groups and shadow economies.

5. DFID, for example, has developed a conflict assessment methodology (Goodhand, Vaux and Walker, 2001).

6. At the time of writing a 'Good Humanitarian Donorship' initiative was supported

by many of the key international donor agencies. However, it appears to have a number of weaknesses, including its narrow interpretation of humanitarian donorship, which in my view reinforces the minimalist position. Also, like the Red Cross Code of Conduct, it lacks teeth and there are no mechanisms for enforcing compliance.

7. MSF maintains a 70 per cent private-to-public ratio, with a strict policy of allowing no more than 50 per cent of their total funds to come from governments (Stoddard, 2003: 29).

Bibliography

Addison, T., Le Billon, P. and Murshed, S.M. (2001) 'Finance in conflict and reconstruction', *Journal of International Development,* 13, pp. 951–64.

Adebajo, A. (2002) 'Liberia: a warlord's peace', in S. Stedman, D. Rothchild and E. Cousens (2002) *Ending Civil Wars. The implementation of peace agreements,* International Peace Academy/Lynne Rienner, Boulder, CO, pp. 599–630.

Allen, T. (1992) 'Upheaval, affliction and health: a Uganda case study', in H. Bernstein, B. Crow and H. Johnson (eds), *Rural Livelihoods. Crises and responses,* Oxford University Press/The Open University, Oxford, pp. 217–48.

Anderson, K. (2004a) 'Humanitarian inviolability in crisis: the meaning of impartiality and neutrality for UN and NGO agencies following the 2003–2004 Afghanistan and Iraq crisis', *Harvard Journal of Human Rights,* 17 (74), pp. 41–74.

Anderson, L. (2004b) 'Antiquated before they can ossify: states that fail before they form', *Journal of International Affairs,* 58 (1), pp. 1–16.

Anderson, M.B. (1996) 'Humanitarian NGOs in conflict intervention', in C.A. Crocker, F. Hampson and P. Hall (eds), *Managing Global Chaos: Sources of and responses to international conflict,* US Institute of Peace Press, Washington, DC, pp. 343–54.

Anderson, M.B. (1999) *Do No Harm: How aid can support peace—or war,* Lynne Rienner, Boulder, CO and London.

Anderson, M.B. and Olson, L. (2003) *Confronting War: Critical lessons for peace practitioners,* The Collaborative for Development Action, Cambridge, MA.

Arendt, H. (1969) 'Reflections on violence', *New York Review of Books,* 27 February.

Atkinson, P. and Leader, N. (2000) The 'Joint Policy of Operation' and the 'Principles and Protocols of Humanitarian Operation' in Liberia, Study no. 2 in *The Politics of Principle: The principles of humanitarian action in practice* series, Humanitarian Policies Group (HPG) Report no. 3, Overseas Development Institute (ODI), London.

Atmar, H. and Goodhand, J. (2002) 'Afghanistan: The challenge of winning the peace', in M. Mekenkamp, P. van Tongeren and H. van de Veen (eds), *Searching for Peace in South and Central Asia. An overview of conflict prevention and peacebuilding activities,* Lynne Rienner, Boulder, CO, pp. 109–40.

Ayoob, M. (1995) *The Third World Security Predicament: State making, regional conflict and the international system,* Lynne Rienner, Boulder, CO.

Ball, N. (2002) 'The reconstruction and transformation of war-torn societies and state institutions: how can external actors contribute?', in T. Debiel with A. Klein (eds), *Fragile Peace. State failure, violence and development in crisis regions,* London, Zed Books, pp. 33–55.

Ballentine, K. and Sherman, J. (eds) (2003) *The Political Economy of Armed Conflict.*

Beyond greed and grievance, Lynne Rienner, Boulder, CO.

Barakat, S., Chard, M., Jacoby, T. and Lume, W. (2002) 'The composite approach: research design in the context of war and armed conflict', *Third World Quarterly,* 23 (5), pp. 991–1003.

Bardhan, P. (1997) 'Method in the madness? A political economy analysis of the ethnic conflicts in less developed countries', *World Development,* 25 (9), pp. 1381–98.

Barnett, M. (2003) 'What is the future of humanitarianism?', *Global Governance,* 9, pp. 401–16.

Bastian, S. (1999) 'The failure of state formation, identity conflict and civil society responses—the case of Sri Lanka', Working Paper no. 4, University of Manchester/University of Bradford.

Bastian, S. (2005) 'The economic agenda and the peace process', A report prepared for the World Bank, DFID, Netherlands Embassy and SIDA.

Bastian, S. and Luckham, R. (eds) (2003) *Can Democracy be Designed?,* Zed Books, London.

Bates, R. (2001) *Prosperity and Violence: The political economy of development,* W.W. Norton, London and New York.

Bebbington, A. (2004) 'Social capital and development studies 1: Critique, debate, progress?', *Progress in Development Studies,* 4 (4), pp. 343–9.

Bellamy, A. (2002) 'Pragmatic solidarism and the dilemmas of humanitarian intervention', *Millennium: Journal of International Studies* 31 (3), pp. 473–97.

Bennet, C., Wakefield, S. and Wilder, A. (2003) 'Afghan Elections: the great gamble', AREU Briefing Paper, November 2003, AREU, Kabul, Afghanistan.

Bentham, J. (2002) 'Humanitarianism and Islam after 9/11', in J. Macrae and A. Harmer, *Humanitarian Action and the Global War on Terror. A review of trends,* ODI, London, pp. 37–48.

Bhatia, M. and Goodhand, J., with Atmar, H., Pain, A. and Suleman, M. (2003) 'Profits and poverty: aid, conflict and livelihoods in Afghanistan', in S. Collinson (ed.), *Power, Livelihoods and Conflict: Case studies in political economy analysis for humanitarian action,* HPG Report no. 13, ODI, London.

Bobbitt, P. (2002) *The Shield of Achilles. War, peace and the course of history,* Penguin Books, London.

Booth, J.A. (1991) 'Socio-economic and political roots of national revolts in Central America', *Latin American Research Review,* 26 (1), pp. 33–74.

Bose, S. (2002) 'Flawed mediation, chaotic implementation: the 1987 Indo-Sri Lanka peace agreement', in S. Stedman, D. Rothchild and E. Cousens, *Ending Civil Wars. The implementation of peace agreements,* International Peace Academy/Lynne Rienner, Boulder, CO, pp. 631–59.

Boyce, J. (ed.) (1996) *Economic Policy for Building Peace: the lesson of El Salvador,* Lynne Rienner, Boulder, CO.

Boyce, J. (2000) 'Beyond good intentions: external assistance and peacebuilding', in S. Forman and S. Patrick, *Pledges of Aid for Post-Conflict Recovery,* Lynne Rienner, Boulder, CO, pp. 367–82.

Boyce, J. (2002a) *Investing in Peace. Aid and conditionality after civil wars,* Adelphi Paper no. 353, Institute of International and Strategic Studies (IISS), September.

Boyce, J. (2002b) 'Unpacking aid', *Development and Change,* 33 (2), pp. 239–46.

Boyce, J. (2002c) 'Aid conditionality as a tool for peacebuilding: opportunities and constraints', *Development and Change,* 33 (5), pp. 1025–48.

Bradbury, M. (2003) 'Living with statelessness: the Somali road to development', *Journal of Conflict, Security and Development,* 3 (1), pp. 7–26.

Bray, J., Lund, L. and Murshed, S.M. (2003) 'Nepal: Economic drivers of the Maoist insurgency', in K. Ballentine and J. Sherman (eds.) (2003) *The Political Economy of Armed Conflict. Beyond greed and grievance,* International Peace Academy, Lynne Rienner, Boulder, CO, pp. 107–32.

Brown, T.L. (1996) *The Challenge to Democracy in Nepal: a political history,* London, Routledge.

Bryans, M., Jones, B. and Stein, J. (1999) 'Mean times. Humanitarian action in complex political emergencies—stark choices, cruel dilemmas', Report of the NGOs in Complex Emergencies Project, 1 (3), January, University of Toronto.

Burke, J. (2004) *Al-Qaeda: The True Story of Radical Islam,* Penguin, London.

Carnegie Commission (1997) *Preventing Deadly Conflict,* Carnegie Commission, New York.

Cerny, P.H. (2000) 'The new security dilemma', *Review of International Studies,* 26 (4), pp. 623–62.

Chambers, R. (1984) *Rural Development: Putting the Last First,* ITDG Publishing, Rugby.

Chambers, R. (1997) *Whose Reality Counts? Putting the First Last,* ITDG Publishing, Rugby.

Chandler, D. (2003) 'Rhetoric without responsibility: the attraction of "ethical" foreign policy', *British Journal of Politics and International Relations,* 5 (3), pp. 295–316.

Chandler, D. (2004) 'The responsibility to protect? Imposing the "liberal peace"', *International Peacekeeping,* 11 (1), pp. 59–81.

Christoplos, I. (1998) 'Humanitarianism and local service institutions in Angola', *Disasters,* 22 (1), pp. 1–20.

Clapham, C. (2002) 'The challenge to the state in a globalized world', *Development and Change,* 33 (5), November, pp. 775–98.

Clausewitz, C. von (1982) *On War,* Penguin, London.

Cliffe, L. and Luckham, R. (1999) 'Complex political emergencies and the state: failure and the fate of the state', *Third World Quarterly,* 20 (1), pp. 27–50.

Cliffe, L. and Luckham, R. (2000) 'What happens to the state in conflict? Political analysis as a tool for planning humanitarian assistance', *Disasters,* 24 (4), pp. 291–313.

Coletta, N.J. and Cullen, M.L. (2000) *Violent Conflict and the Transformation of Social Capital. Lessons from Cambodia, Rwanda, Guatemala and Somalia,* World Bank, Washington, DC.

Collier, P. (2000) 'Doing well out of war: an economic perspective', in M. Berdal and D.M. Malone (eds), *Greed and Grievance: Economic Agendas in Civil Wars,* Lynne Rienner, Boulder, CO and London, pp. 91–111.

Collier, P. and Hoeffler, A. (1998) *On the Economic Causes of Civil War,* Oxford Economic Papers no. 50, Oxford University Press, Oxford, pp. 563–73.

Collinson, S. (ed.) (2003) *Power, Livelihoods and Conflict: Case studies in political economy analysis for humanitarian action,* HPG Report no. 13, ODI, London.

Cooley, A. and Ron, J. (2002) 'The NGO scramble. Organizational insecurity and the political economy of transnational action', *International Security,* 27 (1), pp. 5–39.

Cosgrave, J. (2003) 'The impact of the war on terror on aid flows', Report prepared for ActionAid. Available online at: www.actionaid.org.uk/content_document.asp?doc_id=198.

Craig, D. and Porter, D. (1997) 'Framing participation: development projects, professionals and organizations', *Development in Practice,* 7 (3), pp. 229–36.

Cramer, C. (2002) 'Homo Economicus goes to war: methodological individualism and the political economy of war', *World Development,* 30 (11), pp. 1845–64.

Cramer, C. (2003) 'Does inequality cause conflict?', Special Issue: 'Explaining violent conflict: Going beyond greed versus grievance', *Journal of International Development,* 15 (4), pp. 397–412.

Cramer, C. and Goodhand, J. (2002) 'Try again. Fail again. Fail better? Adventures in war and state-building in Afghanistan', *Development and Change,* 30, pp. 885–909.

Das, V., Kleinman, A., Ramphele, M. and Reynolds, P. (2000) *Violence and Subjectivity,* University of California Press, Berkeley, CA.

Debiel, T. (2002) 'Introduction. Do crisis regions have a chance of lasting peace? The difficult transformation from structures of violence', in T. Debiel with A. Klein (eds), *Fragile Peace. State failure, violence and development in crisis regions,* Zed Books, London, pp. 1–29.

Department for International Development (DFID), Foreign and Commonwealth Office (FCO) and Ministry of Defence (MoD) (2003) 'The global conflict prevention pool: a joint UK approach to reducing conflict', DFID, FCO and MoD, London.

De Torrente, N. (2004) 'Humanitarian action under attack: reflections on the Iraq war', *Harvard Journal of Human Rights,* 17 (74), pp. 1–29.

de Waal, A. (1997) *Famine Crimes: Politics and the disaster relief industry in Africa,* James Currey /African Rights, International Africa Institute (IAI), London.

Donini, A. (2003a) 'Principles, politics and pragmatism in the international response to the Afghan crisis', in A. Donini, N. Niland and K. Wermester (eds), *Nation-Building Unraveled? Aid, peace and justice in Afghanistan,* Kumarian Press, Bloomfield, CT, pp. 4, 117–42.

Donini, A. (2003b) 'The future of humanitarian action: implications of Iraq and other crises', Issues Note, Brainstorming workshop organized by the Feinstein International Famine Centre, Boston, MA, 9 October.

Donini, A., Minear, L., Smillie, I. et al. (2005) 'Mapping the security environment: understanding the perceptions of local communities, peace support operations, and assistance agencies', Feinstein International Famine Centre, report commissioned by the UK NGO-Military Contact Group, Medford, OR.

Downs, G. and Stedman, S.J. (2002) 'Evaluation issues in peace implementation', in S. Stedman, D. Rothchild and E. Cousens, *Ending Civil Wars: The implementation of peace agreements,* International Peace Academy/Lynne Rienner, Boulder, CO, pp. 43–69.

Doyle, M.W. and Sambanis, N. (1999) *Building Peace: Challenges and strategies after civil war,* World Bank, Washington, DC, 27 December.

Doyle, M. and Sambanis, N. (2000) 'International peacebuilding: a theoretical and quantitative analysis', *American Political Science Review,* 94 (4), December, pp. 779–801.

Duffield, M. (1997) 'Evaluating conflict resolution. Context, models and methodology', discussion paper prepared for the Chr. Michelsen Institute in G. Sorbe, J. Macrae and L. Wohigemuth, 'NGOs in conflict—an evaluation of international alert', CMI Report Series, Chr. Michelson Institute, Bergen, Norway, pp. 79–112.

Duffield, M. (1998) 'Aid policy and post-modern conflict. A critical review', Occasional Paper no. 19, School of Public Policy, University of Birmingham.

Duffield, M. (2001) *Global Governance and the New Wars: the merging of development and security,* Zed Books, London and New York.

Duffield, M. (2002) 'Social reconstruction and the radicalization of development: aid as a relation of global liberal governance', *Development and Change,* 33 (5), pp. 1049–72.

Duffield, M. (2004) 'Carry on killing: global governance, humanitarianism and terror', unpublished draft, April.

Duffield, M. and Waddell, N. (2004) 'Human security and global danger. Exploring a governmental assemblage', report completed with a grant from the Economic and Social Science Research Council (ESRC) New Security Challenges Programme (RES-223-25-0035).

Edwards, M. (1999) *Further Positive: International cooperation in the 21st century,* Earthscan, London.

Edwards, M. and Hulme, D. (1996) *Beyond the Magic Bullet. NGO accountability in the post-Cold War world,* Kumarian Press, Bloomfield, CT.

Edwards, M. and Fowler, A. (2002) 'Introduction: changing challenges for NGDO Management', in M. Edwards and A. Fowler (eds), *The Earthscan Reader on NGDO Management,* Earthscan, Sterling, VA, pp. 1–10.

Elbadarwi, I. and Sambanis, N. (2002) 'How much war will we see? Explaining the prevalence of civil war', *Journal of Conflict Resolution,* 46 (3), pp. 307–34.

Ellis, S. (1999) *The Mask of Anarchy: the roots of Liberia's war,* New York University Press, New York.

Feldman, A. (1991) *Formations of Violence: The narrative of the body and political terror in Northern Ireland,* University of Chicago Press, Chicago, IL.

Fetherstone, A.B. (2000) 'Peacekeeping, conflict resolution and peacebuilding: a reconsideration of theoretical frameworks', in Special Issue of *International Peacekeeping,* 7, pp. 190–218.

Fielden, M. and Goodhand, J. (2001) 'Beyond the Taliban? The Afghan conflict and United Nations peacemaking', *Conflict, Security & Development,* 1 (3), pp. 5–32.

Fine, B. (2002) 'The World Bank's speculation on social capital', in J. Pincus and J. Winters (eds) *Reinventing the World Bank,* Cornell University Press, New York.

Forman, S. and Patrick, S. (2000) *Pledges of Aid for Post-Conflict Recovery,* Lynne Rienner, Boulder, CO.

Foucault, M. (2003) *Society Must Be Defended,* Allen Lane, Penguin, London.

Fowler, A. (2005) 'Aid architecture: reflections on NGO futures and the emergence of counter-terrorism', INTRAC OPS No. 45.

Freedman, L. (2004) 'The new security equation', *Conflict, Security & Development,* 4 (3), pp. 245–56.

Galtung, J. (1969) 'Violence, peace and peace research', *Journal of Peace Research* 3, pp. 167–92.

Garilao, E. (1987) 'Indigenous NGOs as strategic institutions: managing the relationships with government and resource agencies', *World Development,* 15, pp. 113–20.

Gilgan, M. (2001) 'The rationality of resistance: alternative for engagement in complex emergencies', *Disasters,* 25 (1), pp. 1–18.

Gilligan, J. (2000) *Violence: Reflections on our deadliest epidemic,* Jessica Kingsley Publishers, London.

Girard, R. (1996) 'Mimesis and violence', in J.G. Williams (ed.) *The Girard Reader,* The Crossroad Publishing Company, New York.

Goodhand, J. (2000) 'Strategic conflict assessment, Nepal', unpublished report for DFID, London.

Goodhand, J. (2001a) *Aid, Conflict and Peacebuilding in Sri Lanka,* Conflict, Security and Development Group, Kings College, University of London, Conflict Assessment, July 2001.

Goodhand, J. (2001b) 'Conflict assessment project: synthesis report', Conflict, Security and Development Group, Kings College, University of London, Conflict Assessments no. 1, July.

Goodhand, J. (2002) 'Aiding violence or building peace? The role of international aid in Afghanistan', *Third World Quarterly,* Special Issue, 23 (5), pp. 837–59.

Goodhand, J. (2003) 'Enduring disorder and persistent poverty: a review of the linkages between war and chronic poverty', *World Development,* 31 (3), pp. 629–46.

Goodhand, J. (2004) 'Afghanistan in Central Asia', in M. Pugh and N. Cooper, with J. Goodhand, *War Economies in a Regional Context: Challenges for transformation,* Lynne Rienner, Boulder, CO, and London, pp. 45–89.

Goodhand, J. (2006) 'Preparing to intervene' in Yanacopulos, H. and Hanlon, J. (eds) *Civil War, Civil Peace,* Open University, James Currey, Oxford, UK, pp. 259–79.

Goodhand, J. with Atkinson, P. (2001) 'Conflict and aid: enhancing the peacebuilding impact of international engagement: a synthesis of findings from Afghanistan, Liberia and Sri Lanka', *International Alert,* London.

Goodhand, J. with Bergne, P. (2003) 'Evaluation of the conflict prevention pools. Afghanistan', DFID, Evaluation Report EV 647.

Goodhand, J. and Hulme, D. (1997) 'NGOs and peacebuilding in complex political emergencies: an introduction', NGOs and Complex Political Emergencies Working Paper no. 1, IDPM, University of Manchester.

Goodhand, J. and Hulme, D. (1999) 'From wars to complex political emergencies; understanding conflict and peacebuilding in the new world disorder', *Third World Quarterly,* Special Issue, 20 (1), pp. 13–26.

Goodhand, J., Hulme, D. and Lewer, N. (2000a) 'Social capital and the political economy of violence: a case study of Sri Lanka', *Disasters* 24 (4), pp. 390–406.

Goodhand, J., Hulme, D. and Lewer, N. (2000b) 'NGOs and complex political emergencies. NGOs and peacebuilding', Sri Lanka Study Discussion Paper, University of Manchester/University of Bradford.

Goodhand, J. and Klem, B. with Fonseka, D. et al. (2005) *Aid, Conflict and Peacebuilding in Sri Lanka, 2000–2005,* AsiaFoundation, US.

Goodhand, J. and Lewer, N. (1999) 'Sri Lanka: NGOs and peacebuilding in complex political emergencies', *Third World Quarterly,* Special Issue, 20 (1), pp. 69–87.

Goodhand, J., Vaux, T. and Walker, R. (2001) 'Conducting conflict assessments: guidance notes', DFID, London.

Gould, S.J. (1997) *Life's Grandeur. The spread of excellence from Plato to Darwin,* Jonathan Cape, London.

Grenier, Y. (1996) 'From causes to causers: the etiology of Salvadoran internal war revisited', *Journal of Conflict Studies,* Fall, pp. 26–43.

Grossman, D. (1996) *On Killing: The psychological cost of learning to kill in war and society,* Back Bay Books, Boston, MA.

GTZ (2003) 'Joint Utstein study of peacebuilding', Report commissioned by the evaluative division of the German Federal Ministry for Economic Cooperation and Development (BMZ), Eschborn, Germany.

Gurr, T.R. (1970) *Why Men Rebel,* Princeton University Press, Princeton, NJ.

Gurr, T.R. (2000) *People Versus States: Minorities at risks in the new century,* US Institute for Peace, Washington, DC.

Gurr, T.R., Marshall, M.G. and Khosla, D. (2001) 'Peace and conflict 2001. A global survey of armed conflicts, self-determination movements, and democracy', Centre for International Development and Conflict Management, University of Maryland, MD.

Hallam, A. (1998) 'Evaluating humanitarian assistance programmes in complex emergencies', Good Practice Review no. 7, ODI, London.

Hanlon, J. (1991) *Mozambique: Who calls the shots?,* James Currey, London.

Harpviken, K.B. (2002) 'Breaking new ground: Afghanistan's response to landmines and unexploded ordnance', *Third World Quarterly* 23, 5, pp. 931–43.

Harrell-Bond, B. (1986) *Imposing Aid: Emergency assistance to refugees,* Oxford University Press, Oxford.

Harris, J. (2002) *Depoliticizing Development. The World Bank and social capital,* Anthem Press, London.

Hegre, H. (2003) 'Disentangling democracy and development as determinants of armed conflict', paper presented to the Annual Meeting of International Studies Association, Portland, OR, 27 February.

Herring, R.J. (2001) 'Making ethnic conflict: the civil war in Sri Lanka', in Milton J. Esman and Ronald J. Herring (eds), *Carrots, Sticks and Ethnic Conflict: Rethinking development assistance,* University of Michigan Press, Ann Arbor, MI, pp. 140–74.

Hilhorst, D. (2003) *The Real World of NGOs. Discourse, diversity and development,* Zed Books, London.

Hirschman, A.O. (1970) *Exit, Voice, Loyalty,* Harvard University Press, Cambridge, MA.

Hirschman, A.O. (1984) *Getting Ahead Collectively: Grassroots experience in Latin America,* Pergamon, New York.

Hirshleifer, J. (1994) 'The dark side of the force', *Economic Inquiry,* 32, pp. 1–10.

Hirst, P. (2005) *Space and Power. Politics, war and architecture,* Polity Press, London.

Hobsbawm, E. (1969, 2001 edn) *Bandits,* Abacus, London.

Hobsbawm, E. (1994) *The Age of Extremes. The short twentieth century,* Abacus, London.

Hock, D. (1995) 'The Chaordic Organization. Out of control and into order', *World Business Academy Perspectives,* 9 (1), pp. 5–18.

Hoddie, M. and Hartzell, C. (2003) 'Civil war settlements and the implementation of military power-sharing arrangements', *Journal of Peace Research,* 40 (3), pp. 303–20.

Hoffman, C., Roberts, L., Shoham, J. and Harvey, P. (2004) 'Measuring the impact of humanitarian aid. A review of current practice', Humanitarian Policy Group Research Report no. 17, ODI, June.

Hopgood, S. (2000) 'Reading the small print in global civil society; the inexorable hegemony of the liberal self', *Millennium Journal of International Studies,* 29 (1), pp. 1–25.

Horowitz, D. (1985) *Ethnic Groups in Conflict,* University of California Press, Berkeley and Los Angeles, CA.

Howard, M. (2002) 'Foreword', in P. Bobbitt, *The Shield of Achilles. War, peace and the course of history,* Penguin Books, London, UK.

Hulme, D. (1995) 'Projects, politics and professionals: Alternative approaches for project identification and project planning', *Agricultural Systems,* 47, pp. 211–33.

Hulme, D. (2000) 'Impact assessment methodologies for microfinance: theory, experience and better practice', *World Devlepment,* 28 (1), pp. 79–98.

Hulme, D. and Edwards, M. (eds) (1997) *NGOs, States and Donors. Too close for comfort?,* Macmillan, London.

Human Development Centre (1999) 'Human development in South Asia. The crisis of governance', Mahbubu ul Haq Human Development Centre, Oxford University Press, Oxford.

Human Security Centre (HSC) (2005) *Human Security Report 2005. War and Peace in the 21st Century,* University of British Columbia, Canada.

International Crisis Group (ICG) (2005a) 'Kyrgyzstan after the revolution', *Asia Report* no. 97, 4 May.

ICG (2005b) 'Nepal: beyond royal rule', Policy Briefing, Asia Briefing no. 41, 15 September, Kathmandu/Brussels.

ICG (2005c) 'Nepal's Maoists: their aims, structure and strategy', Asia Report no. 104, 27 October.

ICG (2005d) 'Nagorno-Karabakh: a plan for peace', Europe Report no. 167, 11 October.

Ignatieff, M. (1998) *Warrior's Honour. Ethnic war and the modern conscience,* Chatto and Windus, New York.

Ignatieff, M. (2003) *Empire Lite. Nation-building in Bosnia, Kosovo and Afghanistan,* Vintage, London.

International Commission on Intervention and State Sovereignty (ICISS) (2001) 'The responsibility to protect', Report of the International Commission on Intervention and State Sovereignty.

Jabri, V. (1996) *Discourses on Violence: Conflict analysis reconsidered,* Manchester University Press, Manchester.

Jackson, R. (1990) *Quasi States: Sovereignty, international relations and the third world,* Cambridge University Press, Cambridge.

Jackson, S. and Walker, P. (1999) 'Depolarising the "broadened" and "back-to-basics" relief models', *Disasters,* 23 (2), pp. 93–114.

Jacobs, S., Jacobson, R. and Marchbank, J. (eds) (2000) *States of Conflict: Gender, violence and resistance,* Zed Books, London.

Jenkins, R. (2001) 'Mistaking "governance" for politics: foreign aid, democracy, and the construction of civil society', in S. Kaviraj and S. Khilnani (eds) *Civil Society. History and possibilities,* Cambridge University Press, Cambridge, pp. 250–68.

Jones, B. (2003) 'Aid, peace, and justice in a reordered world', in A. Donini, N. Niland and K. Wermester (eds) *Nation-Building Unraveled? Aid, peace and justice in Afghanistan,* Kumarian Press, Bloomfield, CT, pp. 207–26.

Kaldor, M. (1999) *New Wars and Old Wars: Organized violence in a global era,* Polity Press, Cambridge.

Kalyvas, S.N. (2000) '"New" and "old" civil wars: is the distinction valid?', paper presented at conference on 'La guerre entre le local et le global: Societies, Etats, Système', CERI, Paris, 29–30 May.

Kaplan, R (1994) 'The coming anarchy: how scarcity, crime, overpopulation and disease are rapidly destroying the social fabric of our planet', *Atlantic Monthly* (February), pp. 44–74.

Keegan, J. (1998) *War and Our World,* Reith Lectures, Hutchinson, London.

Keen, D. (1997) 'A rational kind of madness', Oxford Development Studies, 25 (1), pp. 67–75.

Keen, D. (1998) 'The economic functions of violence in civil wars', Adelphi Paper no. 320, Oxford University Press for IISS, Oxford.

Keen, D. (2000) 'War and peace: what's the difference?', *International Peacekeeping,* 7, (4), pp. 1–22.

Keen, D. (2002) '"Since I am a dog, beware my fangs": beyond a "rational violence" framework in the Sierra Leonean war', London School of Economics (LSE) Crisis States Programme Working Paper no. 14, August.

Kemp, W. (2005) 'Selfish determination: the questionable ownership of autonomy movements', *Ethnopolitics,* 4, 1, pp. 85–93.

Kent, R. (2004) 'Humanitarian futures. Practical policy perspectives', Network paper no. 46, Humanitarian Practice Network, ODI, London.

Keohane, R.O. (2003) 'Introduction', in J.L. Holzgref and R.O. Keohane (eds) (2003) *Humanitarian Intervention. Ethical legal and political dilemmas,* Cambridge University Press, Cambridge, pp. 1–11.

Kiely, R. (2005) *Empire in the Age of Globalization. US hegemony and neoliberal disorder,* Pluto Press, London.

Kissinger, H.A. (1969) 'The Viet Nam negotiations', *Foreign Affairs*, 47 (2), 2 January, pp. 211–34.

Korten, D. (1987) 'Third generation NGO strategies: a key to people-centred development', *World Development*, 15, pp. 145–59.

Kriger, N. (2003) *Guerrilla Veterans in Postwar Zimbabwe*, Cambridge University Press, Cambridge.

Le Billon, P. (2000) 'The political economy of war. What relief workers need to know', HPG Network Paper no. 33, ODI, London.

Lederach, J.P. (1997) *Building Peace: Sustainable reconciliation in divided societies*, United States Institute of Peace, Washington, DC.

Leonard, D.K. (1991) *African Successes: Four Public Managers of Kenyan Rural Development*, University of California Press, Berkeley, CA.

Lewis, D. (2001) *The Management of Non-Governmental Development Organizations: An Introduction*, Routledge, London.

Lewis, D. (2002) 'The rise of non-governmental organizations', in C. Kirkpatrick, R. Clarke and C. Polidano, *Handbook on Development Policy and Management*, Edward Elgar, Cheltenham, pp. 372–80.

Lewis, D., Bebbington, A., and Batterbury, S. et al. (2003) 'Practice, power and meaning: frameworks for studying organizational culture in multi-agency rural and development projects', *Journal of International Development*, 15, pp. 541–57.

Licklider, R. (1995) 'The consequences of negotiated settlements in civil wars, 1945–1993', *American Political Science Review* 89 (3), pp. 681–90.

Lieten, Kristoffel, (2002) 'Multiple Conflicts in Northeast India', pp. 407–32 in Mekenkamp, M., van Tongeren, P. and van de Veen, H. (eds), 2002, *Searching for Peace in Central and South Asia: An overview of conflict prevention and peacebuilding activities*, Lynne Rienner Publishers, Boulder, CO, and London.

Lines, T. (2001) 'At peace but insecure: the paradoxes of post Soviet life', *IDS Bulletin*, 32 (2), pp. 25–34.

Long, N. (1992) 'From paradigm lost to paradigm regained? The case for an actor-oriented sociology of development', in N. Long and A. Long (eds) *Battlefields of Knowledge: The interlocking of theory and practice in social research and development*, Routledge, London, pp. 15–43.

Luckham, R. (2004) 'The international community and state reconstruction in war-torn societies', in *Conflict, Security & Development* 4 (3), pp. 481–507.

Luckham, R., Ahmed, I., Muggah, R. et al. (2001) 'Conflict and poverty in sub-Saharan Africa: an assessment of the issues and evidence', Institute of Development Studies (IDS) Working Paper no. 128, IDS, Sussex.

Lund, M. (2000) 'Improving conflict prevention by learning from experience: issues, approaches and results', in M. Lund and G. Rasamoelina (eds) *The Impact of Conflict Prevention Policy. Cases, measures, assessments. Yearbook 1999/2000*, Conflict Prevention Network (SWP-CPN), Berlin, pp. 63–88.

Lund, M. (2001) 'A toolbox for responding to conflicts and building peace', in L. Reychler and T. Paffenholz, *Peacebuilding. A field guide*, Lynne Rienner Publishers, London and Boulder, CO, pp. 16–20.

Luttwak, E.N. (1999) 'Give war a chance', *Foreign Affairs*, 78 (4), pp. 36–44.

Lynch, D. (2004) *Engaging Eurasia's Separatist States: Unresolved conflicts and de facto states*, United States Institute of Peace Press, Washington, DC.

MacFarlane, N. (2000) 'Politics and humanitarian action', Occasional Paper no. 41, Thomas J. Watson Jr Institute for International Studies and the United Nations University, Providence, R.I., US.

MacFarlane, N. (2001) 'Humanitarian action: the conflict connection', Occasional Paper no. 43, Thomas J. Watson Jr Institute for International Studies and the United

Nations University, Providence, R.I., US.

Mack, A. (2002) 'Civil war: academic research and the policy community', *Journal of Peace Research,* 39 (5), pp. 515–25.

Macmillan, R. and Gartner, R. (1999) 'When she brings home the bacon: labor-force participation and the risk of spousal violence against women', *Journal of Marriage and the Family,* 61 (4), pp.947–58.

Macrae, J. (1999a) 'Foreword', in C. Pirotte, B. Husson and F. Grunewald (eds), *Responding to Emergencies and Fostering Development. The dilemmas of humanitarian aid,* Zed Books, London.

Macrae, J. (1999b) 'Studying up, down and sideways: toward a research agenda in aid operations', in L. Minear and G.W. Weiss (eds), *Humanitarian Action: A Transatlantic Agenda for Operations and Research,* Occasional Paper no. 39, Humanitarianism and War Project, Thomas J. Watson Jr Institute for International Studies and the United Nations University, Providence, R.I., US.

Macrae, J. (2001) *Aiding Recovery? The crisis of aid in chronic political emergencies,* Zed Books, London.

Macrae, J. (2002) in Macrae, J. (ed.) 'The new humanitarianisms: a review of trends in global humanitarian action', HPG Report no. 11, ODI, London, pp. 5–17.

Macrae, J. and Zwi, A. with Duffield, M. and Slim, H. (1994) *War and Hunger: Rethinking international responses to complex emergencies,* Zed Books, London.

Macrae, J. et al. (2002) 'Uncertain Power: The changing role of official donors in humanitarian action', Humanitarian Policy Group Report 12, ODI, London.

Maley, W. (ed.) (1998) *Fundamentalism Reborn? Afghanistan and the Taliban,* Vanguard Books, Lahore, Pakistan.

Mann, M. (1999) 'The dark side of democracy: the modern tradition of ethnic and political cleansing', *New Left Review,* 235, pp 18–45.

Marshall, M.G. and Gurr, T.R. (2005) 'Peace and conflict 2005', Centre for International Development and Conflict Management, University of Maryland, MD.

Miall, H., Ramsbotham, O. and Woodhouse, T. (1999) *Contemporary Conflict Resolution,* Polity Press/Blackwell, Oxford.

Migdal, J. (2004) 'State building and the non-nation-state', *Journal of International Affairs,* 58 (1), pp. 17–46.

Milliken, J. and Krause, K. (2002) 'State failure, state collapse, and state reconstruction: concepts, lessons and strategies', *Development and Change,* 33 (5), pp. 753–76.

Minear, L. (2002) *The Humanitarian Enterprise. Discoveries and dilemmas,* Kumarian Press, Bloomfield, CT.

Mintzberg, H. (1994) *The Rise and Fall of Strategic Planning,* Prentice-Hall, New York.

Moore, B. (1966) *Social Origins of Dictatorship and Democracy: Lord and peasant in the making of the modern world,* Penguin, London.

Moore, M. (2000) 'Political underdevelopment: what causes "bad governance"?', Working Paper, World Bank, Washington, DC.

Moore, M. and Putzel, J. (1999) 'Politics and poverty', a background paper for the World Development Report 2000/01, IDS, University of Sussex.

Moraya, A. (2003) 'Rethinking the state from the frontier', *Millennium: Journal of International Studies,* 3 (2), pp. 267–92.

Moser, C. and Clark, F. (eds) (2001) *Victims, Perpetrators or Actors? Gender, armed conflict and political violence,* Zed Books, London.

Mosse, D. (2004) 'Is good policy unimplementable? Reflections on the ethnography of aid policy and practice', *Development and Change,* 35 (4), pp. 639–71.

Munslow, B. and Brown, C. (1999) 'Complex emergencies: the institutional impasse',

Special Issue, *Third World Quarterly,* March, pp. 207–22.

Nathan, L. (2004) 'The four horsemen of the apocalypse. The structural causes of crises and violence in Africa', paper presented on 24 February 2004 at the Crisis States Programme seminar series, LSE, London.

Nicholds, N. and Borton, J. (1994) 'The changing role of NGOs in the provision of relief and rehabilitation assistance: case study 1—Afghanistan/Pakistan', Working Paper no. 74, ODI, London.

Nordstrom, C. (1999) 'Visible wars and invisible girls, shadow industries, and the politics of not-knowing', *International Feminist Journal of Politics,* 1 (1), pp. 14–33.

Nordstrom, C. (2000) 'Shadows and sovereigns', *Theory, Culture and Society,* 17 (4), pp. 35–54.

O'Brien, P. (2001) *Benefits/harms Handbook,* CARE International, September, Nairobi, Kenya.

O'Brien, P. (2004) 'Politicized humanitarianism: a response to Nicholas de Torrente', *Harvard Journal of Human Rights,* 17 (74), pp. 31–9.

Olson, M. (2000) 'Dictatorship, democracy, and development', in M. Olson and S. Kähkönen (eds) *A Not-So-Dismal Science: A broader view of economies and societies,* Oxford University Press, Oxford, pp. 119–38.

Ondaatje, M. (2000) *Anil's Ghost,* Alfred A. Knopf, New York.

Organization for Economic Co-operation and Development (OECD/DAC) (1997) *Guidelines on Conflict, Peace and Development Cooperation,* OECD, Paris.

Organization for Economic Co-operation and Development (OECD/DAC) (2002) *Glossary of Terms Used in Evaluations,* OECD, Paris.

Ottaway, M. (2002) 'Rebuilding state institutions in collapsed states', *Development and Change,* issue on 'State failure, collapse and reconstruction', 33 (5), pp. 1001–24.

Ottunu, O. and Doyle, M. (eds) (1998) *Peacemaking and Peacekeeping for a New Century,* Rowman and Littlefield, Lanham, MD.

Outram, Q. (1999) 'Liberia: roots and fruits of the emergency', in *Third World Quarterly,* Special Issue, 20 (1), pp. 163–74.

Pankhurst, D. (2003) 'The sex war' and other wars: towards a feminist approach to peacebuilding', *Development in Practice,* 13 (2, 3), pp. 154–77.

Paris, R. (1997) 'Peacebuilding and the limits of liberal internationalism', *International Security,* 22 (2), pp. 54–89.

Paris, R. (2004) *At War's End: Building peace after civil conflict,* Cambridge University Press, Cambridge.

Porter, D., Allen, B. and Thompson, G. (1991) *Development in Practice: Paved with good intentions,* Routledge, London.

Pottier, J. (1996) 'Agricultural rehabilitation and food insecurity in post-war Rwanda', *IDS Bulletin,* 27 (3), pp. 56–75.

Prendergast, J. (1996) *Frontline Diplomacy: Humanitarian aid and conflict in Africa,* Lynne Rienner, Boulder, CO and London.

Pugh, M. and Cooper, N. with Goodhand, J. (2004) *War Economies in a Regional Context: Challenges for transformation,* Lynne Rienner, Boulder, CO, and London.

Putman, D., Leonard, R. and Nanett, R.U. (1993) *Making Democracy Work: Civic tradition in Modern Italy,* Princeton University Press, Princeton, NJ.

Putzel, J. (2004) 'The politics of "participation": civil society, the state and development assistance', Discussion Paper no. 1, Crisis States Development Research Centre, DESTIN, LSE, London.

Rampton, D. and Welikala, A. (2005) 'The politics of the south: a thematic study towards the strategic conflict assessment', report prepared for the World Bank,

DFID, the Netherlands Embassy and SIDA, Sri Lanka.

Ramsbotham, O. and Woodhouse, T. (1996) *Humanitarian Intervention in Contemporary Conflict: A reconceptualisation,* Polity Press, Cambridge.

Reindorp, N. (2001) 'Global humanitarian assistance: trends and prospects', *Humanitarian Exchange* no. 18, ODI, London.

Reno, W. (2000) 'Shadow states and the political economy of civil wars', in M. Berdal and D. Malone (eds), *Greed and Grievance: Economic agendas in civil wars,* Lynne Rienner, Boulder, CO, and London, pp. 43–68.

Richards, P. (1996) *Fighting for the Rainforest: War, youth and resources in Sierra Leone,* James Currey, Oxford/Heinemann/IAI, London.

Richards, P. (ed.) (2005) *No War No Peace. An anthropology of contemporary armed conflicts,* James Currey, Oxford.

Richmond, O.P. (2001) 'A genealogy of peacemaking: the creation and recreation of order', *Alternatives: Global, Local, Political,* 26 (3), pp. 317–32.

Richmond, O.P. (2003) 'Introduction: NGOs, peace and human security', *International Peacekeeping,* 10 (1), pp. 1–11.

Richmond, O. (2005) 'Understanding the Liberal Peace', paper presented at the 'Transformation of War Economies' conference, University of Plymouth, 16–18 June.

Rieff, D. (2002) *A Bed for the Night. Humanitarianism in crisis,* Vintage, London.

Robben, A.C.G.M. and Nordstrom, C. (1995) 'The anthropology and ethnography of violence and socio-political conflict', in C. Nordstrom and A.C.G.M. Robben (eds) *Fieldwork under Fire: Contemporary studies of violence and survival,* University of California Press, Berkeley, CA, pp. 1–24.

Roche, C. (1994) 'Operationality in turbulence: the need for change', *Development in Practice,* 4 (3), pp. 15–25.

Roche, C. (1998) 'Organizational assessment and institutional footprints', in A. Thomas, J. Chataway and M. Wuyts (eds), *Finding out Fast. Investigative skills for policy and development,* Open University/Sage, London, pp. 173–200.

Rogers, P. (1999) *Losing control. Global security in the twenty-first century,* Pluto, London.

Rummel, R.J. (1995) 'Democracy, power, genocide, and mass murder', *Journal of Conflict Resolution,* 39 (1), pp. 3–26.

Salmon, L. and Anheier, H. (1999) 'The third sector in the third world', in D. Lewis (ed.), *International Perspectives on Voluntary Action: Reshaping the third sector,* Earthscan, London.

Sambanis, N. (2003) 'Using case studies to expand the theory of civil war', World Bank Conflict Prevention and Reconstruction Unit Working Paper no. 5, World Bank, Washington, DC.

Saravanamuttu, P. (2003) 'Sri Lanka: the best and last chance for peace?', *Conflict, Security, Development,* 3 (1), pp. 129–38.

Schetter, C. (2001) 'The chimera of ethnicity in Afghanistan: Ethnic affiliation no basis for a new regime', NZZ Online, 10 December; available online at: www.nzz.ch/english.

Schloms, M. (2003) 'Humanitarian NGOs in peace processes', *International Peacekeeping,* 10 (1), pp. 40–55.

Schuler, S.R., Hashemi, S.M, Riley, A.P and Akhter, S. (1996) 'Credit programs, patriarchy and men's violence against women in rural Bangladesh', *Social Science and Medicine,* 43 (12), pp. 1729–42.

Scott, J.C. (1976) *The Moral Economy of the Peasant: Rebellion and subsistence in Southeast Asia,* Yale University Press, New Haven, CT.

Scott, J.C. (1997) 'The infrapolitics of subordinate groups', in M. Rahnema with V.

Bawtree (eds), *The Post-Development Reader,* Zed Books, London.

Scott, J. (2000) 'Hill and valley in Southeast Asia... or why the state is the enemy of people who move around... or... why civilizations can't climb hills', prepared for the 2000 Symposium, 'Development and the Nation State', Washington University, St Louis, MI, February.

Sen, A. (1981) *Poverty and Famines,* Clarendon Press, Oxford.

Shearer, D. (1997) 'Exploring the limits of consent: conflict resolution in Sierra Leone', *Millennium,* 26 (3), pp. 845–60.

Shearer, D. (2000) 'Aiding or abetting? Humanitarian aid and its economic role in civil war', in M. Berdal and D.M. Malone (eds), *Greed and Grievance: Economic agendas in civil wars,* IDRC/Lynne Rienner, London and Boulder, CO, pp. 189–203.

Short, C. (1999) 'Conflict prevention, conflict resolution and post-conflict peacebuilding—from rhetoric to reality', speech of Clare Short, Secretary of State for Development, UK, International Alert, November. Available online at: http://www.international-alert.org/text/short.htm.

Simmons, P.J. (1998) 'Learning to live with NGOs', *Foreign Policy,* 112 (Fall), pp. 82–96.

Slim, H. (1995) 'The continuing metamorphosis of the humanitarian practitioner: some new colours for an endangered chameleon', *Disasters,* 19 (2), pp. 110–26.

Slim, H. (2004) 'A call to alms: humanitarian action and the art of war', Centre for Humanitarian Dialogue, Geneva.

Smillie, I. (1995) *The Alms Bazaar: Altruism under fire—non-profit organizations and international development,* IT Publications, London.

Smillie, I. (1999) 'At sea in a sieve? Trends and issues in the relationship between Northern NGOs and Northern Governments', in I. Smillie and H. Helmich, *Stakeholders. Government-NGO partnerships for international development,* Earthscan, London, pp. 7–35.

Smillie, I. (ed.) (2001) *Patronage or Partnership. Local capacity building in humanitarian crises,* Kumarian Press, Bloomfield, CT.

Smillie, I., Lansana, G. and Hazleton, R. (2000) 'The heart of the matter—Sierra Leone, diamonds and human security', Partnership Africa Canada, Ottawa, Canada.

Smillie, I. and Minear, L. (2004) *The Charity of Nations. Humanitarian action in a calculating world,* Kumarian Press, Bloomfield, CT.

Snyder, Jack (2000) *From Voting to Violence,* W.W. Norton, New York and London.

Soederberg, S. (2005) 'American empire and "excluded states": the Millennium Challenge Account and the shift to pre-emptive development', *Third World Quarterly,* 25 (2), pp. 279–302.

Sorbe, G., Macrae, J. and Wohigemuth, L. (1997) 'NGOs in conflict—an evaluation of International Alert', CMI Report Series, Chr. Michelson Institute, Bergen, Norway.

Sorensen, G. (2000) 'Sovereignty, security and state failure'. Available online at: http://www.ippu.purdue.edu/failed_states/2000/papers/sorensen.html.

Sorensen, G. (2001) 'War and state making—why doesn't it work in the Third World?', paper presented at the Failed States Conference, Florence, 10–14 April.

Spencer, J. (2004) 'The culture, politics and economics of peace in Sri Lanka', paper presented at the LSE /DESTIN Seminar Series, 28 January.

Srivastava, M. (2003) 'Moving beyond "institutions matter". How do the "rules of the game" evolve and change? Some reflections on how institutionalists theorise on institutional development', Crisis State Development Research Centre, Special Seminar, 5 February.

Stedman, S. (1997) 'Spoiler problems in peace processes', *International Security,* 22 (2), pp. 5–53.

Stedman, S. (2001) 'Implementing peace agreements in civil wars. Lessons and recommendations for policy makers', IPA Policy Paper Series on Peace Implementation, New York.

Stedman, S. (2002) 'Introduction', in S. Stedman, D. Rothchild and E. Cousens (2002) *Ending Civil Wars. The implementation of peace agreements,* Lynne Rienner, Boulder, CO, and London, pp. 1–40.

Stedman, S., Rothchild, D. and Cousens, E. (2002) *Ending Civil Wars. The Implementation of peace agreements,* Lynne Rienner, Boulder, CO, and London.

Stepputat, F. (1997) 'Post-war Guatemala: Encounters at the frontier of the modern state', in B. Fredericksen and F. Wilson, *Livelihood, Identity and Organization in Situations of Instability,* Centre for Development Research, Copenhagen, pp. 9–24.

Stewart, F. (1993) 'War and underdevelopment: can economic analysis help reduce the costs?', *Journal of International Development,* 5 (4), pp. 357–80.

Stewart, F. (2002) 'Root causes of violent conflict in developing countries', *British Medical Journal,* 324 (9), February, pp. 342–5.

Stewart, F. and Fitzgerald, V. (2001) *War and Underdevelopment,* Vol. 1, *The Economic and Social Consequences of Conflict,* Oxford University Press, Oxford.

Stoddard, A. (2003) 'Humanitarian NGOs: challenges and trends', in J. Macrae and A. Harmer (eds) (2003) 'Humanitarian action and the "global war on terror": a review of trends and issues', HPG Report no. 14, ODI, London, pp. 25–36.

Stubbs, P. (1995) 'Nationalisms, globalization and civil society in Croatia and Slovenia', paper presented at Second European Conference of Sociology on 'European societies: fusion or fission?', Budapest; 30 April–2 May.

Surkhe, A., Strand, A. and Harpviken, K. (2002) 'After Bonn: conflictual peacebuilding', *Third World Quarterly,* 23 (5), pp. 875–91.

Terry, F. (2002) *Condemned to Repeat? The paradox of humanitarian action,* Cornell University Press, New York.

Tilly, C. (1985) 'War making and state making as organized crime', in P. Evans, D. Rueschemeyer and T. Skocpol (eds), *Bringing the State Back In,* Cambridge University Press, New York, pp. 169–91.

Tilly, Charles (2003) *The Politics of Collective Violence,* Cambridge University Press, Cambridge.

Tschirgi, N. (2003) 'Peacebuilding as the link between security and development: is the window of opportunity closing?', International Peace Academy, Studies in Security and Development, New York.

Tschirgi, N. (2004) 'Post-conflict peacebuilding revisited: achievements, limitations, challenges', Report prepared for the WSP International/IPA Peacebuilding Forum Conference, International Peace Academy, New York.

United Nations (1992) 'An agenda for peace: preventative diplomacy, peacemaking and peace-keeping', Report of the Secretary-General pursuant to the statement adopted by the Summit Meeting of the Security Council on 31 January, UN Doc A/47/277-S/2411, United Nations, New York.

United Nations (2001) *Report of the Panel on United Nations Peace Operations* (Brahimi Report), A/55/305 S/2000/809, United Nations, New York.

United Nations (2004) 'A more secure world: our shared responsibility', Report of the Secretary-General's High-level Panel on Threats, Challenges and Change, United Nations, New York.

United Nations Development Programme (UNDP) (2000) *Towards a Culture of Peace. National Human Development Report Republic of Moldova, 2000,* UNDP, Chisinau, Republic of Moldova.

Uphoff, N. (1992) *Learning from Gal Oya: Possibilities for participatory development and post-Newtonian social science,* Cornell University Press, Ithaca, NY.

Utas, M. (2005) 'The reintegration and marginalisation of youth in Liberia', in P. Richards (ed.), pp. 137–54.

Uvin, P. (1998) *Aiding Violence: The development enterprise in Rwanda,* Kumarian Press, Bloomfield, CT.

Uvin, P. (1999) 'The influence of aid in situations of violent conflicts', draft report prepared for DAC informal taskforce on 'Conflict, peace and development co-operation'.

Uvin, P. (2002) 'The development/peacebuilding nexus: a typology and history of changing paradigms', *Journal of Peacebuilding and Development,* 1 (1), pp. 5–24.

Van Brabant, K. (1998) 'Cool ground for aid providers: towards better security management in aid agencies', *Disasters,* 22 (2), pp. 109–25.

Van Brabant, K. and Killock, T. (1999) 'The limits and scope for the use of development assistance incentives and disincentives for influencing conflict situations: case study, Afghanistan', OECD/DAC, Paris.

Van Roy, A. (ed.) (1999) *Civil Society and the Aid Industry,* Earthscan, London.

Varshney, A. (2002) *Ethnic Conflict and Civic Life: Hindus and Muslims in India,* Yale University Press, New Haven, CT.

Vaux, T. (2001) *The Selfish Altruist. Relief work in famine and war,* Earthscan, London.

Vaux, T. and Goodhand, J. (2001) 'Disturbing connections: aid and conflict in Kyrgyzstan', Conflict, Security and Development Group, Kings College, University of London, Conflict Assessment 3, July 2001.

Vaux, T. and Goodhand, J. (2002) *War and Peace in the Southern Caucasus. A Strategic Conflict Assessment of the Armenia-Azerbaijan Conflict,* Humanitarian Initiatives, Oxford, UK.

Voutira, E. and Brown, S.A.W. (1995) *Conflict Resolution: A Review of Some Non-Governmental Practices—'A Cautionary Tale',* Studies on Emergencies and Disaster Relief, Report no. 4, Refugee Studies Programme, University of Oxford.

Walkup, M. (1997) 'Policy dysfunction in humanitarian organisations: the role of coping strategies, institutions and organisational culture', *Journal of Refugee Studies,* 10 (1), pp. 37–60.

Wallensteen, P. (2002) *Understanding Conflict Resolution: War, Peace and the Global System,* Sage Publications, London, Thousand Oaks and New Delhi.

Wallensteen, P. and Sollenberg, M. (1998) 'Armed Conflict and Regional Conflict Complexes, 1989–97', *Journal of Peace Research,* 35, (5), pp. 621–34.

Weick, W.E. (1995) Sensemaking in Organizations, Sage, London.

Weiss, T. (2001) 'Researching humanitarian intervention: some lessons', *Journal of Peace Research,* 38 (4), pp. 419–28.

West, K. (2001) *Agents of Altruism. The expansion of humanitarian NGOs in Rwanda and Afghanistan,* Ashgate, Aldershot.

White, P. and Cliffe, L. (2000) 'Matching response to context in complex political emergencies: relief, development, peacebuilding or something in-between?', *Disasters,* 24 (4), pp. 314–42.

Wickramasinghe, N. (2001) *Civil Society in Sri Lanka. New circles of power,* Sage, London.

Wolf, E. (1971) *Peasant Wars of the Twentieth Century,* Faber and Faber, London.

Wood, G. (1997) 'States without citizens: the problem of the franchise state', in D. Hulme and M. Edwards (eds), *NGOs, States and Donors. Too close for comfort?,*

Macmillan, London, pp. 455–72.

Woodhouse, T. (1994) *Conflict Resolution and Ethnic Conflict,* Working Paper, Department of Peace Studies, University of Bradford.

Woodhouse, T. (1999) *International Conflict Resolution: Some Critiques and a Response,* Working Paper no.1, Centre for Conflict Resolution, Department of Peace Studies, University of Bradford.

Woodward, (2000) *Moldova Strategic Conflict Assessment,* Unpublished report for DFID.

Woodwell, D. (2002) *The 'Troubles' of Northern Ireland—Civil Conflict Within an Economically Well-Developed State,* Paper prepared for the Yale University/World Bank Case Study Project on Political Economy of Civil Wars.

World Bank (2003) *Breaking the Conflict Trap: Civil war and development policy,* World Bank, Washington, DC.

Yannis, A. (2002) 'State collapse and its implications for peace-building and reconstruction', *Development and Change,* 33 (5), pp. 817–36.

Zartmann, W. (1996), *Elusive Peace: Negotiating an end to civil wars,* Brookings Institute, Washington, DC.

Index

accountability, 164–166, 169; future directions for donors, 184–185; humanitarian aid, 89, 91–92

actors: case studies, 64–70; conflict assessment methodology, 29–30, 43–45; greed models, 38–39; grievance models, 37–38; individual choices, 7–8; international, 128; intervention, 132–134; leadership, 158–160; security dimension, 52–53; staff, 160–161

adaptability, 192–193

adhocracies, 41, 122, 162–163

advocacy, 15–17

Afghanistan, 17–18, 25; accountability, 165; actors, 64, 67–68, 70, 132–133; agency-community relationships, 167–169; aid conditionalities, 143–144; aid market, 144–146, 176; assessment of international peacemaking, 130, 132; coherence of international intervention, 138; conflict assessment framework, 18; conflict-fuelling programmes, 109–115; data collection, 157–159; dynamics of conflict, 71–72, 102; economic dimension, 61, 111–113, 114, 121; holding operations, 110; impact of conflict on NGOs, 104–108; international intervention, 132–133, 134–135, 135–138, 141; international political landscape, 128; minimalism, 189; NGO leadership, 158–160; NGO organizational culture, 155–156; peacebuilding context, 127; peacebuilding programmes, 110, 117–118, 119; political dimension, 54–58, 109, 111, 117–118; programming mix, 150–153; security dimension, 50–54; social and cultural dimension, 62–64; social dimension, 115, 121–123; Soviet occupation, 4; timing of international intervention, 139; war-peace continuum, 49

age, 65

agency, 7–8, 44–45

aid: conflict assessment framework, 18–24; fuelling conflict, 109–115, 173; international intervention, 140–146; international political landscape, 128. *See also* development aid; humanitarian aid

aid conditionalities, 85, 143–144, 185

aid market, 6–7, 144–146, 176

aid regime, definition of, 15

Anderson, M. B., 40

Angola, 82

armed conflict. *See* conflict

Armenia-Azerbaijan, 19; actors, 63, 66–67, 133; assessment of interna-

About the Book

As nongovernmental organizations play a growing role in the international response to armed conflict, tasked with mitigating the effects of war and helping to end the violence—there is an acute need for information on the impact they are actually having. Addressing this need, *Aiding Peace?* explores just how NGOs interact with conflict and peace dynamics, and with what results.

Jonathan Goodhand compares the programs of international and national NGOs in seven conflict arenas: Afghanistan, Armenia-Azerbaijan, Kyrgyzstan, Liberia, Moldova, Nepal, and Sri Lanka. His multilevel approach is well grounded in an analysis of the political-economy context of each conflict. His important and perhaps unexpected results point to essential policy and practice changes in the interest of enhanced NGO peacebuilding efforts. Not least, they also highlight the need for a fundamental adjustment of expectations.

Jonathan Goodhand is senior lecturer in the Development Studies Department at the School of Oriental and African Studies, University of London